DATE DUE

JUL 13 2000	SEP 27 2004
AUG 08 2000	FEB 21 2006
SEP 06 2000	SEP 19 2006
OCT 07 2000	OCT 23 2006
OCT 26 2000	
NOV 17 2000	
DEC 26 2000	
JAN 02 2001	
MAY 23 2001	
AUG 08 2001	

GAYLORD · PRINTED IN U.S.A.

SEP 04 2001	
JUN 26 2002	
JUL 03 2002	
JUL 24 2002	
NOV 21 2002	
SEP 03 2003	
NOV 28 2003	
Dec 17	
MAR 10 2004	

GAYLORD · PRINTED IN U.S.A.

FINDING
YOUR
RELIGION

FINDING YOUR RELIGION

When the Faith You Grew Up with Has Lost Its Meaning

~ ᘓᘔ ~

Scotty McLennan

HarperSanFrancisco
A Division of HarperCollins*Publishers*

Grateful acknowledgment is made for permission to reprint material copyrighted by the following authors or publishers:

From *Sadhana* by Rabindranath Tagore (New York: Macmillan, 1913). Copyright © 1913 by Rabindranath Tagore. Reprinted by permission of Simon & Schuster.

From *InterVarsity's Code of Ethics for Christian Witness.* Used by permission of InterVarsity Christian Fellowship, USA. P.O. Box 7895, Madison, WI 53707.

From "i thank You God for most this amazing" copyright © 1950, 1978, 1991 by the Trustees for the E. E. Cummings Trust. Copyright © 1979 by George James Firmage, from *Complete Poems: 1904–1962* by E. E. Cummings, Edited by George J. Firmage. Reprinted by permission of Liveright Publishing Corporation.

From *Rebecca: A Father's Journey from Grief to Gratitude* by Robert A. Jonas (New York: The Crossroad Publishing Company, 1996). Copyright © 1996 by Robert A. Jonas. Used with permission of The Crossroad Publishing Company.

From *Zen Comics, volume 1,* by Ioanna Salajan (Rutland, Vermont: Charles E. Tuttle Co., 1974). Copyright © 1974 by Ioanna Salajan. Used by permission of Charles E. Tuttle Co., Inc. of Boston, Massachusetts, and Tokyo, Japan.

From *Doonesbury* comic strip by Garry Trudeau. Copyright © 1971, 1975, 1978, 1984, 1987, 1994, 1995 by Garry Trudeau. Reprinted by permission of Garry Trudeau.

Cover illustration: *Doonesbury* © G. B. Trudeau. Reprinted with permission of Universal Press Syndicate. All rights reserved.

HarperCollins Web Site: http://www.harpercollins.com
HarperCollins®, 📖®, and HarperSanFrancisco™ are
trademarks of HarperCollins Publishers Inc.

FIRST EDITION
Designed by Joseph Rutt

Library of Congress Cataloging-in-Publication Data
McLennan, Scotty.
Finding your religion : when the faith you grew up with has lost its meaning /
Scotty McLennan. — 1st ed.
p. cm.
Includes bibliographical references and index.
ISBN 0–06–065347–7 (cloth)
ISBN 0–06–065346–9 (paper)
1. Religious life. I. Title.
BL624.M3977   1999
291.4—dc21   99–27147

99 00 01 02 03 ❖/RRD(H) 10 9 8 7 6 5 4 3 2

To Will and Dan
May you find the kind of joy and love my father had.

Table of Contents

Acknowledgments

I am indebted to many wise guides, starting with my mother and father, who prepared me to write this book. If it weren't for the members of my Jung group and Holy Spirit group in Boston, few of the ideas and little of the passion that animate this text would have coalesced. Most of all, though, it has been the students, professors, chaplains, staff, administrators, and alumni (including my agent, Gail Ross) of Tufts University who have made this effort possible. Tufts has been my primary community for the past fifteen years, and many of its members are in this book. Since those relationships are confidential, I have received written permission from each of these Tufts people, and from a number of other wonderful colleagues and friends, to include their disguised stories here. Thank you very, very much. I'm particularly obliged to the students and guest lecturers who examined this book in its infancy in my spring 1998 course in the Tufts Experimental College.

Then there are those others who have been kind enough to read and comment on various drafts of the book: Miriam Acevedo, Martha Ajami, Brent Coffin, Elizabeth Ellis, Anita Farber-Robertson, Peter Haines, John Jenke, Robert Jonas, Maria Karagianis, Linda Karpowich, Jane LaRoque, Mohamed Mahmoud, Thomas Mikelson, David O'Leary, Charlie Pillsbury, Gail Ross, Dawn Sangrey, Edith Stead, Jeff Summit, Barry Svigals, Garry Trudeau, Bob Turner, Joseph Walser, Bill Webb, Kate

Wheeler, Joe Wheelwright, and Howard Yoon. I am very grateful to each and every one of you. I also want to thank my editors at HarperCollins, Mark Chimsky and Doug Abrams, who worked with me painstakingly, chapter by chapter, to make this a much better book than when it started. Finally, though, my appreciation and love are unbounded for my wife, Ellen, who has inspired me from the start and gently helped me every step of the way.

Introduction

Of all the impressive characters I encountered in college in the late sixties, the most unsettling—by far—was the author of this book. It wasn't just the sweep of his erudition; it was its maddening functionality—the quiet certainty with which he linked the acquisition of knowledge to his personal goals, which were fixed and true. This would be merely commendable in an aspiring engineer, but Scotty McLennan was a student of faith and philosophy, traditionally treacherous territory for the empirically-minded. What the rest of us learned in order to pass exams, Scotty harnessed and put right to use, working one loamy pasture after another, confident of the harvest ahead. He had come to Yale to be outfitted, and he emerged from seminar rooms grinning, stuffing his rucksack with tools he had seemingly longed for since birth. So certain was he that life revealed its mysteries in ways that could be wholly anticipated, he once planned his entire fall semester social schedule in advance, cross-referencing potential dates with big weekends, thereby delivering to his grateful friends a full season of hilarity.

Of course, unearned scorn only strengthened him. As Scotty looked at a world gone mad around him, his passion for social justice carried him into divinity school and law school (simultaneously!), and then out into a challenging legal aid ministry—just as planned. For those of us with broken rudders and low draft numbers, Scotty's direct path seemed unreal, all the more so because it was illuminated by a faith that so many of us had long ago abandoned.

If you were twenty-three, and it was 1971, you couldn't make up someone like this, so as an aspiring artist, I didn't try. I simply appropriated him, ordaining him on the spot (so as to fulfill one of his personal goals before he could). And in filling out the character of Scot Sloan, I also borrowed from Scotty's mentor, the Reverend William Sloane Coffin, a campus hero and antiwar activist of near-mythic reputation. But the caricatured likeness was of Scotty himself, and in my mind, it was him I dragooned into service as the "fighting young priest," dropping him into a coffeehouse where the other cast members could come for spiritual, temporal, or caffeinated sustenance.

With this preface, I repay my debt—if only by confessing how miserly was my portrayal. If you haven't guessed by now, the journey that Scotty had embarked on all those years ago was imperfectly observed, to say the least. My view had been one of moral glamour without the struggle. It didn't account for the ferocious integrity with which he had always challenged his most cherished articles of faith, and it certainly didn't anticipate the collapse of spiritual goals and loss of heart that beset him as he approached thirty. Scotty, as it turned out, was human, and it's his humanity that's at the core of this book. Having stumbled, badly, on the mountain, Scotty picked himself up, and in the long but fruitful process of exploration and recovery, he began to notice how much company he had.

He was uniquely well positioned to do so. As the chaplain at Tufts University for fifteen years, Scotty has ministered to a generation of students and faculty, many of them discouraged by failures of faith similar to his own. Some of them were rebelling against the suffocating embrace of family traditions, some had had their beliefs shaken by their study of modernists and skeptics like Freud, and some had been overtaken by the pervasive secular humanism of their times. Yet all felt empty and hungry and ready to approach the mountain once again. Their stories of reengagement and renewal are what give this book such power, especially when viewed as stages of faith-building. Take a step forward, the author exhorts. Now take another. Don't worry about the auspices—the mountain is criss-crossed with an infinite variety of paths, some more traveled than others. But all of them lead to glory.

I grew up in the Episcopalian faith—the "best religion money can buy," it was joked—and my family worshiped at the small, wooden, rural church my great-grandfather had helped found. A block down the street was a far more imposing structure, the town's Catholic church, and to me, it was terra incognita. Since the church was dark and vaulted and built of stone, and since it was always leaking incense and Latin into the street outside, Catholicism remained shrouded in otherness the whole of my childhood. My faith home was St. Luke's—home in the same way that the Yankees, not the Dodgers, and Ike, not Adlai, were home. In a small town, no one takes you by the hand and says, "You may not be from our tribe, but here you are welcome. Here you are free to seek grace—or not."

When the faith of one's youth loses its meaning, there is no ingrained cultural habit of looking elsewhere. Indeed, in much of the world, where religious freedom is all but unknown, the strictures against straying make it unthinkable. But in millennial America, there are, to paraphrase Paul Tillich, many windows through which to see God at work. This book frees you to gaze through all of them, to drink in the light until you find the clarity that gives life meaning.

Garry Trudeau

The Mountain Beckons

_രൂ ൭_

T he mountain beckons. This book
is intended for personal exploration. It is full of stories of seekers on the
spiritual mountain. My hope is that each and every one of these stories
can be of assistance to you, because of the important discoveries these
individuals have made about religion in their lives. I assume that you are
no longer happy with the religion of your childhood, or never had one in
the first place. This book does not offer answers. Instead, it offers a
method of exploration, as the chapter titles suggest. The journey must be
yours, but there is a lot of help available along the way from others who
have found new meaning for their lives within the major religious traditions of the world.

I am a university chaplain. For the past fifteen years I've had the good
fortune of getting to know students, faculty, staff, alumni, and local community people from a wide variety of backgrounds: Protestant, Catholic,
and Eastern Orthodox Christians; Jews and Muslims and Bahá'ís;
Hindus, Jains, and Sikhs; Taoists and Confucianists; Buddhists and
Shintoists; Marxists and secular humanists; agnostics and atheists. I've
celebrated with them and learned from them; taught, counseled, advised
and been helped by them; sung and danced, laughed and cried, discussed
and argued with them; solemnized their marriages, dedicated their children, and memorialized them after death.

My own denomination is Unitarian Universalist, but as the university chaplain at Tufts I am responsible to the entire community. I serve as an umbrella for all campus ministries and try to keep everyone talking to one another. I also teach and am available to anyone as a sounding board. My other professional experiences include practicing law for a decade before I came to Tufts, and moonlighting as a visiting lecturer on ethics for the past ten years at the Harvard Business School.

Starting with my own experiences in college in the 1960s and divinity school in the early 1970s, I have learned a great deal about how people lose and find their own religion. I've come to see it very much as an ongoing process that never stops. For many people, the faith they grew up with loses its meaning during adolescence. Others who never had any faith in childhood begin exploring religion for the first time in adolescence or young adulthood. I've come to realize that there are identifiable stages of spiritual development that people go through, no matter what their religious tradition is or isn't. Just as we grow emotionally and intellectually over the years, so we grow spiritually, if we allow ourselves. In my experience, religious faith is not an "on-off" button. It naturally changes over time. The feeling of having arrived or of being sure almost never lasts, no matter how old we get. (That's what the chapter "Opening" is all about.)

So, discovering our religion should be an exciting, dynamic process that ebbs and flows with the seasons of our lives. At the half-century mark myself, I can personally vouch only for the decades through the forties. Yet, during some twenty-five years of ordained ministry, I've had the opportunity to know people well at all ages and stages.

I've come to feel like a kind of mountain guide. There is a spiritual mountain that all of us (or at least a lot of us) are trying to climb. There are many paths up that mountain—many paths that can reach the top, although very few people actually get to the summit of this very high mountain. Those paths may be rough or smooth, steep or easy, boring or colorful, tiring or exhilarating. Yet, they are all on the same spiritual mountain, and, ultimately, they all converge at the very top, as mystics of all religions have told us.

Most of us aren't mystics, though, and for us the point is to enjoy the journey—to find fulfillment in our pilgrimage on the mountain itself—rather than to miss everything along the way in pursuit of the summit. As I've heard from the great mystical guides, it can be very cold and breath-taking up there. Few people are able to stay there very long. In moun-taineering language, it's the difference between trekking and peak-bagging. Trekkers tend to experience a lot more of the flora and fauna. Peak-baggers report a glorious view.

I've spent a lot of time on the mountain under a wide variety of condi-tions. I know well-worn paths as well as hidden trails. I'm familiar with the flora and fauna. I've studied the mountain's history. I know streams and falls, cliffs and caves, passes and ridges, meadows and snowfields. I love the mountain. As a guide, though, I also want to be sensitive to differ-ent climbers' interests and abilities. That's what the next three chapters are all about. They will help the hesitant and the dubious to view the spir-itual mountain from a distance, getting ready to pick a path and start walking. If this book is to do any good, it must support many different travelers at various stages of their journeys. And it will need to be a resource you can keep returning to as you explore different aspects of the mountain at different altitudes over time. Read each of the accounts of other people's experiences with that in mind. Savor their stories and store them in the back of your mind—and deep in your soul—for use as much in the future as in the present.

After the next chapter describes the stages of spiritual development, the "Thinking" chapter urges you to open your adult mind to religious inquiry—to start thinking about religion. I report some insights from my spending more than twenty years in a "Jung Club." Religious myths and symbols from around the world have taken on new meaning for each member as we've seen them first as internal constructions of the human mind and then asked what relation, if any, they bear to external reality. I recount how one of our members became a Buddhist. I describe a trip of mine through the desert to Mount Sinai, where three major religious traditions hold that Moses received the Ten Commandments from God. Profound lessons were learned there by all of us travelers, whether we were modern secularists, Jews, Christians, or Muslims.

The next chapter suggests that you begin *experiencing*—opening your senses along with your mind as you begin your religious search. As you become more awake and alert to the environment around you—to your own bodily sensations of sight, hearing, smell, taste, and feel—you will also become more spiritually perceptive. New ways will emerge to see the sunrise, hear the birds sing, smell the flowers, taste food, and feel the wind in your face. In any case, you can't find your way if you're asleep.

What can a Russian atheist, for whom religion is "unintelligible," learn floating down a river on a boat at night with his eyes and ears open? Why do huge crowds gather in Japanese parks each evening during cherry blossom season to picnic and light colorful lanterns? How did Ralph Waldo Emerson challenge the "decaying church" and "wasting unbelief" of his day by his love of "the splendor of nature"?

The following chapter suggests that each reader now pick a religious path and start *walking*. Even if it turns out not to be the right way later on, you won't get anywhere spiritually without starting. Spiritual life of necessity requires exertion and effort. It withers on the couch and in the armchair. I understand how frightening and difficult it is for many people to commit themselves to a religious tradition before they think they've gathered enough experience and knowledge about what they're getting into. Yet I see this as a process, not a final decision.

I know a lot of people who are spiritually paralyzed inside of their heads. They think, read, and talk about religion, yet they are incapable of acting and feeling. Their heart has not been touched. They are afraid of taking risks. "There are always two sides, or many sides, to any question," they opine. "It's hard to choose. It's hard to know where to start." Start anywhere that looks interesting, I respond, but start. Act. Do. Make some mistakes and get knocked down. Pull yourself up and start again. Real learning requires an interplay between action and reflection, between heart and head.

The next chapter, "Joining," encourages you to join with fellow travelers on the path you've chosen. You can discuss your doubts and discoveries, your hopes and fears, your ideas and feelings. You're not alone in your search, and traveling companions will help you see and experience a lot along the way that you'd otherwise miss. Your questions will challenge and help them, just as their perceptions will widen your perspective and deepen your practice. Keep communication open! Some fellow travelers on your path may be "experts" with names like "clergy," "gurus," or "masters." Be certain that the experts are guides who enhance your journey, though, rather than substituting themselves for your own fresh sensations of the mountain itself.

The "Crossing" chapter extols the value of a comparative approach in which you learn from trail crossings even as you have set off on a particular path. Experimenting with Buddhist and Hindu meditation can enhance Christian and Jewish prayer life, and vice versa. Understanding how different traditions grieve their dead can make it easier for you—in giving and receiving sympathy and help—to mourn the loss of someone close to you. Learning about the spiritual experiences of Muslims during the month-long fast of Ramadan can help Jews to find new meaning in keeping kosher, Christians to use Lent as a rich period of self-examination when they haven't reflected for years, and Hindus to emulate Gandhi's use of fasting at times of profound personal and social turmoil. Appreciating the similarities and differences between various celebrations at the time of the vernal equinox—such as Passover, Easter, and May Day—can enliven the season for all.

The next chapter, "Sitting," emphasizes the power of meditation and prayer in the spiritual life, as I encourage readers to take some time to sit alone under a tree in the midst of the trek. The Buddha achieved enlightenment sitting alone under the *bodhi* tree. Direct experience of the Ultimate Reality (whatever he, she, or it is called) is reported most often in these very private moments. Meditation and prayer are also quite literally good for your health. An initially skeptical physician, Herbert Benson of Harvard Medical School, studied a form of Hindu meditation in the 1970s; quite to his surprise, he found that it had demonstrably positive medical benefits. His best-selling book *The Relaxation Response* noted that similar health advantages could be achieved through other forms of meditation or prayer in almost any tradition.

The "Suffering" chapter grapples with the role suffering plays in religion and the spiritual life. "There are no atheists in foxholes," as the old saying goes. Many people find their religion in times of crisis. It's inevitable that there will be upsetting incidents, unpleasant surprises, injury, illness, and loss along each of our life paths. One can either fall apart at these times or see them as opportunities—for personal deepening, for closer relationships with family and friends, for a deeper connection with what Paul Tillich called "the Ground of our Being." All the major religious traditions have paid particular attention to the question of suffering and offer significant resources to help searchers at these times.

The final chapter is entitled "Rejoicing." So much of the religious life in all traditions has involved singing and dancing, eating and drinking together, and enjoying life in all of its wonder. A sense of humor can also produce more insight than virtually anything else. Religious holy days become the culture's holidays—times of recreation, entertainment, and gaiety. In America, for example, we celebrate at least three festivals of light during the darkest days of the year: Hanukkah, Christmas, and Kwanza. Religious rites of passage such as namings and baptisms, bar or bat mitzvahs and confirmations, and weddings joyously mark the great occasions of our life journeys. Religion at its best also helps us appreciate small, everyday joys that renew us and help us get through the day with some sense of fulfillment.

So, this book is a guide for those who are at a spiritual turning point—for those who are not satisfied with the faith they grew up with, or who grew up without a faith, but want to find a meaningful way to express their spirituality. It's intended for readers who feel a stirring in their soul but don't know where it's pulling them. If that's you, then this book is for you. It should help you identify what stage you're at in the development of your faith. It may point you in the direction of a new religion to help you grow, or you may discover new meaning and depth within the religion in which you grew up. What's most important is that this book give you hope that you can find a religion that will get you moving again on the spiritual mountain.

Opening

—᧔᧓—

Donna Radley[1] lost her religion as a teenager. Her childhood prayers had been tidy and polite when she was growing up as a Protestant Christian in an affluent suburb of Los Angeles. She went to Presbyterian Sunday school every week and Bible camps every summer. She thought what it meant to follow Christ was to be good: "Dear God, please God, thank you, God, I'm sorry, God." In high school she found a boyfriend and began drinking—as she put it, "doing a few things I didn't want God to know about." She began distancing herself from God, "figuring that if I couldn't see Him, He couldn't see me." As she put it, "I adopted an all-or-nothing philosophy" because "I didn't see any way to follow Jesus and still do what I wanted."

Through college and into her mid-twenties she had nothing to do with religion. She engaged in other forms of behavior she knew would not be acceptable to her church. She experimented with drugs and became sexually active. Donna grew up emotionally and intellectually, but she still viewed God through her high school eyes as a strict, moralistic parent. She didn't want Him hovering around telling her what to do and making her feel guilty.

Donna married her college sweetheart soon after graduation. Some years later when her husband suggested that they find a church to go to with their children, it felt as if he was inviting her to visit an old grandfather she hadn't seen in years. The church they settled on was a liberal and open Presbyterian congregation, and with her life more settled, she began to feel a renewed spirituality and a reconnection with God.

But things got harder over time. She started feeling guilty in this congregation, which she felt was focused too heavily on social justice and not enough on worship. She felt she wasn't writing enough letters to her representatives in Congress or attending enough rallies. She came out of services depressed rather than nurtured. With two small kids and a part-time job, she found her relationship with God increasingly strained. "Everything felt like a laundry list, including any attempt at prayer. I'd try to pray in the morning or evening, but it wasn't remotely spiritual. It was more like God and me checking our plans for the day, deciding who would do what. I'd take care of my kids, and he would watch over the big stuff." So increasingly, religion went on the back burner.

Part of the problem was her troubled marriage. Ten years after she married, she decided to take her two kids and leave her husband. It was the most difficult period in her life, a time when she desperately searched for a way to help her cope with the hardship. The adolescent came out in her again, as she explains it: "I crossed faith off my list until further notice . . . I assumed God would disapprove entirely, and I figured I had enough to do without convincing Him."

Within a year after her divorce, Donna began reading about Buddhism and meditating. In this nonjudgmental context "there was the feeling of some doors opening." Then a friend suggested she attend Quaker meeting. At first, the services gave her exactly what she needed: "just some quiet and an acknowledgment of a presence." Later she felt the desire to add music, incense, communion, and ritual to her worship, and she became a regular at an Episcopal church. She came away with a feeling of being fed. Soon she began rethinking her adolescent relationship to God as a strict parent. As she puts it, "I began to see not only that my being good wasn't God's chief concern, but that, in an entirely different way, *God* was good. Not good as in 'behave yourself,' but *good*. Like pizza and beer for dinner when you're tired and hungry. Like a hot bath, or a great day, or holding your kids: that kind of good. And I wanted more of Him."

Donna bought a Bible and began browsing around in it for something helpful. This is what she found: "Do not be afraid." She discovered this message again and again in many parts of the Bible. Her life fears eased and her self-confidence grew. She read, "You shall love the Lord your God with all your heart and with all your soul and with all your might." This verse she'd known since childhood now began sounding different. She saw it not as a command but as a promise. As she put it, "I was beginning to want to love this God, and that verse seemed to tell me that I would learn how."

She read the richly sensual love poetry of the Song of Songs, and something new began to stir within her. The book begins, "Let him kiss me with the kisses of his mouth!" Donna thought, *That's You? That's what You're like?* She explains, "There was a passion and an intimacy I hadn't known, as though that distant family member I'd imagined wasn't so, but a lover—a case of mistaken identity. I felt I was being not called so much, but beckoned—a hard-to-resist and provocative 'Come over here. Come here. Come.' And I began falling in love with Him."

Finally, with a new boyfriend, she started going to Catholic Mass. She was transported. Here's how she described it: "I was always amazed afterward! I found the Mass beautiful and powerful, and the presence I sensed there was so different from who I'd thought God was. It was as though I'd had everything upside down. At Mass, God was a mystery, and it seemed we were called not to figure Him out, but simply to experience Him. We didn't go to please Him; we went to feed ourselves. . . . And I began to feel loved."

Looking back, did Donna need to leave the Protestantism of her child-hood to become a Roman Catholic? No, in the abstract. Yet, yes, con-cretely, for her. Protestantism, through her child's eyes, had been judgmental, frightening, and guilt-producing. Her adult Catholicism was warm, loving, and liberating. As a young girl she hadn't even known many Catholics, except an uncle and four cousins who lived next door. On the Christmas Eve after she became a Catholic, she went to her first Mass with her uncle. As they received the sacrament of communion together, she felt overwhelmed by love and joined to him in mature faith. She expe-rienced this even though she knew full well that this was his first time at Mass in years. You see, he had matured in his faith too—by going the other way. He had become a Protestant.

Donna Radley's journey took her along paths that she sequentially labeled Presbyterian, Buddhist, Quaker, Episcopalian, and Roman Catholic. However, many people I've known reject all denominational labels and say, "I'm spiritual, but I'm not religious." By this they usually mean that they have a personal vitality and energy deep within them-selves that relates them to the world in an essential way, but they don't think that quality has anything to do with institutions or traditions. They aren't interested in buildings, clergy, denominations, and groups of people who gather in formal worship. They don't want to have much to do with scripture, theology, doctrine, or authoritative teachings and practices.

Theirs tends to be a pick-and-choose approach: say, putting together meditation from one tradition with nature appreciation from another, phi-losophy or psychology from a third tradition, and social activism or com-munity service from a fourth. These people are drawn to teachers who move easily between science and the occult, East and West, theory and practice. They tend to think that their own experience is unique and that they're involved in a search for self that admits of no limits or boundaries.

It is my experience, though, that the spiritual mountain is best climbed along marked trails and paths. Of course, it's possible to make progress by striking out on one's own and bushwhacking through the brambles and undergrowth. That may also seem a lot more exhilarating and much more fun—for a while, anyway. It's also a lot easier that way to get lost, exhausted, and burned out. This can be lonely and frightening if you're by yourself. If you're hiking with others, arguments tend to develop about what to do and where to go next. Frustrations build, nerves fray, and tempers rise. Too often the journey is abandoned entirely.

There are major world religions that have been around for millennia and have had billions of followers. These great religions offer wide paths that have accommodated the individual needs of radically different people. They have included mystics and intellectuals, artists and professional people, social activists and common laborers. They have spoken in a wide variety of ways to people of all ages and all stages of spiritual development. From my perspective, none of these religions is inherently any more "right" than another. None has a lock on "salvation," insight, community, creativity, or meaning. On the other hand, it is through established religions that we encounter much of what is called "spirituality," and spirituality can best be developed along one of their paths. It is to this end that this book takes a look at the major traditions of Christianity, Judaism, Islam, Hinduism, and Buddhism, along with some smaller religions such as the Bahá'í faith.

All of this is not to say that in mountain climbing one might not want to try different paths at different times. Donna found the Buddhist way helpful to her when she had abandoned the Christian. Even on one route, it's helpful to talk to pilgrims on other paths at trail crossings about what they've encountered and seen. Traveling companions on the same path may also have very different personal experiences, depending on who they are and what they're looking for. Nonetheless, there are good reasons trails have been worn on a mountainside: they help the hiker progress without unnecessary obstacles and injury, they lead to points of interest, they facilitate camaraderie among fellow travelers, and the many feet that have gone before have kept the trails maintained for the next generation of venturers.

Another way to look at explorations on the spiritual mountain is to notice common experiences at different altitudes, no matter what path you are on. If you're an alpine hiker, you know there are different bands of vegetation from the base to the summit of a mountain. Topsoil gives way to rock. The air gets noticeably fresher by stages as you ascend. At some point you enter the clouds and start walking in mist. And ultimately, you have to pay more attention to your breathing. Similarly, there are distinct stages of spiritual development that occur at different levels on the spiritual mountain. From my experience in counseling people of different ages from diverse religious backgrounds, I've fashioned a working understanding of how people change throughout their life. My understanding is also grounded in more than twenty years of research in the field of developmental psychology. I've learned especially from James Fowler and Fritz Oser, who have written about stages of faith and stages of relationship to God, respectively.[2]

Although Donna Radley did, there is certainly no need to leave one's childhood denominational home as one passes through different faith stages. Some find it a developmental necessity, while others stay quite happily within their tradition as they grow and mature. Many people, though, become fearful that they're losing their faith entirely as they move from stage to stage. They aren't prepared for how significantly their spiritual outlook and their understanding of God can change. Others, who are spiritually stable—having stayed at a particular stage for an extended period—are made very uncomfortable, sometimes to the point of defensiveness, by what they see as the unsteadiness of their friends and loved ones. For reasons I don't understand, the academic research on stages of faith has not made its way into popular culture. I think it would make a big difference for both groups of people.

Lots of us have heard of the "identity crisis" and the other inner crises, largely emotional, identified by psychologist Erik Erikson. He described stages during the human life cycle from childhood through adolescence and adulthood to old age.[3] Likewise, many know about the work of another psychologist, Jean Piaget, who explained that there are standard stages of cognitive development for all human beings.[4] People learn about the research of psychologist Lawrence Kohlberg on stages of moral development.[5] Why aren't the stages of spiritual development common knowledge along with the stages of emotional, intellectual, and moral development?

There are also individuals who say their education has convinced them of the folly of spirituality and religion. It's all superstitious nonsense, they explain—illogical, senseless, and useless. Often, a closer analysis reveals that these individuals' spiritual understanding hasn't kept pace with their emotional, intellectual, and moral development. They ask how any mature, educated adult could think there's an old man with a beard looking down at us from the sky. Of course, that's not the way most religious adults understand God either. But many of these critics still look at God through the lenses of childhood, when they were last involved with religion. This isn't to say that there aren't mature, conscientious atheists who live fulfilling lives without a belief in God. Of course there are, and I'll speak of atheism in relation to one of the stages later in this chapter. However, some adults are deeply conflicted, their spiritual side having been freeze-dried in childhood or early adolescence. Some of them, otherwise intelligent and capable, are then drawn to the rigidities of authoritarian religious leaders and unequivocal teachings. Involvement in a cult—a psychologically destructive group—becomes a significant risk for them. Others reject religion entirely, without realizing that a spiritually mature person can combine what he or she knows logically, scientifically, and practically with a rich life of faith.

Kevin Gallagher is one of those who rejected religion entirely as he matured intellectually through high school and college. He remembers the first time he formally learned about heaven. He was in the second grade and one of the nuns in his parochial school drew a diagram on the chalkboard. Heaven was at the top of the board and human beings at the bottom. There was a straight line between the two. The nun then drew several jagged up-and-down lines that ascended toward heaven like a stock market index.

"This," she said pointing to the straight line, "is Catholicism. These lines are other denominations. They all get to the top, but tell me, class, which one is *the best?*" Kevin had often wondered about other religions. Why were there so many? Does God rule over all of them? Does everyone in every religion get to go to heaven? Now the answer was in front of him, drawn up on the chalkboard and so easy to see. The class responded in unison. Even Kevin knew the answer.

As the youngest of six children growing up in the late 1950s, Kevin was secure in his Catholic identity. His father had studied to be a priest. His mother attended Mass every day. His oldest sister, Sylvia, had joined a Dominican convent when she was eighteen, and his oldest brother, Dan, had graduated from seminary. No matter where he turned, Catholicism was present in so many forms in his life.

At an early age, Kevin tried to use his religion to his advantage. "Catholics around me believed that not just God but Jesus and the Virgin Mary and the saints all had special powers for us," he said. "It was a panoply of supernatural beings. I remember going to piano lessons and not wanting the nuns to rap my knuckles with a ruler when I made a mistake on the keys. So I would pray to the Virgin Mary to help me make it through because I never practiced. It worked!"

Confession also played a major role in Kevin's childhood. His teachers taught him that sins are "blots" on your soul, and that these blots get darker and darker unless you go to confession. "I remember walking out of confession when I was six or seven thinking that I had a scrubbed soul. I thought it was pretty easy—I could commit a small sin and make up for it the next week by saying a couple of Hail Marys."

Yet as he grew older, Kevin found it harder to deal with the problems he had with the Catholic Church, such as the notion that Catholics are somehow better than those of other religions or denominations. During high school, Kevin began to retreat from his Catholic upbringing. Thanks to the influence of several young Jesuit teachers, he was drawn to other traditions, such as existentialism and Buddhism. He read Albert Camus and Hermann Hesse. The priests also involved him in social issues such as civil rights and environmentalism.

He still attended Mass every week, but only to appease his parents. He stopped praying and going to confession. Kevin began having trouble with the idea of miracles, and he lost the sense that Jesus was literally and uniquely God. Catholicism always had seemed like a package to him— "You buy all the dogma or none." As he put it, "Once there were a couple of loose threads, the whole thing unraveled like a theological double-knit suit." By the time he went to college, he wasn't attending church at all. Although in his rational mind he retained some notion of a divine power or force somewhere out there, it had no connection to institutional religion.

When he married a Jewish woman and they had their first child in the mid-1980s, Kevin decided not to have his baby daughter baptized within the Catholic Church. He couldn't believe that the destiny of his daughter's soul would hinge on this Christian ritual. How can a loving God condemn those who aren't baptized, he asked himself. Then, since he wasn't actively involved in a religious tradition himself, but his wife still felt some connection to Judaism, he had no objection when she wanted to raise their children Jewish.

A few years ago Kevin and his wife, Susan, bought their dream house in Chicago. By then they had two children, a girl and a boy. Susan's only connection to Judaism, it turned out, had been lighting Sabbath candles on Friday night and celebrating Hanukkah along with Christmas. When she decided to start going to the local synagogue with her kids because of its outstanding reputation, Kevin was struck by the sincerity and energy of the congregation, and especially of the young rabbi. As his growing family settled into their new home and this new synagogue, Kevin found himself attending more and more Jewish functions with his wife and children. He found the spiritual community comforting and appealing.

Reading Martin Buber's *I and Thou* built a bridge for him to Judaism from Christianity, existentialism, and Buddhism. A German Jewish theologian who spent the last third of his long life in what became Israel, Buber wrote expansively of Jesus, Nietzsche, and the Buddha while developing his humanistic Jewish philosophy. He saw human existence at its core as being grounded in relationships and felt that we betray ourselves every time we treat others as objects or things. The sacred for Buber was here and now between people, primarily. The door was opened for Kevin to study the tenets of Judaism more closely, and they spoke directly to his heart. Finally, after many years of floating at sea without a spiritual port, Kevin decided to convert to Judaism.

His decision resulted from a number of factors. Above all else, the recent death of his father had put his own mortality into focus. Also, he had just turned forty, and with the new house, a beautiful family, and a job he loved, he realized that he wanted to have a spiritual grounding to make his life complete. Something had been percolating on the right side of his brain without any meaningful expression for the past twenty years. Within his family of origin, his sister Sylvia had left the Dominican convent after ten years and married, but remained a committed Catholic. His brother Dan did not become a Catholic priest after seminary; he also married and then found a spiritual home with his wife in the Methodist church. His middle sister had become a Buddhist after spending a lot of time at the Naropa Institute in Colorado and taking periodic trips to Nepal. Kevin no longer saw religious traditions as boxes with impenetrable walls. His other siblings and his mother remained Catholic, but Kevin did not see himself so much as moving away from Catholicism as moving toward Judaism. For example, this tradition emphasized "living right, choosing well, and understanding the importance of every deed." In fact, that was a confirmation of what the priests had taught him in high school about living out one's faith in action.

After deliberating by himself for several months, Kevin finally told his wife of his decision. She was surprised but supported him. After a year of classes with the rabbi, Kevin had his conversion ceremony at their synagogue.

Like Kevin, most people go through different spiritual phases in life. We need to be open to change because it's virtually inevitable. As I see it from the psychological literature I've read and my own counseling experience, there are six distinct stages of spiritual development possible from birth to death. Most of us don't make it completely to the sixth stage, which is the domain of the mystics, but almost all of us move through at least three or four different types of spiritual understanding during our lifetimes. Some scholars[6] believe that spiritual stages are a human universal that can be described with a fair degree of precision; levels are also accompanied by different, stage-appropriate, perceptions of God or Ultimate Reality. They happen sequentially, and most of us have to reach a certain chronological age before the next stage is a possibility for us. However, there is no guarantee that we will change. That is, many of us remain perfectly happy at a particular stage throughout our lives, while others continue moving on.

FAITH STAGES

Stage	Experience of God
Magic	All-powerful God
Reality	Cause-and-effect God
Dependence	Parent God
Independence	Distant God (or atheism)
Interdependence	Paradoxical God
Unity	All-pervasive God

The first stage, Magic, can occur anytime after the first two years of life and usually concludes by age ten. The world is perceived magically: full of fairies and demons, superheroes and villains. It is hard to separate sleeping and waking states, nightmares and daydreams. Children in this phase speak of God as all-powerful—someone who is responsible for everything that happens internally and externally, usually including both good and ill, from good health to plane crashes. God can create ghosts and destroy dragons. A five-year-old I know described God as having the power to disappear and reappear anywhere in the world in an instant to "do good" and "fight monsters and dinosaurs."

Usually sometime after the age of six, however, children begin to separate fact from fantasy. They enter the stage of Reality, in which they learn to think logically and order their world with "scientific" categories such as number and time and causality. "Is it real?" becomes the refrain. Santa Claus no longer brings presents on Christmas Eve, because kids now realize how impossible it is to visit so many children with so many presents in one night and get down chimneys. In this reality-based spiritual stage, God begins to be imaged more tangibly as a person—in Western culture, often as an old man with a long white beard. The Bible and other scriptures are read concretely and literally, rather than as mere tales. Moral rules begin to have an impact. Now there is a cause-and-effect relationship to God or Ultimate Reality. God can be influenced by good deeds, promises, and vows. People have some degree of free will and choice, which also means some control over good and bad results.

At this stage in his life, Kevin prayed to the Virgin Mary to help him make it through piano lessons without getting his knuckles rapped, and it worked. At six or seven he was convinced that he could easily make up for sins by saying a couple of Hail Marys. Similarly, before she was a teenager, Donna Radley was convinced that she could influence the Director of the Natural Order by saying "please," "thank you," and "I'm sorry."

Yet, before they get to this Reality stage, most children go through a transition period during which they still hold onto fragments of their Magic stage. For example, a child may believe more strongly in Santa Claus when she starts to believe that God has moral rules that reward or punish her for being "naughty or nice." The transition usually takes place after the age of six, when some children are more oriented toward one stage and some toward the other. Therefore, I find it useful to describe childhood as a period of spiritual tension between the stages of Magic and Reality.

Most adolescents, by contrast, struggle with a very different spiritual dynamic: the tension between Dependence and Independence.[7] The need for dependence, which starts around age twelve, stems from a number of unavoidable factors in both psychological and physiological development. The first and most important factor is puberty, which can be a confusing and painful time for girls and boys. Around this age, children also become affected more by peer pressure and are more easily influenced by the leadership of respected older people, such as the priests who introduced Kevin to Buddhism and environmentalism during high school. These factors contribute to the period of dependence, during which time an individual is susceptible not only to cult involvement and brainwashing but also to the development of a meaningful outlook on life.

In the Dependence stage, the young person hungers for a very personal relationship with God—the One who knows the individual and loves him or her unconditionally. God then helps and directs the person as an idealized parent, often replacing the actual parents, whom the adolescent begins to see as flawed. Jesus himself at the age of twelve stays behind in the temple in Jerusalem after the festival of Passover, when his parents head home toward Nazareth. After they realize he's missing and go back to find him, his mother says, "Child, why have you treated us like this? Look, your father and I have been searching for you in great anxiety." Jesus has been sitting among the teachers in the temple, listening to them and asking them questions. He responds, "Why were you searching for me? Did you not know that I must be in my Father's house?" The account in the gospel of Luke says that his parents didn't understand what Jesus was saying to them.[8]

Donna Radley had a different kind of Dependence reaction. When she found a boyfriend and began drinking in high school, she began distancing herself from God as she would from a parent, because she was doing some things she didn't want God to know about. She somehow figured, just the way she might with her own parents, that if she couldn't see God, He couldn't see her.

Another example is a college undergraduate I knew who taught nine-year-olds in a Baptist Sunday school class. Tom considered it very important to "teach by the book." He didn't want to question church doctrine or go beyond the lesson plan for the day. If something came up about sexuality, for example, he would refer it to the minister or say, "Let me get back to you on that next week after I've checked with Reverend Johnson."

Often I heard him say how the minister is "a really great guy." I also observed how intent Tom was on saying and doing the right things in front of Reverend Johnson. Clearly, Tom was in the Dependence stage of his spiritual development, with his minister a central authority for him.

One's spiritual Independence stage, by contrast, can begin as early as age sixteen. Instead of relying on outsiders, social conventions, and spiritual advisors to define one's religious orientation, the late teenager or young adult begins to find spiritual authority within. This is a common time for the individual to say, "I'm spiritual, but I'm not religious," not wanting to be part of any institution or under anyone's control. At the same time, God or Ultimate Reality tends to become more impersonal and distant. Even for those who find in effect that the kingdom of God is within them (Luke 17:21), and in that sense close at hand, the internal God is usually described as *soul* or *spirit*. This form of God is not something with whom one interacts interpersonally in the way one would with a parent. Instead, God lies buried, waiting to be found as an animating force, deep beneath layers of one's personal psychology and various kinds of self-deception.

Some people become functional deists during the Independence stage. Deists feel that a Supreme Being may have created the universe but has long since retreated and left the universe subject to the forces of natural and human laws. Perhaps this God or Force remains present in the form of energy or electricity, but certainly not as a person who intervenes to break natural laws with miracles or as someone who carries on conversations with us. A common analogy for the absent deist God is that of a clockmaker, who constructs and winds up the clock but lets it run on its own. Thomas Jefferson and Voltaire were deists throughout most of their lives.

Some people in the Independence stage demythologize religious symbols, rituals, and stories. They search for historical background, literary function, and conceptual meaning. That also means that sacred power is muted or lost. Instead of experiencing the holy directly, these people have trouble getting beyond critical examination of the rituals, symbols, and myths that mediate the sacred. Harvard Divinity School professor Harvey Cox once described a demythologizing experience he had. A college friend whispered to him as he was about to receive the body and blood of Jesus through the Communion bread and wine at a Christmas Eve service, "That's just a primitive totemic ritual, you know. Almost all premodern religious and tribal groups have them. They are ceremonies where worshipers bind themselves together and to the power of the sacred by a cannibalistic act of ingesting the *mana* of a dead god." Cox says Communion was forever changed for him after that.[9]

By the time he went to college, Kevin had apparently reached the Independence stage. He no longer believed in miracles, and he had lost the sense of God as a person—in particular, of God in the person of Jesus. Instead, he had an impersonal notion of a divine power or force at some considerable distance from himself. In his mind that force had nothing to do with institutional religion, and he stopped going to church. Similarly, Donna Radley's move to Buddhism and Quakerism in her thirties rings of Independence. There was no judgmental God for her anymore, and "presence" was enough of a definition of the divine. Even the positive experience of the music, incense, and ritual of the Episcopal church she started attending was a far cry from the strict parent God who disapproved of so much of her life.

Since many adults never reach the Independence stage, and for a large number it does not emerge until the mid-thirties or forties, the tension between Dependence and Independence can cause considerable stress and strain in social and religious settings. A Protestant I know, whom I believe is at the Independence stage, explains that he no longer feels comfortable or welcome at most Christian services. He sees Jesus as a great historical teacher and exemplar, but not as identical with God and not as his personal Lord and Savior. When he expresses these thoughts, he gets in arguments and feels excluded by many other Christians. He finds institutional religion rigid and judgmental, pietistic and moralistic. Rejecting dogma and doctrine, he says, "There's a river of spirit deep within each of us that can't be named, that's completely nondenominational, and that doesn't require any labels like 'God' and 'Jesus.' There's no one right way to find that river and get into its flow."

I would not be surprised if this same Protestant, years from now, opens up to his religion and accepts much of the dogma and doctrine of his once-rejected faith. He would then be categorized in the next stage of faith development, which is usually reserved for people well into their adult life. The *Interdependence* stage has been called a "second naivete"[10] because it is a time when religious symbols become sacred once again and are found to have new power. As the name suggests, this stage of Interdependence is the reconciliation of the previous stages of Dependence and Independence. People at this spiritual level live in a dialectical yin-and-yang world, in which they are able to tolerate ambiguity and seeming contradiction and enjoy complexity. God or Ultimate Reality is experienced paradoxically. For example, many people at this stage can pray to God the person, even though they intellectually understand the divine as an impersonal force in the universe. Instead of taking an either-or approach to life, people at the Interdependence stage are able to see all sides of an issue at the same time. As with the onion-peeling effect of discovering symbolic depth in great literature, adults at the Interdependence stage are able to read scripture simultaneously at the literal, allegorical, historical, conceptual, poetic, and inspirational levels.

Religiously, people at the Interdependence stage are open to dialogue between different traditions because they understand that truth is multidimensional. Any particular religious symbol, myth, or ritual is necessarily limited and incomplete, bound by the follower's personal experiences. This is not a purely relativistic approach, however, as it is in the

Independence stage. People in the Interdependence stage know the value of picking a particular path.

Kevin as he converted is a good example of someone at this stage, because he understood that there was more than one way to get up the mountain, but he chose Judaism as his path. Also, those in the Interdependence stage do not demythologize religion, because critical analysis is tempered by spiritual awareness. For example, someone at this level recognizes that Communion, on the surface, is a totemic ritual but still feels the sacred meaning of the Eucharist. Donna Radley was at this stage when she took the Eucharist with her uncle at the Christmas Eve Mass.

Psychologist James Fowler is one of the leading theorists of spiritual development. In his seminal 1981 book, *Stages of Faith*, he describes a seventy-eight-year-old woman named "Miss T"[11] who had reached the stage I call Interdependence some twenty years earlier. She was a Quaker but was profoundly influenced by the Hindu teacher Krishnamurti and the psychologist Carl Jung. Miss T had grown up as a Unitarian Christian and described her confirmation at age twelve as "a religious experience." In college she became a pacifist and left the Unitarian church altogether after her minister tried to "correct" her opposition to war. After working in the theater for thirty years and suffering an acute midlife crisis, she rediscovered Christianity as a Quaker in her fifties. She became involved in camp work, especially in recruiting inner-city children of color and promoting positive interracial relations. She described her understanding of Ultimate Reality in several ways: as God, Jesus, the Light Within, Cosmic Flow, Love, and simply Reality. However, she also said, "It doesn't matter what you call it. It is there. And what you learn directly from that source will not tie you up in creeds."

Miss T sounds like she may be edging toward the final spiritual level, populated by the mystics. Sometimes they emerge in their thirties, but usually not until ripe old age. While people at the Interdependence stage recognize partial truths and their limitations, people at the stage of Unity feel unconditionally related to the Ultimate. In other words, they have a direct awareness of the oneness of all existence. I have had such experiences, but they have happened rarely and lasted only a few minutes. People at the Unity stage have these kinds of experience much more often, and these experiences continually inform the rest of their understanding.

Yin and yang and all other forms of paradox now disappear into undivided unity. People at this stage speak of God in an all-pervasive sense: God is felt to be in everything, and everything seems to exist in God. As a result, they possess a universalizing compassion and a vision of universal community beyond all forms of tribalism.

Personal security also ceases to be a concern at the stage of Unity, and virtually all forms of ego attachment disappear. One is now ready for deep relationships with individuals at any of the other faith stages and from any other religious tradition. These mystically aware people can be seen to be subversive of structures and organizations (including institutional religion). As a result they can become targets of misunderstanding and conflict. Some have died at the hands of others, such as Mohandas Gandhi, who was assassinated by a fellow Hindu for his openness to Muslims. Often these figures are more revered and respected after they are dead. Two modern examples of those revered well before their death are Mother Teresa, a Catholic, and the fourteenth Dalai Lama, a Buddhist.

When I teach the stages of spiritual development at Tufts University, students have a lot of questions. They often resent the notion that their own particular experience can be categorized into six universal stages. As Jim put it in one class, "The journey is a personal, creative, and undefined one that cannot be outlined by attempted clinical or scientific research." Evan added, "Religion isn't an instinct, like other theories we deal with. Each individual has his or her own special way of dealing with it, regardless of whether they are two people on opposite sides of the world, or identical twins."

Mary responded, "But I could relate to many of the stages described. With some stages that I feel I have not reached yet, I recognize friends and acquaintances who have, and so I understand more where they lead." Joan added: "I was so glad to be able to see myself through the stages. For example, going from Magic to Reality, I remember being about nine or ten. I knew, inside me, that there was no such thing as Santa Claus. I hoped with all myself that he existed, and so I wrote one last Christmas Eve letter, hoping he would respond and somehow this 'reality' would be wrong. My mother wrote me back. It was a disappointing Christmas."

By the end of the discussion, Jim had relented: "I can see that I have experienced bits of each of the stages, and right now I would probably place myself in the Independence stage. I do also remember a time during junior high and my first year of high school when I was relatively 'religious' and felt that God/Jesus was like an idealized parent, always protecting me."

Tony had a different critique: "This discussion excites in me, as I'm sure it does in many of us, an immediate self-reflection and categorization of myself. But I don't think this is beneficial in and of itself, and we should be warned against it. I think stage theory can be very dangerous, especially to people who are unsure of their path and only have a cursory knowledge of it." Jane elaborated on Tony's point: "This may not only be detrimental and possibly discouraging to individuals in terms of their own growth, but it misses the real point of spiritual development. It makes the reader become goal-oriented and it may undermine the importance of nurturing the spirit at whatever stage it happens to be, rather than looking further along the path."

In fact, Roger wondered why, once he was aware of "the strange, but interesting, idea" of religious development within himself, he shouldn't "be able to sort of speed up the process and skip ahead." As he put it, "After all, if I can recognize where I am and know where I am going, why shouldn't I be able to just go?" He also felt that stage theory is judgmental, implying that later stages are better than earlier ones and that some people are more religiously developed than others.

A professor of psychology and ordained Episcopal deacon, who was visiting the class, pointed out how religion is often perceived through nondevelopmental lenses, so that many people speak of religion as if it were something one either "gets" or "doesn't get"—as if it were some one thing to be fully embraced or rejected. The stage approach, by contrast, allows us to see religion quite differently—"as a process rather than a product, as something continuously changing and hopefully developing." She also explained that stage theory presents the opportunity to discover similarities among various religious traditions and among various spiritual lives. "Making such discoveries is no easy achievement, for what strikes us first are differences between religions, not similarities." The stages, then, help prevent judgmentalism, by pointing to "deep-structure similarities between the spiritual paths taken by people from various religious traditions."

WHAT STAGE ARE YOU IN?

A Faith Stage Checklist

Stage One (Magic)

1. Is your world full of spirits and demons?
2. Are fairy tales your favorite kind of literature?
3. Do you think God makes everything happen, for good and bad?

Stage Two (Reality)

1. Do you spend a lot of time trying to determine what's real and what's not?
2. Are scriptures true in a concrete and literal sense, rather than being stories and maxims that may or may not be real?

3. Do you feel you can influence God's actions by being good?

Stage Three (Dependence)

1. Do you have a very important peer group or leader who is primarily responsible for shaping your faith?
2. Is it important to you to understand and follow religious doctrine and moral rules?
3. Is your main image of God that of a perfect parent?

Stage Four (Independence)

1. Is your spiritual life unique and personal?
2. Do you often find yourself wanting to demystify scripture?
3. Do you think of God or Ultimate Reality primarily as an impersonal force or spirit (or as nonexistent)?

Stage Five (Interdependence)

1. Do you find a spiritual community important to you at the same time that you maintain your own distinctive faith?
2. Do you experience spiritual power in religious symbols and myths that you can also analyze objectively?
3. Do you conceive of God or Ultimate Reality both as a person and as an impersonal force?

Stage Six (Unity)

1. Do you sense yourself in community with religiously committed people of any and all traditions?
2. Is your consciousness ego-free and beyond paradox and ambiguity?
3. Do you often feel that God or divine spirit is in everything and that everything exists in God or divine spirit?

It is important to explore fully the place where you find yourself on the spiritual mountain, rather than trying to look behind or ahead, up or down the slope. Just as F. Scott Fitzgerald's novel *The Great Gatsby* will be experienced very differently in high school at sixteen, at business school at twenty-six, and on the beach in one's thirties or forties, so a religious tradition will be encountered quite distinctly at different ages. There should be no judgment involved, because one will necessarily have different kinds of engagement with *The Great Gatsby* or Buddhism, say, at different times in one's life.

The romantic relationship of Gatsby and Daisy may resonate the most for a teenager, the vision of the American Dream for a business student, and discovering Gatsby's character as visionary or crook for the beach reader. None is less valid as a point of concentration than the other. One can't go back from one's forties to recapture the feelings of adolescent romanticism any more than a teenager can leap forward to understand how a business graduate student contextualizes the American Dream or how one discerns character after four decades of life experience. One must savor each era in one's life fully. How unfortunate it would be not to appreciate the distinctive gifts of each age and the particular perspective each offers. And how unfair and disrespectful it is to judge one period from the viewpoint of another.

Kevin's conversion to Judaism looked a lot different to his married Methodist brother Dan in his forties than it would have to his celibate Catholic seminarian brother Dan in his twenties. His Buddhist sister of thirty-five was fascinated—also reacting differently from the way the same sister would have when they were attending parochial school together. Kevin's brothers and sisters who remained Catholic turned out to be curious, rather than condemning, about what had happened. His mother had the most trouble, seeing the conversion as a personal rejection of her. Yet her own relationship to Catholicism had also altered significantly from her childhood days. It's obvious that their reactions would be different at different stages of their lives, and in the same way, our reactions to our own religion will evolve as we mature.

Open yourself to change as you face the spiritual mountain. You may soon find yourself in another stage of your life—one that you'd never imagined. As a result, God will start looking quite different to you; religious people will, too. Then the next step is to open your mind and begin thinking differently about religion itself. You'll be amazed by how fascinating it will be when approached afresh.

Thinking

~~~⑶⑵~~~

I've long been a member of a monthly reading group that calls itself The Jung Club of Boston. Of course our little group of inquiring agnostics, dubious Christians, and budding Buddhists knows that the title we've given ourselves is ridiculously presumptuous. We're friends without particular expertise who happened to come together over twenty years ago because we were fascinated by the writings of psychologist Carl Jung (1875–1961). Jung has intrigued a lot of people in the twentieth century, from anthropologists and artists on through the rest of the alphabet to zealots of many stripes. I recommend his writings as a starting point for people wondering if they really want to begin a religious search.

Jung is a master at opening closed minds. When the Jung Club first met, I remember us devouring the hardback version of his 1964 book, *Man and His Symbols*, as if we were eating candy. It was hard to get to the text, in fact, because the pictures and illustrations were so compelling. Through them we traveled the world, from prehistory to modern life on all continents, across every imaginable religious tradition, and deep into the human psyche. Jung is known for his psychological studies of religious "archetypes," which he claimed are found in all people, cultures, and times. For example, he and one of his students, Joseph Campbell, studied the hero archetype extensively and discovered a universal form of this archetype represented as much by the Osiris-Horus myth of ancient Egypt as by the story of the Christian Jesus.

Another of Jung's students, Mircea Eliade (for thirty years a historian of religion at the University of Chicago, until his death in 1986) wrote extensively of the *axis mundi* image as a universal. Every culture has had a sacred place that it considers to be the center of the world. For example, sacred mountains like Mount Meru for Hindus and Golgotha for Christians are places where earth and heaven are said to meet and through which the axis of the world (*axis mundi*) is believed to pass. This single world center archetype has many local variants.[1]

I once had the opportunity to visit a widely revered *axis mundi*, and it was definitely a mind-opening experience. The place was Jebel Musa (the Mountain of Moses) in the Sinai Desert. Tradition holds that this is Mount Sinai, the great mountain where Moses received the Ten Commandments directly from God around 1300 B.C.[2] Three religious traditions speak of it with awe: Judaism, Christianity, and Islam. I reached it after several days of hot, gritty travel from Israel in a huge, open-sided, four-wheel-drive Mercedes truck, along with a couple dozen other pilgrims. We spent our nights in sleeping bags on the sand in what we called "The Million-Star Hotel." Without lights and pollution, the heavens came down to earth and gently kissed our faces. The Milky Way was a broad white road leading out of the galaxy.

During the day we traveled from oasis to oasis, mesmerized by the crisp, clean edges of sand drifts until a few date palms came into view across the vast expanses. Eventually we began to look to the hills—sandstone, limestone, and finally, red granite—thrusting up from the desert floor. The only other signs of life were proud camels carrying turbaned men through the relentless heat and bejeweled Bedouin women shepherding their flocks of goats, their faces hidden behind black.

Mount Sinai lies within a rugged region in the southern part of the desert peninsula that is surrounded by the Red Sea. The sun was setting as our four-wheeled behemoth lumbered to a stop at its base. We bedded down in the broad Plain of Raha, where the children of Israel are said to have camped, awaiting Moses' return from the heights and fashioning a golden calf to while away the time.

The next morning we awakened before 3:00 A.M. to begin climbing before the desert sun could wilt and wither our fragile "civilized" bodies. The way we chose was a wide path on the lower part of the mountain, narrowing to what seemed to be a stairway to heaven higher up. More than three thousand steps had been cut into the rock by monks centuries ago. Breathing heavily and drenched with perspiration, we finally made it to an arch of stone at the top of the steps. The landscape by now looked like the moon, not the earth. The steepest part of the climb to the 7,455-foot summit still lay ahead over bare rock. When we made it, we were greeted by a small chapel, perched at the highest possible point.

The rising sun accentuated the deep fissures and rifts in the surrounding mountains. All was empty red wilderness as far as the eye could see. We stood at the top of the world, imagining what Moses must have felt here when "the glory of the Lord was like devouring fire on the top of the mount."[3] Even the utterly unreligious among us spoke only in whispers as the rest sat scattered about in stunned silence. I don't think any of us doubted for that moment that we were on the axis of the world.

When we made it back down to the bottom we began to realize what a multireligious context we were in. Jung's broad view was palpably present. Many in the group were Jews for whom Mount Sinai was central to self-understanding. For not only the Ten Commandments but also the Torah—the first five books of the Bible, with hundreds of rules that were to govern the Jewish community—is said to have been given to Moses at Sinai. From the Jewish perspective, here also God made his covenant with all Jews through Moses: If the laws of the Torah were obeyed, blessings would follow for the Jews as a people. If they were broken, the people as a whole would suffer.[4] Modern Jews who keep a kosher diet and observe holidays like Passover and Yom Kippur are said to be honoring elements of this covenant, which is over three thousand years old.

Others of us who came panting off Mount Sinai were Christians. We found one of the oldest surviving monasteries in the world nestled at the bottom of the mountain. The Eastern Orthodox monks who live there let us in for a visit. They explained that St. Catherine's monastery had been built on the orders of the Emperor Justinian in 530 A.D. Its chapel is constructed around the reputed burning bush, where Moses on his first visit to Sinai was called by God to lead the exodus of Jews out of slavery in Egypt. How amazed we were to come in out of the desert sun into a richly ornate church, scented with incense, lit by a firmament of silver and gold chandeliers, and decorated with floor-to-ceiling mosaics and white icon-adorned granite columns extending the length of the sanctuary. Christian pilgrims started coming to the *axis mundi* that is Mount Sinai in the early centuries of the church and have been here ever since.

Christianity and Judaism are not the only religions that recognize what happened on Mount Sinai. Next to the church, inside the walled compound, we found a mosque. It was erected in the eleventh century, since which time the whole area surrounding Mount Sinai has been Islamic (or Muslim).[5] Mount Sinai is specifically referenced in the Qur'an (or Koran), the Muslim scriptures, written down in the seventh century A.D.[6] Moses is one of the great prophets for Islam as well as for Judaism and Christianity. The story of his receiving the Book from God on the top of the mountain while the people at the bottom fashioned a golden calf to worship is told and retold in the Qur'an.[7]

What's unique about Moses in the Qur'an, though, in comparison to his treatment in the Hebrew Scriptures, or Old Testament, and the Christian New Testament, is that he received only a preliminary and partial understanding of God's law at Sinai. According to the Qur'an, Muhammad (570–632 A.D.) is the seal of the prophets, and only his revelation is complete and final. Muslim law alone, the *shari'ah*, grounded in the Qur'an, is authoritative. The Qur'an also recognizes Jesus as a prophet—one who came with the holy spirit and a message of love rather than the law—yet he too is a teacher preliminary to Muhammad and certainly not identical with God.[8]

As we left Mount Sinai and rumbled back across the desert's central plateau toward Israel, we began finding millennia-old rock drawings left by other pilgrims to the holy mountain. How many millions of journeys have been lost in the sands of time? And how many seekers have been lost all over the world because they couldn't find the equivalent of a Mount Sinai to begin their spiritual climb?

Consider Jung's example. He grew up in Switzerland. In his autobiography he tells of a lovely summer evening in the late 1870s when he was around four years old, in what I would call the Magic stage of spiritual development. An aunt said to him, "Now I'm going to show you something," and she took him outside to show him the chain of the Alps on the far horizon, bathed in glowing sunset reds. The mountains could be seen very clearly that evening; it was the first time he consciously saw the Alps.

Jung was excited to learn that the next day the village children would be going on a school outing to a panoramic viewing point called the Uetliberg on the outskirts of Zurich, close to the range he was seeing. He wanted so much to go and was deeply disappointed when told that he was too young for the trip. There was nothing he could do about it, but the incident took on symbolic importance: "From then on the Uetliberg and Zurich became an unattainable land of dreams, near to the glowing, snow-covered mountains."[9] They held a magic for him that he couldn't touch.

Jung grew up tall, broad-shouldered, and strong.[10] When he was fourteen and probably almost at the end of the second stage of spiritual development, the Reality stage, he finally got his chance: magic became reality. His minister father took him to a mile-high mountain called the Rigi near Lake Lucerne. A cog railroad ran up it, and his father pressed a ticket into his hand, saying, "You can ride up to the peak alone. I'll stay here, it's too expensive for the two of us." Jung writes, "I was speechless with joy. Here I was at the foot of this mighty mountain, higher than any I had ever seen, and quite close to the fiery peaks of my faraway childhood. . . . With a tremendous puffing, the wonderful locomotive shook and rattled me up to the dizzy heights where ever-new abysses and panoramas opened out before my gaze, until at last I stood on the peak in the strange thin air, looking into unimaginable distances."

There he said to himself, "Yes, this is it, my world, the real world, the secret, where there are no teachers, no schools, no unanswered questions, where one can *be* without having to ask anything." His mind was wide open. He explains that he kept carefully to the paths, though. There were tremendous precipices all around, and his father had warned him of the risks of falling. Most important, however, it was a deeply spiritual experience: "It was all very solemn, and I felt one had to be polite and silent up here, for one was in God's world. Here it was physically present. This was the best and most precious gift my father had ever given me."

The impression of this experience stayed with Jung for the rest of his life: "[T]his image rose up whenever I was wearied from overwork and sought a point of rest. In real life I have promised myself this splendor again and again, but I have never kept my promise."[11]

The institutional church, however, was another matter. His father was not the only Protestant parson in his family. So were two paternal uncles and six relatives on his mother's side![12] Within a year after his journey up the Rigi, after years of "torment" in the Christian faith in which he grew up, Jung had left the church. Just as I think his private moments on the Rigi may resonate with those who have found a spiritual opening in the mountains, so his devastating description of his First (and last) Communion may be a reminder of the ways our childhood faith can fail us.[13]

His father personally gave him instruction for the confirmation of his faith (of which Jung said, "It bored me to death"). Jung made every effort to believe and prepared himself especially carefully for the sacrament of Communion, on which his father seemed to place a very high value. He was sure that some great mystery must lie behind it, although at first he just thought of it as a memorial meal, "a kind of anniversary celebration for Lord Jesus." He learned instead that he should eat the Communion bread as if it were Jesus' flesh and drink the wine as if it were his blood, and in this special way incorporate Jesus into himself.

On the appointed day for the First Communion, Jung was picked up at his home by a member of the church committee who had been appointed godfather to him, as was customary. This nice old man was a wheelwright in whose workshop Jung had often been. When he arrived at the church, the altar was covered by a white cloth. On it were large trays filled with small pieces of bread and a pewter cup of wine. He noticed that the bread came from the local baker, whose goods were generally of poor quality. He was also familiar with the tavern from which the wine had come.

His father conducted the service in his black ministerial robes, giving the bread and wine first to all the old men present. "All were stiff, solemn, and, it seemed to me, uninterested. I looked on in suspense, but could not see or guess whether anything unusual was going on inside the old men." Then his turn came to take the body and blood of Christ: "I ate the bread; it tasted flat, as I had expected. The wine, of which I took only the smallest sip, was thin and rather sour, plainly not of the best." His expectant mind was disappointed. "Then came the final prayer, and the people went out, neither depressed nor illumined with joy, but with faces that said, 'So that's that.'"

As he walked home with his father after the service, even though the reality of the experience had been disappointing, Jung himself felt a certain elation. He felt that he had been accepted into the society of adults. And the Sunday dinner that day was an unusually good one. Only gradually, over several days, did he realize how profoundly disillusioned he was: "I had reached the pinnacle of religious initiation, had expected something—I knew not what—to happen, and nothing at all had happened. I knew that God could do stupendous things to me, things of fire and unearthly light; but this ceremony contained no trace of God—not for me, at any rate. To be sure, there had been talk about Him, but it had all amounted to no more than words."

Jung goes on to explain, "I had observed no sign of 'communion,' of 'union, becoming one with'. . . With whom? With Jesus? Yet he was only a man who had died 1860 years ago. Why should a person become one with him? He was called the 'Son of God'—a demigod, therefore, like the Greek heroes: how then could an ordinary person become one with him? This was called the 'Christian religion,' but none of it had anything to do with God as I had experienced Him. . . . [W]hat was the purpose of this wretched memorial service with the flat bread and the sour wine? Slowly I came to understand that this communion had been a fatal experience for me. It had proved hollow; more than that, it had proved to be a total loss. I knew that I would never again be able to participate in this ceremony. 'Why, that is not religion at all,' I thought. 'It is an absence of God; the church is a place I should not go to.'"

Jung wondered if the failure of Communion to affect him was his own fault. Yet as he thought about it, he realized that he had prepared in all earnestness. He had hoped for an experience of grace and illumination, perhaps like what he had known in the Alps. Nothing had happened, though. He felt God had been absent. "For God's sake I now found myself cut off from the Church and from my father's and everybody else's faith. Insofar as they all represented the Christian religion, I was an outsider." Dependence on trusted adults had not worked, and Jung was thrown headlong into spiritual Independence.

Jung was far from an outsider to religion in general, though. He always knew there was a mountain to climb, figuratively as well as literally. He remained open; he maintained an active, inquiring mind about religious traditions all over the world. There are a couple of reasons Jung's ideas are particularly helpful to people at the beginning of a religious search. First of all, as he opens his mind, all the religions of the world come together in his view. He sees fundamental connections among them and moves easily between traditions in his explanations and theorizing. For people not wanting to commit themselves to a religious path without knowing their options, he provides a wonderful introduction. Second, in reading Jung one can finesse the question of whether there is really a God at all. He often seems ambivalent about whether archetypes are merely psychological constructs within the human mind or expressions of a divine reality transcending and deep within each of us. He provides a good entree into spirituality, then, for people who no longer find meaning in their childhood faith or who don't have a religious background at all. You don't have to commit to any reality besides that of the human psyche to engage with Jung.

Clara Boatman is a member of our Jung group who has found religion without God, but with a very active interest in the human psyche. She's become a Buddhist. It all began in South America, where she grew up surrounded by Protestant Christian missionaries. Although her parents were not particularly religious, Clara was touched and troubled by the stories she'd heard of North Americans being martyred as they tried to convert

native peoples in Colombia. In eighth grade she began consciously inviting Jesus into her heart and reading the New Testament from cover to
cover. She prayed and prayed, tried and tried, but nothing happened.
Jesus didn't come. She began feeling like a terrible failure, and she wondered if something was deeply wrong with her.

Another influence working on Clara during her childhood was Mrs.
Taylor, a friend of her mother's who had grown up in Thailand and knew
about Eastern religious traditions. She taught yoga, and her children
spoke of having visions and out-of-body experiences. Clara especially
remembers reading one of Mrs. Taylor's yoga texts; it featured a girl who
looked just like Clara in a sitting posture for meditation called "the pose of
the hero." Since most of Clara's childhood books depicted girls being res-
cued by princes and white knights, she appreciated this new, self-assured
image of femininity. By high school she was practicing yoga regularly,
and by the time she was in college in Texas she was virtually living on the
fourth floor of the library among the books on Hinduism and Buddhism,
while also assiduously pursuing esoteric Eastern practices like walking
through walls (that didn't work any better than opening her heart to
Jesus, though).

In her adolescent years Clara was searching for authentic religious
experiences, rather than simply reading words. She wanted to recognize
something real happening to her in her body and mind as a result of her
spiritual practices. Presumably in transition from the Reality stage to the
Dependence stage of faith development, Clara also desperately wanted to
find a teacher in whom she could believe. When a Hindu holy man visited
her college campus, she carefully prepared a necklace of small items from
her childhood and presented it to the guru in return for a blessing in front
of hundreds of people in the room. He refused it, looked disgusted, and
swatted her on the head with a peacock feather. Publicly humiliated, she
later found solace in a charismatic professor who taught myth and symbol

in the visual arts. He was a Buddhist who used to attend long silent retreats. After returning from one lasting two weeks, he projected two slides side by side on the screen in front of the class and asked, "What do these two men have in common?" The starving Buddha (when he was an ascetic, eating only one grain of rice a day) was pictured next to the nineteenth-century Hindu saint Ramakrishna, both sitting cross-legged in meditation. After a long silence greeted his question, he exclaimed, "They are trying to live right!" and stalked out of the room, literally leaving the class in the dark.

The words "trying to live right" resonated deeply in Clara and deepened her commitment to the Buddhist and Hindu traditions. Yet the critical experience for her didn't come until after college during a two-week Buddhist retreat in California. She was very grateful when her teachers there encouraged her simply to be herself and to follow her own experience. Through detailed attention to her own body sensations and to her breath during spiritual exercises, she began to undergo a number of altered-state experiences. For example, time would stop and become contained entirely within the present moment. When it started up again, she felt as if she were not the same person she had been minutes before. Scales seemed to be falling from her eyes and ears—colors becoming more and more vivid, sounds (even of silence) reverberating deep within her. Eventually it felt as if she were in a state of permanent exultation.

She wasn't. The two weeks ended and the intensity faded. In one sense she spent the next decade trying to recover the initial bliss of that two-week retreat. Yet, in another sense she felt much more open and capable of living fully in the present moment. She kept speaking of "reality as it is" and appreciating how all spiritual truth seemed to be contained in the here and now, rather than in some other world to come. She found a job writing for a newspaper for the next six years, but she kept using her vacations for Buddhist retreats. Then, after two years in graduate school, Clara began a successful career as a fiction writer. Meanwhile, she weathered misfortunes like her mother's fatal battle with cancer, major surgery of her own, and a failed love relationship. Daily meditation and routine retreats centered her life and gave her strength.

In her early thirties, after editing the writings of a Burmese master, Clara received a visa to go to Burma and ended up spending half a year in a Buddhist monastery. At long last she felt the kind of exultation she had known in California. She shaved her head and took her vows to become a Buddhist nun. The practice was rigorous and demanding, but to her it was also fun—of a very deep sort. She might never have left if she had not found herself in the midst of a revolution. Troop truck movement and machine-gun fire became the regular din outside the monastery walls. As a resident Westerner she was putting monks and nuns around her at risk, so she decided she needed to leave the country.

When she fled Burma, though, she still wanted more: "Truth or bust," as she put it. Writing short stories that ultimately won her national awards back home, she headed straight for the place where the Buddha is said to have become enlightened—under the *bodhi* tree in Bodh Gaya, India. After meditating there every day for two weeks, she found herself with a Hindu teacher who radically redirected her life so that she could come home again. In an audience with this master, named Prakash-ji, he asked her, "What exactly have you figured out so far?" She stammered a bit, and finally said, "Nothing." She felt embarrassed and exposed as a fraud. "Good!" he responded. "Good—stay there."

Clara stayed with him for six weeks, trying to figure out what he meant, but knowing somehow that she had been deeply freed. Her mind had been opened again. She realized that her life's pursuit of perfection was the problem. He kept telling her to stop thinking that there's somewhere to go: "There is no 'there' there." So she crawled back down her ladder and began life on earth. She became "ordinary" again. She returned to the United States. She completed her first book and got it published.

Yet she didn't stop being a Buddhist. In fact, now she realized that she understood being Buddhist better than ever. Life became an adventure. Everything always felt new. Meanwhile, the evidence for suffering being a result of ego attachment seemed compelling, going back to her feeling publicly humiliated by the guru at college. Her personal realization of freedom meant that there were no more masters to whom she was beholden. On a later trip to Nepal she was able to help a woman suing a lama, a Tibetan Buddhist teacher, who had become corrupt, even as she was criticized for her actions by Buddhist authorities. She continued a daily practice of meditation and began leading retreats herself. Her writing became better than ever.

Clara began telling others that she was no longer striving to get to the top of the spiritual mountain, but instead trying to enjoy the journey, minute by minute ("The path is the goal"). She was amazed that life could be so fascinating and new all the time, while also so familiar and so often painful. Her religious Independence then began merging with a need for community to help her reflect upon and cultivate her awareness. She came to appreciate organizations and institutions that preserved Buddhist scriptures and practices. She led retreats but also participated regularly in those led by others. She came to see a continuum between teachers and students, rather than projecting onto others some kind of ultimate awareness and insight into life's mysteries. She now wanted teachers who could admit their flaws—who could serve as guides to specific techniques and perceptions while realizing that there were others of equal value to which they did not have access.

Part of Clara's new religious Interdependence was a respectful give-and-take with people of other traditions. When a New York psychiatrist invited her to teach with him, she refrained from using traditional Buddhist terms about enlightenment in those sessions and grappled with emotions like anger and anxiety, asking what it takes to live a good human life. She insisted that the capacity for wisdom is not confined to special people at the top of the spiritual mountain, and certainly not just to Buddhists. Everyone is capable of flashes of genuine insight, especially when they speak from the heart.

She taught with Christians too, explaining that since her childhood she had remained Christian in many ways. For example, her ethics were still grounded in the Golden Rule propounded by Jesus: "Do unto others as you would have them do unto you." She found the question "What would Jesus do?" useful in many difficult situations; it provided a way to get beyond one's own ego and guide oneself by something transcending the self. God language came to have a place for her, too. Since connection with reality was the touchstone of her Buddhist understanding, perhaps God was simply a name for reality. In any case, religious arguments came to seem like a total waste of time, since life is always bigger than we think and there's so much to learn from others if we'll only listen.

Clara learned a lot by growing up in several countries in South America, moving to the United States, and then traveling through Burma, India, Nepal, and other parts of Asia. Similarly, Jung's insights about religious archetypes came from study and experience all over the world. Travel helps tremendously in opening your mind, if you're able to do it. Personally, I was lucky enough to do so in my first sabbatical year.

For me, thirty started off as a cruel year. "Don't trust anyone over thirty," we used to say in college. My thirtieth birthday was the low point of my life. Divorced two weeks before. Spiritually fragmented in my work as a church-sponsored poverty lawyer in Boston. Suffering from an ulcer. My existence in tatters. What to do?

My birthday often falls during Thanksgiving week, and my thirtieth was no exception. Throughout my life the Thanksgiving season has been a time of transition. There's something about knowing the harvest's gathered or watching leafless trees merging into bleak gray skies that sets my imagination free. I can remake myself! *Why not take a year off and travel?*

I dared to imagine one morning on the subway. (*Well, there are actually a lot of reasons why not . . . Repress them.*) *Why not head west around the globe until I return, hopefully a changed person?* It would be a spiritual odyssey. I had studied comparative religion in divinity school and had made many contacts from my participation in major international religious conferences. I would live in temples, shrines, ashrams, religious communities of all kinds—wherever they would take me. It could be done on a shoestring—the simpler the better.

So, that same evening I bought a map of the world on the way home from work. I made a blazing fire in my fireplace and spread the world out on the floor of my lonely apartment. In my wildest dreams, where would I like to go? My red marker skimmed across the United States and out into the Pacific. *Does the equivalent of Gauguin's Tahiti still exist?* I wondered: the simple life, I thought, of women in grass skirts and men in loincloths, savoring fresh fish and coconut milk on white sand beaches under green palm trees. My marker sailed on across Micronesia to Bali, in the midst of the Indonesian archipelago. I'd heard that this Hindu island contained exquisite beauty—natural, human, and spiritual.

From there, where? How about China, which Nixon had just opened up to Americans a few years before? The home of Confucianism and Taoism, and of imported Buddhism and Marxism. I'd spent my childhood trying to dig holes in my backyard to get there. Finally, this was my chance. Also nearby was Japan, which had been locked in mortal combat with my father several years before I was born. As a baby boomer, I'd heard years of war stories from this PT boat captain. His brother, a marine flyer, had been shot down over Guadalcanal. I now bore my dead uncle's nickname, Scotty. And I was fascinated by Zen.

My red pen kept moving. What could be more romantic than taking the Trans-Siberian railroad all the way across Russia, from the Pacific to the Baltic Sea? Then there were Eastern European countries I'd never visited, like Hungary and Romania. What about the Middle East as the spiritual center of three great world religions? (My pen was doubling back now.) And Africa? How many times had I dreamed of the animal kingdom—of lions and tigers, elephants and giraffes, zebras and antelope? I had friends in Europe—in Odysseus's Greek Isles and Van Gogh's Holland. (The marker lines were zigging and zagging south and north now.)

From the eastern shores of the Atlantic I could look back at America now. It's a big hemisphere over there, and I'd never been to half of it: Central and South America. Now was the time. I'd heard of a great Spanish language school in Guatemala, and I had church contacts in Panama. Countries like Colombia, Ecuador, and Peru didn't seem that far away. Then a straight line north to Boston went right through that neme- sis nation nipping at our southern coast, Cuba. My passport had always excluded travel there. Was it still forbidden fruit?

I fell back against my apartment couch, head reeling and heart racing. Whew! What a wild dream. What a far-fetched adventure.

And then I did it. It took more than a year of planning and saving. It meant a lot of research and conversations and letters abroad. It involved listening to a lot of people (with the notable exception of my Jung group) who said I was crazy. Yet during one incredible year I went everywhere in the world I had traced out that night in my apartment, and to even more places. The year I returned, I married a wonderful woman. Our first child was conceived. I started a new kind of law practice, which I loved—a "legal ministry"—in a low-income Boston neighborhood. I was meditat- ing daily, and my ulcer had disappeared for good.

Now, this all sounds a little too neat and tidy, even contrived, doesn't it? A glimmer of the biblical Job—who suffered personally, was challenged by his friends who didn't approve of the way he was dealing with it, and then was blessed by God in the end. My experience was a lot more com- fortable along the way, without Job's horrible body sores and family deaths, and with a year of globe-trotting thrown in. The key to it all for me, though, lay in opening my mind, thinking, and challenging the conventional wisdom of my life. It brought me to Mount Sinai and many other places I'll describe in this book. It brought me to a new level of faith. It worked.

The Jung Club of Boston also welcomed me back with open arms. We still meet over dinner in one of our homes every month. Three of the other members, besides the writer Clara, are artists, whose imagination and vision seem unbounded. Our leader is a very perceptive and well-read former publisher; he keeps us on the breaking wave of new literature in art, religion, and science, along with Jung and plenty of fiction. They all keep me thinking about what is most important in life. What they cannot provide directly, though, is data of the senses, which play such a central role in the spiritual life. Before one is ready to pick a religious path up the mountain and start walking, eyes and ears must be open, and the senses of taste, smell, and touch must be aroused, in order fully to experience one's surroundings. As I'll discuss in detail in the following chapter, mountain climbing is done as much by the body as by the mind.

Experiencing

─·◌◌·─

Colors were everywhere and always. The afternoon's rainbow had been a double one, spewing out of green volcanic mountains and plunging into the blue sea. Flowers sprinkled pathways and bushes and walls. They ran up into the fabric of women's sarongs in infinitely varying designs. Early this morning their petals had been lovingly and ritualistically arranged on the doorstep of a batik store I entered, then swept away by a customer's feet before I left. My bus had screeched to a halt in the countryside more than once, to allow women to leave flower offerings at roadside shrines. Multicolored piles of fruits and vegetables in the marketplace had taken my breath away, so lush and lovely. A resplendent ceremonial procession had appeared out of nowhere around a corner. Translucent umbrellas had sheltered white swathed heads alongside shimmering green fields of rice through my bus window. And now the sea itself was red, the beach black, as the sun slipped beneath the earth to end another day.

I was sitting cross-legged on the edge of a circle of strikingly beautiful people in eastern Bali. The day's farm work was over for the three dozen ashram residents, aged ten to sixty. They had gathered to play music, sing, dance, and tell stories. "Chak-a-chak, chak-a-chak . . ." Men's voices joined in rhythmic monkey sounds at the beginning of the *kecak* dance. Then the storyteller's melodic voice emerged from the cacophony. He was telling a tale from the *Ramayana*, one of the great Hindu epics. The god-king Rama was trying to rescue his wife, Sita, from the demon-king Rawana and had gained the assistance of the monkey-general Hanuman and his army.[1] The cross-legged men began swaying from their waist, and from time to time their arms shot up into the air. They seemed to be in a trance. As the throbbing voices droned on, my reality slowly began to pulsate as I had these thoughts:

Where am I, really? How did I get here? It's 1980 and I'm a thirty-one-year-old American lawyer and minister, trained at Harvard. I've been practicing law as a "minister at large" in a low-income neighborhood of Boston for the past five years. Now I've left it all for a year to take a religious pilgrimage. I'm halfway around the world and no one back there knows exactly where I am. I don't really, either.

My spiritual life was in disarray. How could I put it back together? I had no real religious community back home and seemingly little time for reflection, meditation, or prayer. I tried to follow Jesus' injunction to feed the hungry, clothe the naked, and visit prisoners and the sick. Yet my days were increasingly filled with acrimonious exchanges with other lawyers and judges, creating mountains of paper, and responding to my clients as "eviction cases," "welfare hearings," and "commitment procedures," rather than as whole people.

The shouting voices had started to become overwhelming, frightening. I remembered that the purpose of the chorus of monkey sounds is to resist Rawana, to drive out evil. *Am I part of that evil? Is there evil within me? (Of course). Can the monkeys drive it out without destroying me? Can I find my spiritual center again?*

My jangled mind coursed back over my weeks at the ashram. Up every day at 3:30 A.M. for an hour-long ritual of meditation and chanting, followed by yoga on the beach to greet the rising sun. A communal breakfast, like all meals. Daily chores. Then morning and afternoon farm work for the ashram members and for me a regimen of reading, visits, and touring, punctuated by lunch. Worship again at 5:00 P.M. Supper. The evening gathering.

Life is colorful in Bali and life is rhythmic. Hinduism infuses every minute of every day in the most public of ways, from those doorstep flower-petal arrangements to the impromptu processions to the bus stops at roadside shrines. The Balinese have a habit of building temples at the site of virtually any natural wonder: volcanoes, bat caves, and peninsulas that become islands at high tide, to name a few. Back in America we always kept religion in its place: personal, private, on the weekend, and clearly separated from the state. Here spirituality was around-the-clock, explicit, and assumed. I had begun to feel blessed virtually all the time.

Except tonight. "Chak-a-chak. Chak-a-chak. Chak-a-chak." It was becoming deafening. My head was splitting. The dying pink embers in the sky now generated little light. It was pitch black under the palm trees behind the undulating torch-lit bodies. There was a shadow side to this Balinese paradise. A number of the ashram members suffered chronically from malaria. They were poor. Natural disaster was only as far away as the next tropical storm or the next volcano eruption. And the ashram's spiritual progenitor, Mahatma Gandhi, had been shot to death by a fellow Hindu. How could I put it all together spiritually? My head was splitting.

The *kecak* dance is unnerving, but it is also ecstatic. The individual is progressively engulfed and transformed by the group. Beyond the group lies mystical unity with creation itself, in all its glory and its anguish. The *kecak* uses no instruments beyond the human voices, which in turn simulate animals and, by implication, all of nature. The dance builds into an ecstatic frenzy of waving torsos that can transport all within the circle—cross-legged participants and observers alike—into a sense of union with all that is.

I found myself thinking more deeply now about this ashram community of which I was temporarily a part. It was founded on Gandhian principles of nonviolence, truth, and humanitarianism. That means respect for the individual, self-sufficiency for the community, and compassionate outreach to neighbors. Every ashram member is cared for from birth to death. The farm provides for virtually all of its members' needs. There is a supplementary diet outreach program for two hundred children attending the village elementary school. The ashram clinic also serves village families, emphasizing the use of local medicinal herbs. And the ashram houses transients and pilgrims like me. Gandhi was convinced that one's spirituality must be translated into action that affects social and political life. How could I bring the spiritual discipline and values of this ashram back into my poverty law work in America?

The storyteller's voice was becoming clearer above the monkey chanting now. He was telling of Sita's deliverance from the forces of evil. I imagined his voice as Gandhi's, not understanding the local language of either. I remembered some of Gandhi's words from books in English I'd been reading in the ashram library, and I put them in the storyteller's mouth:

"Service which has not the slightest touch of self in it is the highest religion."[2] (*When I return, I'll have to guard against ego attachment as I crusade for my low-income clients.*)

"I do not believe in people telling others of their faith, especially with a view to conversion. Faith does not admit of telling. It has to be lived, and then it becomes self-propagating." (*I should be careful never to proselytize my religion. Just live it.*)

"Our prayer for others must not be 'God, give him the light that Thou has given me,' but 'Give him all the light and truth that he needs for his own highest development.'" (*Respect the spiritual development of every individual. It goes through stages, and he or she may be having a very different experience than I am.*)

Finally all the voices fell silent and the *kecak* dance ended. I felt exhilarated, even without experiencing the mystical ecstasy that the dancers seemed to have achieved. I was in love with Bali. Its color and energy had woken me up and opened my eyes. I'd become more alert and aware. I could look into my soul here. Bali's rituals connected me with the natural rhythms of my body, of nature, of the circle of day and night. I felt more compassionate as all of life became sacralized around me.

I began to visualize a new kind of law practice for myself that would promote conciliation rather than adversary relations. I dared conceive of talking to lawyers as humans about the real needs of our clients rather than playing procedural games. Most important, I pictured my clients not as specific legal problems but as whole people, which means as holy people. Gandhi would help me. The Balinese would help me. Rama would help me. I would find people back home with whom to share a daily spiritual discipline. Love would have new dimensions. And I would revere all of our spiritual journeys.

To find one's religion, it's not enough just to open one's mind and think deeply. Each of us must also open all of our senses and experience the world. Religion grows from the heart as much as from the head, and it cries out to fuse body and mind. Faith, as a divinity school professor of mine used to insist, is an orientation of the whole personality, a total response. It's not just belief—the holding of certain ideas—which is a function of the mind alone. Beliefs can be expressed in propositional form, to which the adjectives "true" or "false" may be attached. Faith, by contrast, is the opposite of nihilism and despair. It may or may not include beliefs, but it is much larger; it is the ability to experience the universe as meaningful. Having faith means that our lives hold together and make sense at a deep level, rather than seeming ultimately awry, askew, or absurd.[3] Therefore, your religion is something you not only think about but also dance, sing, eat, paint, and sculpt. To find your religion you must engage all of your senses. You should feel it as well as explain it, hear it as well as see it, taste it as well as smell it.

That wasn't the way Peter Mikhel learned about religion growing up in the Soviet Union. All he knew was that "religion is unintelligible." Peter is now a thirty-two-year-old engineer working in Germany. I first met him when he was a graduate student at Tufts. His parents never went to church in Moscow, and they claimed Jesus never existed, much less God. His maternal grandfather was brought up as a Jew but abandoned religion by the time he was twenty. In elementary school this was the message Peter received: Science gives you all the answers, except the moral ones. There the Communist Party fills in and tells you how people should behave. It was hard for him to understand how anyone could believe "fairy tales" like "there being some guy with a beard who will send you to a place called heaven or hell."

When Peter was sixteen, his parents took him for a boat trip along the Volga River. A major incident sticks in his mind from those three days on the water. It occurred on the third night as he was sitting out under the stars on the upper deck. No one was around. Everything was very quiet, except for the gentle slapping of small waves against the bow. For at least an hour he sat alone, deeply breathing in the night air and feeling a slight chill that made his spine tingle. Hills he describes as "very boring," with nothing growing on them, were slowly slipping by as the boat moved upstream. He kept staring at them, lost in thought. Suddenly, as he puts it, he lost all personal boundaries and merged into the hills.

Peter immediately had a clear sense that he and those hills were made of the same stuff. At that moment he had absolutely no doubt of this truth: "We're both part of each other. There's no essential difference between myself and nature, even inanimate nature. It's quite natural to go to the hills, lie down with them, and become one with them. It makes no difference whether I'm inside the hills or on top of them." Peter isn't sure how long this feeling lasted—maybe only a few minutes. All he knows now is that it was a very powerful event.

These days he describes what happened as a mystical experience. When he came back to everyday reality, his rational mind saw that the whole world has a logic behind it that's manifested equally in nature and in human beings. As a scientist, he could have cited Einstein: $e = mc^2$. Peter came to call it God. He saw it as a kind of energy that included everything within it, from the hills to the stars to himself to the boat he was traveling on. Later, when he learned about pantheism—the doctrine that everything is part of God, and God is present in all things—he began to apply the pantheist label to himself.

What happened that night, as Peter looks back, was that he opened all of his senses: breathed in the night air, felt the coolness against his skin, listened to the wavelets gurgling at the bow, and watched the hills as they passed by. That was his part. He did it for a long time. Then something far outside of himself or deep within himself did the rest, for which he takes no credit and has no satisfactory explanation. Yet from that night on, religion no longer was unintelligible.

The American poet and essayist Ralph Waldo Emerson (1803–1882) had a profound understanding of the role the senses play in finding one's religion. Because of his love of nature, many now look to him and his younger colleague, Henry David Thoreau, as founders of the environmental movement. Emerson was once an ordained minister, but his address to the graduating class of Harvard Divinity School in 1838 was found so objectionable by so many of the local clergy that the school made a public disclaimer of responsibility for it. Emerson was banned from Boston church pulpits and not invited to speak again at Harvard for almost thirty years.[4] His spiritual openness and insistence on experiencing nature as part of religion were clearly not as appreciated then as they are now.

Emerson begins his Divinity School address directly with an appeal to the senses: "In this refulgent summer, it has been a luxury to draw the breath of life. The grass grows, the buds burst, the meadow is spotted with fire and gold in the tint of flowers. The air is full of birds, and sweet with the breath of the pine, the balm-of-Gilead, and the new hay." He goes on to explain, "One is constrained to respect the perfection of this world in which our senses converse. How wide; how rich; what invitation from every property it gives to every faculty of man."

Emerson explains that the "religious sentiment" is engendered by openness to nature and the language of the senses, and in turn reflects nature back: "Wonderful is its power to charm and to command. It is a mountain air. . . . It makes the sky and the hills sublime, and the silent song of the stars is it. By it is the universe made safe and habitable, not by science or power."

Then Emerson starts to get himself into trouble as he criticizes clergy who are tied to dogma, prayer books, rituals, and sermons that explicate scripture without a hint of the preacher's own personal biography and passion for the beauty of the earth. He explains that "the faith should blend with the light of rising and of setting suns, with the flying cloud, the singing bird, and the breath of flowers. But now the priest's Sabbath has lost the splendor of nature; it is unlovely; we are glad when it is done."

The next step to Emerson's being banned is his challenge to any authority but the self, since he sees the religious sentiment as an intuition that cannot be received secondhand. The Spirit is indwelling in every person. For Emerson, Jesus can help, because he "belonged to the true race of prophets." He saw the Spirit within more clearly than most of us: "ravished with its beauty, he lived in it, and had his being there." However, any of us can learn to see the Spirit within us, just as Jesus did. Emerson's

Jesus says, "I am divine. Through me, God acts; through me speaks. Would you see God, see me; or see thee, when thou also thinkest as I now think."

Perhaps Emerson's crowning blow was his claim that the "divine impulses" of Americans and Europeans are derived historically not only from Israel and Jesus but also from Egypt, Persia, India, and China. That means people can be helped to connect with the indwelling Spirit not only through the resources of Judaism and Christianity but also through those of ancient Egyptian religion, Zoroastrianism, Islam, Hinduism, Buddhism, Taoism, and Confucianism.[5]

For a couple of years, starting in 1841, Emerson and his wife, Lydian, gave the bedroom at the top of their front stairs to a young unemployed Harvard graduate named Henry Thoreau. After college, he had taught school for four years in Concord, Massachusetts, where the Emersons lived. Now he wanted to become a writer. Fourteen years younger than his host, he had been deeply influenced in college by Emerson's book *Nature*. As a child he had loved the outdoors and spent as much time as he could in the woods and fields and hills. He knew plants and animals much better from experience than from anything he had learned in the classroom.

Emerson gave Thoreau another perspective, though: the inner meaning of nature. He wrote of people finding solitude and peace in nature, and ultimately of finding God there. Thoreau had started keeping a journal after graduation and had published some poetry and a few articles, such as "A Winter Walk" and "Natural History of Massachusetts," in *The Dial*, the mouthpiece of Emerson's transcendentalist movement.[6]

In 1845 Thoreau moved to the fifteen acres of woods bordering a Concord pond that Emerson owned about a mile from his house. He wrote about his two years there in *Walden*, explaining, "Every morning was a cheerful invitation to make my life of equal simplicity, and I may say innocence, with Nature herself. I have been as sincere a worshipper of Aurora as the Greeks. I got up early and bathed in the pond; that was a religious exercise, and one of the best things which I did."[7]

One of Thoreau's lasting legacies was his counsel to live fully in the present moment: "In any weather, at any hour of the day or night, I have been anxious to improve the nick of time, and notch it on my stick too; to stand on the meeting of two eternities, the past and future, which is precisely the present moment; to toe that line." He asked, "Why should we live with such hurry and waste of time? We are determined to be starved before we are hungry." For himself, he explained that "time is but the stream I go a-fishing in. I drink at it; but while I drink I see the sandy bottom and detect how shallow it is. Its thin current slides away, but eternity remains." Put most simply, this was his understanding: "We should be blessed if we lived in the present always, and took advantage of every accident that befell us . . . and did not spend our time in atoning for the neglect of past opportunities."[8]

A similar understanding seems to be sewn into the fabric of Japanese culture. I spent April there on my year's journey, just as the cherry blossoms were coming into bloom. Huge crowds gathered in public parks each evening in Tokyo to picnic, drink, and celebrate the appearance of the delicate pink and white blossoms. They lit colorful lanterns and hung banners. I asked people why this was such an important event. Part of it was simply that this was a spring festival, like all of those observed archetypally around the world, as nature stirs again after a long winter.

Yet, another part of it, they explained, was related to Zen—a form of Buddhism that developed in Japan after being imported from India via China. I was given this Zen story to contemplate: "A monk asked Master Seppo, 'What is the First Word?' The Master was silent. The monk went on to another Master, Chosho, and told him the story. Chosho said to the monk, 'You are already the man of the second word.'"[9] Zen stresses living fully in the present and savoring every moment as if it were the last (or the first). It's had an enormous influence on Japanese art, landscape architecture, literature, and consciousness itself. Cherry blossoms are not only very beautiful; they are also very delicate. One rainstorm or a night of strong wind will plaster all the petals to the ground. The Japanese demonstrate their awareness of nature and its transitory beauty by their nightly visits to the parks, always assuming that this night may be their last to sit with the cherry blossoms. Zen encourages precisely this kind of opening of the senses to the exquisite and ethereal, which surround us all the time, if only we can be awake and alive to them.

I went out and found some books on Zen, because I now began to see its influence in carefully raked Japanese rock gardens, the slowly unfolding tea ceremony, the simplicity of the traditional Japanese home, and many other places. I also spent a week visiting Zen temples in Kyoto, no doubt the most concentrated domain of Zen sensibility in the world. Zen, like all forms of Buddhism, is centered in a meditation practice, *zazen*—daily sitting, still and quiet. That meditational attitude is then to be brought into other activities, such as walking in an intentional and alert way, listening and speaking attentively, and eventually opening all of one's minute-to-minute existence to appreciative awareness.

I read about one Western student who had been practicing for seven years in Kyoto. When asked what Zen training leads to, he replied, "No paranormal experiences that I can detect. But you wake up in the morning and the world seems so beautiful you can hardly stand it."[10] Zen has infused Japanese culture, even for those without any formal training. I was told that the ideal is to carry out daily duties, no matter how large or small, with the perception that each is equally a manifestation of infinite joy in its particular time and place. The Zen position is that if I can't find the ultimate justification of existence in an act as simple as doing the dishes, and relish each soapy part of it, then I won't be able to find it anywhere.

This sounded to me a lot like what Thoreau had written in *Walden:* "God himself culminates in the present moment, and will never be more divine in the lapse of all the ages. And we are enabled to apprehend at all what is sublime and noble only by the perpetual instilling and drenching of the reality that surrounds us."[11] Similarly, I remembered these words of Emerson's: "These roses under my window make no reference to former roses or to better ones; they are for what they are; they exist with God today. . . . But we postpone or remember. We do not live in the present, but with reverted eye lament the past, or, heedless of the riches that surround us, stand on tiptoe to foresee the future."[12]

After a week's introduction to Zen in Kyoto, I decided to try to spend an afternoon with my senses fully open, simply experiencing my environment. Leaving the Buddhist temple where I was staying, I started walking, just watching where my feet and spirit led me. I tried the discipline of going in a straight line at first, partially so that I wouldn't get lost and could find my way back to the temple. As I reached the top of a highway overpass, though, I spied a nearby hillside. Since I have a certain affinity for hills, I headed directly for it. The first path up that I found was steep, and I climbed until the way became choked with underbrush. Tired, I lay down in the warm, sweet-smelling leaves, watching sunbeams filter through the branches. As I quieted down, I noticed birds singing, near and far. They sang me to sleep, in fact. When I awoke, my feet led me back down the path to the bottom of the hill.

What to do now? My spirit said not to leave the hill behind, so I followed along its bottom edge, which led to another hillside and then another. The valley to my right was crowded with industrial sites at first, but gradually they gave way to farmlands, and then I found myself in a wildlife refuge. Here I was completely alone, first in bamboo thickets and then in pine forests, following a small trail. When I came to a lake, I sat for a while. The birds started singing to me again, and a gentle breeze wafted the fragrance of pine needles through my being. Realizing, after some time, that there were no other people around, I felt safe enough to slip out of my clothes and into the lake. The cool water transformed my frame. I let all my muscles go limp and floated face up. The words *peace* and *renewal* welled up within me, flowed through my veins, and then emptied back out into the water.

After I had dried off in a spot of sun along the shore, I started walking again—first around the lake and then following any path that looked interesting and seemed to be going up. By now my thoughts were getting more expansive: *How does this experience relate to what I was feeling in Bali during the* kecak *dance? What, again, am I really supposed to be doing with my life? Where am I going? Where will I end up?*

Suddenly I realized that I had left any semblance of Zen consciousness. Was I aware of my feet, my labored breath, my fast-beating heart? Was I noticing my surroundings and appreciating what was there? I slowed down and became more deliberate and mindful. Feeling each step, I became more attentive and observant. Just as I was beginning to become connected to my own body and to nature around me again, the path reached the top of the hill. I stumbled into a large Shinto shrine, open to the elements! Red and black post-and-lintel gates, grass-skirted rocks, and wild cat statues seemed to be guarding it all.

Shinto is the original, indigenous religion of Japan, centered around the *kami:* gods or spirits of water, rocks, plants, trees, animals, certain human figures, and hundreds of other natural objects and beings. Zen Buddhism comfortably coexists with it, and Japanese people are often affiliated with both—say, being married in a Shinto shrine and buried in a Buddhist temple. But today there wasn't another soul around (except the *kami*), and yet there were tables set up, along with booths and festive flags. Working my way through the shrine area, I came to a stairway leading up to an observation deck, flanked by two fully blooming cherry trees. Standing at

the top of it, I had a spectacular 270-degree view of the valley and surrounding mountains. Awe is what I felt.

In fact, I felt a bit like Moses, being led up to look over the promised
land after wandering in the desert for forty years, long after his encounter
with God on Mount Sinai. As I gazed back behind me at the shrine, it
seemed like paradise: bright colors, beautiful flowering trees, and statues
and offerings to the gods. I began thinking back over my afternoon's journey. I hadn't known where I was going, but just followed my feet and my
spirit. I was careful to try to keep my senses fully open. I took my time. I
slept when I wanted. I swam when I felt like it. I reached for the unknown,
without a map, without looking back, and without a destination. I tried to
stay in the present moment's experience. The journey was its own reward,
step by step. Then, unexpectedly and surprisingly, in the middle of the
woods, I was graced with a view of the likes of the promised land and of
paradise. There wasn't anyone else around, and it seemed it had all been
set up and provided just for me.

Spontaneously I knelt down and sent a prayer of thanks off somewhere.
Then I walked back down the steps into the shrine. There was a fountain
there, and I had learned that all worshipers or visitors to a Shinto shrine
should purify themselves by dipping the ladle provided into the water,
pouring it over their hands, and touching the water to their lips. I then
walked over to the main altar, put a hundred yen in the box, bowed,
clapped my hands twice, and rang the bell, thanking what I know as the
one God—in the Shinto manner—for bringing me here, teaching me Zen
lessons, and filling me with tears of joy.

Then I slowly and consciously walked down the stone steps leaving the
shrine, under literally hundreds of red and black gates that overarched the
pathway down. It was significant, I thought, that many of the gates were
too low for my height, so I had to concentrate, watch closely, and bow at

appropriate moments. I grazed my head once, demonstrating how my mindfulness could slip, and how the next miscue could be painful.

More than a decade before, on the slopes of another mountain, I had learned decisively where carelessness could lead. I was backpacking with a good friend in the high country of the Teton Range in Wyoming. As I climbed across a rock face without ropes, my backpack became stuck on an outcropping behind me. Each time I tried to free it, I started to be thrown forward, away from the rock face, toward a pile of huge boulders a couple of hundred feet below. I was slipping and struggling to hold on, and my friend was on the other side of a crevasse, too far away to help

This is it! I thought. *How incredibly stupid to die this way!* Then, as the adrenaline started rushing through my veins, each of my senses seemed to expand many-fold. I became hyperalert. It became a Technicolor day. Everything went into slow motion, including the hawk circling overhead. I could taste the bitter saltiness of my own sweat. My heart was pounding through my chest. Van Gogh could not have painted the sky more blue, the far-off trees more green, the rock face more luminescently white. My voice moved away from my body and sounded like thunder, echoing off the cliffs. Life became so precious, second by second.

Probably it was only a minute or two before my by-then very strong, perfectly balanced body was able to free the pack, and I was able to move to safety. It felt like eternity. Yet, for that minute or two, I was more alive and more aware than I have ever been. I followed every breath in and out, every muscle tightening and loosening. It seemed as if I saw the face of every friend and family member with me. I ran through the gamut of emotions, from fear to anger to sadness to ecstasy.

Why is it that it takes a near-death experience to wake us up so completely? Isn't there a way to experience more deeply and appreciate more poignantly in our day-to-day lives? What can make time stand still without risking our lives? Does it really matter how long we live—another half century, decades, a few years, or even months or weeks? Isn't the real point *how* we live those weeks or months or years? Zen seems to point in the right direction. So do Emerson and Thoreau. Once our senses are open, a number of religious paths can look more inviting.

That's what happened to Peter Mikhel around the time of his Volga River experience. Yet it happened differently than through nature mysticism another time. He came to appreciate Protestant Christianity through his ears—through music. During high school in Moscow, Peter was learning German when he first heard the organ—playing the St. Matthew and St. John Passion music of Johann Sebastian Bach (music that Bach composed within a Lutheran church context about the last days of Jesus' life). He fell in love with the sound of the organ accompanying the singing, and he began to pick up some of the words of the gospel story in German. To him it was very moving to hear of Jesus' Last Supper with his disciples, his betrayal to the Roman authorities, his challenge to the governor, and his painful execution. Before long, he began reading the Bible in Russian.

Most of all, though, Peter wanted to learn how to play the organ. He felt that music on this instrument projected a "great, transcendental, eternal quality." He saw organ music as a dialogue between human beings and God. As he listened to Bach, it seemed that people were being pushed to embrace and devote themselves to the ultimate beauty and power that is God, rather than to their minuscule selves. At the age of seventeen, Peter joined an organ class in Moscow. He spent years at it and had become an accomplished performer by the time he showed up at Tufts as a graduate student in his mid-twenties. Bach was still his favorite; he got more power and volume out of the chapel organ than I ever thought our century-old instrument could produce.

Peter spoke to me about organ music as the essence of spirituality. Its sound—sometimes grand, sometimes meditative—seems to have no beginning and no end. He began playing for a Protestant church in

Boston. There he found himself drawn into the sermons, too. Christianity became an important anchor for his life. He began reading the Bible again, now using computerized versions in English, Russian, and German. As he put it, he became "more and more comfortable with Jesus." Now in Germany, he's in church every Sunday, and still playing the organ.

If you open your eyes and ears, if you taste and smell and feel the world around you, you never know what might happen—on the Volga River or while listening to your favorite music. Open your senses and experience all that is there.

Walking

Now it's time to pick a religious path and start walking. Once you are open to change, and you've opened your mind and senses, the mountain beckons. Enough time sitting at home, or even crossing deserts, with the peaks always on the horizon. No more walking around the base trying to decide on the best way up. No matter how many guidebooks you read and how many pictures you take of its majesty from a distance, you'll know very little of the mountain until you begin climbing and feel its slopes under your own feet. You might be tempted to avoid any of the well-trodden paths, but bushwhacking usually doesn't get you very far, especially if you are an inexperienced climber. Committing yourself to one trail instead of another need not be forever. There will be trail crossings ahead, and you'll become aware of other options as you climb that you couldn't see from the bottom. There's no chance of getting out of the valley and gaining any perspective, though, until you start walking up and get to your first vista.

There is a novel I read in college in the 1960s that still has great power for the students I teach now at the brink of the millennium. Whether they are undergraduates or graduate business students, Hermann Hesse's *Siddhartha* never fails to have a potent effect on the vast majority of them.[2] I believe that's because Siddhartha has the courage to pick a path and start walking, and then pick another path and keep walking, and then do it again, until he finally reaches the top of the mountain. First published by its Swiss author in 1922, the story is set in the era of the historical Buddha, around 500 B.C. Although he shares the same given name, this Siddhartha is not the Buddha. In fact, when he meets the Buddha during the tale, he chooses not to become a disciple.

Hesse's Siddhartha was born the son of a Hindu priest, a Brahmin, and practiced the art of meditation while growing up, along with the rituals of his faith. He was handsome and intelligent, a delight to both his mother and his father, to all of his friends, and indeed to everyone who met him. As a teenager, though, he became unhappy. He came to feel that all the love he felt from his family and friends was not enough. The religious teachings and practices he had learned were not enough. He wanted to reach the depths of his own soul, called *Atman* in the Hindu tradition. The priests he knew, including his father, didn't seem to have stretched all the way down and couldn't help him to do so.

One day some wandering ascetics, called Samanas, passed through Siddhartha's town. They were practically naked, sun-scorched, and strange-looking. Yet they had around them a mood of quiet passion and of committed service to the world. Siddhartha looked at his life of relative ease and knew that he could grow up to be a respected and learned man, a prince among Brahmins, but that something would always be missing on a deeper level. Or he could decide to give up everything except a loincloth and cloak and follow the Samanas. He didn't know where their path would lead, but at least he would be actively engaged in his search, rather than just sitting in comfort, wondering and wishing.

Siddhartha chose to follow the Samanas. There was a major problem, though. What would his parents say? He had never disobeyed his mother and father; he had always done what they told him. With a lot of trepidation, no doubt, he went to the room in his house where his father was sitting and said, "With your permission, Father, I have come to tell you that I wish to leave your house tomorrow and join the ascetics. I wish to become a Samana. I trust my father will not object." His father remained sitting silently for a long time before responding, "It is not seemly for Brahmins to utter forceful and angry words, but there is displeasure in my heart. I should not like to hear you make this request a second time."

I have found in my counseling work that telling your parents about a change in your religious life is perhaps the most difficult step of all. Kevin Gallagher was sad that his mother saw his conversion to Judaism as a personal rejection of her. Try as he would, he couldn't convince her that this was not a move away from Catholicism as much as a move toward something that was completely enthralling for him. Carl Jung worried that it was his own fault when he found himself cut off not only from the church but from his father after his disastrous First Communion. He could only be grateful for the gift of the cog railroad ticket up the Rigi that his father had given him. It was at the top of that mountain that he discovered "God's world," but his father had been left at the foot of the mountain. Each of these two approaches sometimes works for my counselees, though: helping parents understand that your religious conversion is not a rejection of them, and expressing gratitude for the spiritual gifts your parents continue to give you.

I've spent time with a Lutheran student from the Midwest who converted to Judaism while at Tufts. Harriet worked hard to convince her parents that she was not spurning them. In the fundamentalist environment where she grew up, it was unambiguously stated that if Jews didn't convert to Christianity, they would go to hell. Now she was converting to Judaism. Because she was so worried about failing her family's and friends' expectations of her, she spent a lot of time with them explaining why. For example, she felt she was finally living the words that were so often on Jesus' Jewish lips about loving God and neighbor. The warmth of the Jewish community, especially in its respect for families, had become utterly compelling to her. That meant, though, that being comfortable with those closest to her—her parents, siblings, and old friends—was infinitely more important, she explained, than following every aspect of Jewish law. Over a year or so, her parents came to believe that this change was very important for her, that she had achieved happiness of a sort they had never seen in her before, and that far from rebelling, she still loved them very deeply. Although they didn't really like her Judaism or understand it, they communicated to Harriet that their love was unconditional; they would never think of forsaking or abandoning her.

In Michael's case, he converted from Catholicism to the Bahá'í religion in college. To his parents, he kept framing his new orientation as part of a continuum with his childhood faith. Jesus was undoubtedly a Manifestation of God, but there have been some others throughout history, including Bahá'u'lláh, the nineteenth-century Persian prophet who had founded Michael's present religion. Michael continued to revere the Bible as sacred scripture. It was only because of the loving and devoted way he was raised, with a deep spiritual dimension in his family life, that he was able to continue the religious journey that led to his becoming a Bahá'í. Bahá'u'lláh had even written that if one must choose between serving one's parents or following him, then one must serve one's own parents. Michael explained how thankful he was for all of their Sundays in church (which he continued attending when he was home), for the countless evenings of bedside prayers, for the many years of parochial school. Even now, Michael affirmed, his parents' faith continued to be a source of inspiration for him, and he enjoyed spending spiritually oriented time with them. They came to reciprocate, impressed by the depth of his religious commitment and his continuing openness to them.

Hesse's Siddhartha took yet another tack. He didn't want to confront or disobey his father directly, so essentially he exercised patience until his father came around and bestowed his blessing. He did this in a vivid and potent way, perhaps steeped in the Hindu tradition of nonviolent protest. He remained standing silently where he had asked for permission to join the Samanas, even after his father had left the room and gone to bed. Several times during the night his father got up and found Siddhartha still standing there with his arms folded, unmoving. Just before dawn he asked, "Siddhartha, why are you waiting?" "You know why," was the response. "Will you go on standing and waiting until it is day, noon, evening?" his father asked. "I will stand and wait," Siddhartha replied.

So, after daybreak, his father realized that Siddhartha had truly made up his mind to follow a new path and had essentially already left him. He touched Siddhartha's shoulder and said, "You will go into the forest and become a Samana. If you find bliss in the forest, come back and teach it to me. If you find disillusionment, come back, and we shall again offer sacrifices to the gods together. Now go, kiss your mother and tell her where you are going." I'm sure many of us long for such a response from our parents—and for the patience to wait for it.

Siddhartha inspired his best friend, Govinda, to come along when he joined the Samanas. Their new discipline included fasting and other forms of self-denial. They also learned to practice yoga and to meditate in such a way that the mind was emptied of all images, while the breathing rate and heartbeat slowed to almost nothing. They lived outside and begged food from villagers in order to eat. Progressively they were able to conquer pain and become less attached to things.

As time went on, though, Siddhartha began asking questions of this friend, Govinda: "Are we on the right road? Are we gaining knowledge?

Are we approaching salvation? Or are we perhaps going in circles?" Govinda responded, "We have learned much, Siddhartha. There still remains much to learn. We are not going in circles, we are going upwards. The path is a spiral; we have already climbed many steps." Yet Siddhartha pointed out that their oldest and most venerated teacher had not yet attained Nirvana—final emancipation from the suffering of the world and union with God. Siddhartha began to doubt that this teacher or any of the Samanas would ever reach Nirvana. What was the point, then, of following them?

After three years with the Samanas, Siddhartha and Govinda began to hear of the Buddha—one who was reported to have attained Nirvana and truly conquered the sorrows of the world. He was traveling throughout the land, surrounded by disciples, preaching wisdom and healing the afflicted. He modeled a "middle way" between the asceticism of the Samanas and materialistic living in the world. Govinda and Siddhartha by that time had become thoroughly disillusioned with the Samanas and were ready to hear about a different path. They traveled to the town where the Buddha was staying.

Once in his presence, both Govinda and Siddhartha sensed the elevation of the Buddha. He was quiet and unassuming, begging his own daily food and dressing in saffron-colored robes just like his monks. He seemed to be smiling gently, inwardly, and he walked as if he sought nothing and imitated nothing. He reflected an aura of utter peacefulness. They heard him preach about the Four Noble Truths and the Eightfold Path, lessons about overcoming the suffering caused by ego attachment that were destined to become the centerpiece of a new religious tradition called Buddhism. Siddhartha found the Buddha's teachings and character flawless, like a clear light from the heavens: "Never had Siddhartha esteemed a man so much, never had he loved a man so much."

This time, though, Siddhartha took a different path than his friend,

Govinda, who became a lifelong disciple. Siddhartha had a private audience with the Buddha. He explained how much he admired the Buddha's teachings but ironically took from them a message that no one can find salvation through another's teachings. Each must achieve enlightenment through personal experience: "That is why I am going on my way—not to seek another and better doctrine, for I know there is none, but to leave all doctrines and all teachers and to reach my goal alone—or die." The Buddha's final words to Siddhartha were these: "You are clever, O Samana. You know how to speak cleverly my friend. Be on your guard against too much cleverness." Siddhartha said to himself as the Buddha walked away, "A man only looks and walks like that when he has conquered his Self. I also will conquer my Self."

Hesse's book powerfully demonstrates the struggle between Dependence and Independence in spiritual development. In fact, the newly independent Siddhartha stumbles and soon becomes caught in dependent relationships with a prostitute, a gambler, and a troubled businessman. Later in the novel we see Siddhartha achieve Interdependence as he overcomes acquisitiveness, works selflessly alongside a ferryman, and begins to listen to all river passengers without praise or blame. He develops a capacity for love he never had—one that allows him paradoxically to appreciate other people as much in their pride and vanity as in their moral courage and humility, as much in their warring as in their peacemaking. He finds truth in the flowing river, which "was not just water, but the voice of life, the voice of Being, of perpetual Becoming." In the last couple of chapters, it is clear that Siddhartha has reached the final stage of spiritual development, marked by continuous consciousness of the unity of all life. He becomes a Buddha in his own right.

Siddhartha never would have gotten anywhere spiritually, though, if he hadn't picked a path and started walking. Yet I know how difficult that is to do. In a Tufts course I taught on finding one's religion, a number of students described themselves as "mentally paralyzed," as locked up inside their heads and unable to start moving. One student, Beth, explained: "I can think, I can read, and I can talk. But I often lose the capacity to act on my beliefs. I know what I have to do, but it is the next step that I have the most trouble with. I don't know if I have the strength to discontinue my procrastination." Another student, Amir, added: "I empathize with Siddhartha. I know his journey is a lonely one. It is scary to ask the questions he is asking. I do feel the loneliness, and sometimes I want to forget these questions and drown myself in work or something else."

How much does one need to know before picking a path? That worried more than one student. Josh summed up the struggle: "The idea of just choosing a path and going with it is very appealing, but difficult. For me, in order to choose a path I must believe it. Or is that exactly the choice I have to make? To believe it? I can't see how I could follow a path without believing it. Since at this point I don't really believe in any of them, I must make myself believe one first. Maybe this can be done while experimenting with the path, or maybe it's a prerequisite. The goal is to find a religion that I can believe in, so I can't demand of myself that I believe in something before I do it. So, it seems the only option I have is to go with a path—whatever grabs me, I guess. But how can I fully follow a path if I am in constant doubt?"

We do need to pick a path to make spiritual progress. You and I can't get anywhere without putting one foot in front of the other. Yet how does that happen? By putting on a blindfold, spinning around, and pinning our hopes on whatever direction in which we happen to stumble? Perhaps we could call that blind faith. Another way, which would interest me, is to be taken by the hand by a friend. Say you know a Christian who has been trying to get you to attend a Quaker meeting, a Jew who wants to invite you to a Passover Seder, or a Buddhist who would like to teach you how to meditate. Then at least you have companionship and some degree of trust. It is true that while hand-holding can work pretty well at the Dependent and Interdependent stages of spiritual development, it is virtually useless at the Independent stage. People establishing their own spiritual autonomy like to keep both hands free. Seeing the effects of faith in someone else, though, may open you to try out what they do.

A third way, which I've also used, is to research all paths as thoroughly as possible before setting foot on any one. Potential problems here include terminal paralysis, separation of the mind from body and soul, and the gap between what one can discover on paper and what one learns through personal experience. A fourth way is to follow your instincts about what path looks immediately inviting, knowing you can turn back later or veer off onto another intriguing trail along the way. Obviously, in any case you won't want to abandon common sense about signs of danger and false friends.

One of my students, Karen, took my advice to start walking by visiting a local church one evening with a friend. She was told it was a Bible study and to bring hers along. Karen thought this was an especially good idea since she was taking a New Testament course at the university. "This will be a great chance to gain insight," she thought.

Here's what happened, in Karen's words: "The pastor began his lesson by holding up two flags, the United Nations and the Rainbow [gay] flag. He began by saying that the United Nations was the instrument of Satan. He said it was bringing about the new world order, which would surely mean the end. He urged us to write and protest the United States's involvement with the U.N. Then he moved on to the other flag. He went on about how he constantly sees women wearing hats and men wearing scarves. He condemned them for doing 'what is abominable before God' and then continued to tell us to seek these people out and tell them about their sinful ways."

Karen had been very impressed by the work of the United Nations, especially in its peacekeeping operations, and she had several gay and lesbian friends (with whom she had been working on being more tolerant and open). Needless to say, she quickly determined that this path was not for her: "I won't be back there again!" As she politely put it, "I just think it's odd that a church that bases itself on love and forgiveness would be so quick to judge those whom they have not even met."

So, the question remains: How do you pick a religious path to begin with? Especially when some seem to lead people to be bigoted and destructive? I think the answer is to start with something that seems intriguing and engaging. Let your heart lead you into something that resonates deep inside you, even if it's not the path you know best. Use your head, though—your common sense and your judgment—just the way Karen did, when it looks like an approach might be hurtful and damaging to yourself or others. Stay away from paths where someone's pushing you too hard, misleading you, or causing pain. It won't do you any good to start walking a path that you know isn't any fun. You won't get very far that way.

This is how it happened for me in college. There I rediscovered the path on which I'd begun walking as a child, and I've managed to stay on it, or at least within sight of it, ever since. When I arrived at Yale at eighteen, I had rejected my childhood Christianity and was convinced God didn't exist. How else could there be natural disasters and horrible tragedies, like children dying in earthquakes and hurricanes? But a noncredit Seminar for Friendly Disbelievers with the chaplain, along with several courses I took in my freshman year, began rebuilding my religion. "Signals of transcendence," as Peter Berger put it in *A Rumor of Angels*, began to creep into my world through my academic studies.

In mathematics I was fascinated by the almost theological debate between Georg Cantor (1845–1918) and Leopold Kronecker (1823–1891) about the existence of infinite numbers. Kronecker argued that all of mathematics should be reduced to positive whole numbers that can be counted. I came to side with Cantor, who claimed that infinite numbers actually exist. Next, in a philosophy course I became intrigued by the limits on what formal logical systems like computers could do. When a professor explained how "infinite proofs" could resolve some of the logical problems, I found infinity making its way into my consciousness in new and enthralling ways.

Meanwhile, I was taking courses in anthropology and art, where I was learning about the role of myth and symbol in human society, and what they may point to beyond. I was especially taken by how similar they could be across cultures and throughout history. Later, in a psychology course, I first encountered the universal religious archetypes of Jungian theory, which I have discussed in the "Thinking" chapter. I also began reading about Eastern traditions like Hinduism and Buddhism. Maybe there was more to religion than I had thought! Perhaps God did not have to be conceived of as a person who arbitrarily intervened in history or neglected us as He chose, but more as a life force with which we could align ourselves to live meaningful lives. Perhaps science itself pointed to trustworthy natural laws by which we could predict and avoid earthquakes and hurricanes, rather than blaming God for them. By the end of the year I was convinced I had to go to India that summer to explore a different kind of spiritual awareness than I had known to date.

I traveled with a dozen Americans visiting South Asia as part of a theology group. We stayed with families from different religious backgrounds. Indian Muslims taught me how to prostrate myself in prayer, facing Mecca. Jains fed us their diet of milk, fruits, vegetables, nuts, and berries, based on their religion of strict nonviolence. Forbidden to destroy any animal or even any growing plant, they could not harvest potatoes or carrots, because this would kill the plants' roots. Sikhs showed me how they wrapped and turbaned their uncut hair. Zoroastrians explained the towers of silence where they placed their dead to be consumed by birds to avoid defiling the sacred elements of earth, water, air, or fire through an act of burial or cremation. It made ecological sense. On a field trip I sat near a *bodhi* tree said to be descended from saplings of the original tree under which the Buddha achieved enlightenment.

Hinduism, as the world's oldest religion, seemed to have spawned virtually all of these traditions, or at least tolerantly encompassed each of them sooner or later within its ever-embracing arms. I spent the monsoon season with a Hindu Brahmin priest and his family in northeastern India, some two hundred miles from Calcutta. As the rains poured down, I passed a lot of time inside—reading, talking, and learning how to meditate with the priest. Standing six feet two inches and weighing well over 200 pounds, he cut a huge figure compared to his compatriots (and to me at 175 pounds, although I measured six feet four inches). Those few weeks spent with him had a huge effect on the direction of my spiritual life. Each morning I woke up to the sound of the names of 108 deities being chanted through the wall that connected my room to the *puja* room, or chapel. Incense wafted around me and filled my lungs, and I felt spiritually transported even before I climbed out of my mosquito netting to start the day. In the *puja*, the priest and his family said their daily prayers and draped flower garlands over statues and pictures of Krishna, Ganesh, and other gods. It all seemed very exotic and I felt so far from home. Yet India was planting its roots deeply into my soul.

It turned out that this priest knew the Bible better than I did. Even though he was Hindu, he kept a copy next to his bed. He'd also read the Qur'an from cover to cover and recited passages from its suras (chapters). He seemed as familiar with the Buddhist scriptures as the Hindu. He spoke of many avatars—incarnations of divinity—throughout history, including Krishna, Buddha, and Jesus. As I sat cross-legged each day in my white cotton *dhoti* and *kurta*, I began to think, *Maybe this is the way to spiritual maturity. Be open to all religious traditions. Pick and choose from what rings true for me in each.* Yet the priest kept emphasizing getting on a path, following a discipline, becoming committed to a teacher and a set of teachings. "There are many paths up the mountain," he would say, "and they all reach the top, but you need to follow a path and you can't be on more than one at a time."

By the end of the summer I had decided I wanted to become a Hindu. On the morning I approached the priest with my request, he took me to sit with him in the front room on a Persian rug. The rain was coming down in sheets and banged loudly against the roof. I was stunned by his response. "No, no!" he chided. "You've missed the point of everything I've taught you. You've grown up as a Christian and you know a lot about that path. It's the religion of your family and your culture. You know almost nothing of Hinduism. Go back and be the best Christian you can be."

I remember how the rain against the roof seemed to rattle my brain. I was upset. "But I don't believe Jesus was any more divine than Krishna or the Buddha," I pleaded. "And Christians would condemn you for knowing about Jesus and not accepting him uniquely as your Lord and Savior." His response was simple: "Then go back and find a way to be an open, nonexclusive Christian, following in Jesus' footsteps yourself, but appreciating others' journeys on their own paths." The more I could learn about others' paths, he explained, the more it would help me to progress along my own and deepen my understanding of it. Those words have remained my marching orders for life.

Hard rain always reminds me when I forget.

Perhaps my mirror image is another Hindu I now know here in America. He also struggled with the faith of his childhood when he arrived at college. Arvind grew up in a Hindu household in suburban St. Louis. His parents, an engineer and a teacher, had emigrated from India just a few years before he was born. Religion was always familial and pleasant—children playing at their parents' holiday gatherings and watching Hindu rituals performed. Yet, by the end of high school in his middle-class white community, he had drifted into agnosticism. There weren't many Indians around, and his religion seemed so disconnected from his daily reality. Christian figures like Martin Luther King, Jr., who had made a difference in his society, made more sense to him than the colorful Hindu gods with whom he had grown up.

He arrived at college a secularized American kid, far from the Hinduism of his parents. Then, in his freshman year, he saw the Hollywood movie about Mahatma Gandhi. He'd seen it before as a child, but now it was as if the scales fell from his eyes. He was hooked by this powerful figure in the loincloth. He started to read every book he could find by and about him. Arvind made a personal connection to Hinduism for the first time in his life. However, this was not the Hinduism of 108 deities, or of Brahman and Atman—the Transcendent and Immanent, which merge as the one Godhead in the Upanishad scriptures. This was an activist Hinduism of militant nonviolence and commitment to social change.

College was the first place where Arvind began meeting a critical mass of other Indian Americans like himself. He quickly got involved with the South Asian Club and by sophomore year was president. He set to work addressing minority needs, especially those of Muslims, within the organization. He knew how hard Gandhi had worked to promote understanding between Hindus and Muslims, and to prevent the partition of the Asian subcontinent into two countries—India and Pakistan. This labor of love had cost Gandhi his life at the hands of a Hindu extremist assassin. Arvind also encouraged the South Asian Club to join with other people of color on campus to challenge the rest of the university to examine institutional racism.

He used the Gandhian spiritual discipline of fasting to raise money on campus during Hunger and Homelessness Week for Oxfam America. For three years Arvind was the main organizer of the twenty-four-hour Fast for a World Harvest. He personally fasted longer than one day each year, stressing its spiritual value in helping to produce a greater clarity of consciousness—making our minds more lucid, sharp, and efficient and enhancing our inner life as we challenge the power of materialism within ourselves. He also reminded others that this was a method of Gandhi's nonviolence—what Gandhi called *satyagraha,* or truth-force, based on a deep respect for the equality of all people and the spark of the divine that could be kindled in each of us through love. For Arvind, self-restraint and self-denial were ways to transcend the ego in dedication to something higher and more all-encompassing.

Arvind became involved in many other social issues from his Gandhian perspective. For example, he joined an organization called the American Anti-Slavery Group, pointing out that slavery in the world has been largely neglected by the human rights community. He organized a panel discussion on campus concerning the atrocities of slavery in third-world countries. He worked with a pacifist organization, the American Friends Service Committee, to abolish nuclear weapons and was selected to attend a week-long conference in Tahiti to promote the end of these weapons of mass destruction by the year 2000. He spent the summer before his senior year in India working on a nutrition project. After college he went back to India for a year to do health education and community organizing in rural villages.

What is most striking about Arvind is his quiet passion and his deep commitment both to nonviolent social change and to self-purification in the process to remove all traces of ego attachment. His Hindu life philosophy includes service, compassion, and good stewardship of his talents. A chemistry major in college, he is now in medical school. He wants to join medicine with community development in low-income communities and in the developing world. Arvind worked with socially committed people of all religions during college, but Gandhian Hinduism had clearly become his personal path. He quotes the Mahatma: "Wake up with me. Walk where I walk." By this, Arvind means that actions speak louder than words or beliefs. His Hindu path turned out to be very different from the familial and ritual-based one of his parents. Yet, he found Hinduism anew as an adult, and it became the source of integrity for his life.

For many Americans, though, Hinduism conjures up cult images. Arvind himself worried about other young adults he met in American airports and shopping malls, dressed in saffron robes, chanting and dancing, asking for money, and handing out copies of the same Hindu scripture, the Bhagavad Gita, that had meant so much to Gandhi, and later to Arvind himself. He had heard that many of them had cut off contact with their families and old friends and had generally limited their reading and learning to the sources authorized by their group. Were they a cult, and how would members feel if and when others decided to leave?

So-called cults are certainly not limited to Eastern traditions. America has had a long history of new movements within Christianity that others characterized at first as cults." In this chapter it's worth looking briefly at how religious practices can become dangerous to your health, since I'm advising you to pick a path and start walking.

Take the case of Barbara Smith, for example. She was a sophomore at Tufts when I first met her—an older student who had taken several years off to work in the middle of college. She was deeply involved in the Church of Jesus United[1] and wanted it to become a recognized campus organization. She handed me a one-page statement that explained, "The church's only book and creed is the Bible." It went on to describe beliefs and practices: "We search the Bible diligently for the truth, and submit to its authority. Christ taught that every person must believe, confess, repent, be baptized and live faithfully to his teachings. Through group

Bible studies, one-on-one discipling, and retreats, we are able to meet each student's personal needs. Throughout the semester we also participate in social functions such as international dinners, movie nights, and sports activities."

I later came to learn what wasn't in that statement. The charismatic founder had set up a rigid hierarchy of authority through elders and deacons down to the individual "disciplers," who acted as twenty-four-hour big brothers or big sisters and oversaw every activity of new members. In turn, each discipler had someone always looking over his or her shoulder, and that someone was also watched, all the way back up. The only mission of the church was to be a "multiplying ministry"—recruiting as many people as possible to join. Even if someone was already a baptized Christian, he or she had to be rebaptized by the Church of Jesus United, because this church alone understood "the truth." All nonmembers were condemned to the eternal fires of hell.

Members were asked to restrict their involvement with their parents, other family members, and prior friends, if after a reasonable time they were unsuccessful in converting those people. All waking hours were to be spent with other church members, primarily in proselytizing activities. In fact, the church was meant to be a total experience around the clock: eating, socializing, and traveling together, studying together (although grades often suffered because of lack of attention), attending church functions together, and saving souls for Jesus together. There were also strict rules about never criticizing the church or its leaders, reading only authorized literature about religion, and examining only those Bible passages that were accompanied by church interpretation and instruction.

Eventually the church was duly registered as a student organization, based on considerations of religious liberty and freedom of association. The officers also assured the university that there would be no door-to-door solicitation in dormitories or harassment of people not wanting to join or later wishing to leave. The next thing I heard was that the church was working inside the dormitories and many students felt either harassed or deceived. They would be offered ice cream in student lounges or asked to go out to social events without being told the real nature of the group, whose members would claim they were "just a bunch of us getting together as friends." When confronted on this, Barbara claimed, "The church is being persecuted by the authorities again, just like Peter and Paul and the early church were in the New Testament." A couple of years later Barbara left Tufts, and the church became less active on campus.

Five years after I first met her, Barbara showed up in my office as an alumna one day out of the blue. "I'm out!" she exclaimed.

"What do you mean?" I responded.

"The Church of Jesus United. I'm done with them."

I asked what had happened.

"I completely lost myself and was in a fog for two years," she explained. "I thought I'd been born again, but in fact it was the death of my true self. I lost my freedom and autonomy. I basically stopped thinking for myself. All my doubts went up on the shelf. The leaders told me who and how to date, what to wear, and how to act. I became a really tough person, manipulating others into joining us and preventing them from being baptized in other churches—things I wouldn't have thought were ethical before I joined. Well, I went ahead and did them. There's one message to the outside before you join, and then another one on the inside as you move up the ladder. We lie."

She continued: "Then one day all of those doubts up on the shelf came crashing down. I realized I had wasted years of my life. But then I had to struggle to get out. After I told my discipleship partner, who was my roommate, that I'd decided for sure, and there was nothing she could do about it, I found the locks changed on our apartment when I returned at the end of the day. All my clothes and belongings were still inside. I was told I could have them back only if I agreed to one more talk, this time with church leaders. At that point I walked away from everything I owned."

Barbara went on to describe what had been the most difficult part of leaving: "You know, I've been really lonely. The church was my whole life, and people inside who I thought were personal friends dropped me like a lead balloon after I left—they shunned me, really. Was I stupid not to realize that this was all for the group and wasn't real friendship? I don't know who to trust anymore. I feel betrayed. It's really been devastating. I left all my old friends years ago, and I stopped relating to my parents after I joined the church. It's hard to repair all the damage and start again. I'm having trouble with Jesus right now, too, although I think I'll get over it. Sometimes I can't help wondering whose side he's on; every so often I have these fears that I'm going to hell after all. It's like a double whammy: losing all my friends *and* going to hell. But I've found a normal church in the community now, where I'm trying to put it all back together."

Before you get worried about churches with members who say they've been born again, though, I want to make it crystal clear that this book is not trying to warn you off conservative, evangelical Christian churches. Half of the Protestant congregations in America today may fall into that category, and many of them are just as concerned about Christian cults and dangerous religious practices as I am as a liberal Christian. There are also large evangelical "para-church" organizations like the InterVarsity Christian Fellowship, which is active on college campuses across the nation, that have created codes of ethics on proselytizing to prevent abuses.

InterVarsity's code respects "the individual integrity, intellectual honesty, and academic freedom of other believers and skeptics." It affirms "the inalienable right of every person to survey other options and to convert to or choose a different belief system." Disavowed is "the use of any coercive technique or manipulative appeals which bypass a person's criti-cal faculties, play on psychological weaknesses or mask the true nature of Christian conversion." There will be "no false advertising" and "no overly emotional appeals which minimize reason and evidence." InterVarsity will always "reveal our own identity and purpose, our theological position and sources of information, and will not be intentionally misleading." Wanting to relate to people of other religions, it will also "divest our witness of any stereotypes or fixed formulas which are barriers to true dialog."

Charlie Wright is an evangelical business leader in his seventies who has long been involved with InterVarsity programs. His spiritual journey has been very different from Barbara Smith's. He grew up in a Methodist family and attended Sunday school faithfully until age ten. Then he joined a famous Episcopal boys choir that went to Carnegie Hall to sing during the 1939 World's Fair. Once his voice changed early in high school, though, he stopped going to church. The next time he thought seriously about religion was in a thatched hut in the Marshall Islands just after the end of World War II. As a supply officer he was somehow bunked in with the two base chaplains—Roman Catholic and Baptist. They talked late into the nights about the meaning of life and death.

Within six months, as officers who had overstayed their tour of duty during wartime began returning home, this nineteen-year-old became the one and only supply officer for the naval air base, with some five hundred people reporting to him. It was great experience for launching a business career! Then, after almost three years in the military, he went to college in Virginia and "became an intellectual." His religious development was put on hold as his mind soared and as he spent six years in school getting both a B.A. and an M.B.A. He also became fascinated by the political issues of the day, especially McCarthyism in the early 1950s. Charlie emerged from that era a lifelong liberal Democrat, putting him at political odds with many of his business associates.

He then worked outside Washington, D.C., where he had two Catholic girlfriends. He took a summer trip to Europe and was astounded by the beauty of the cathedrals and their ethereal music. As the procession of monks passed into the golden-altared church of Assisi, carrying candles, spreading incense, and chanting, surrounded by Giotto paintings on the life of St. Francis, Charlie felt "it was enough to send you straight to heaven." Back home he began attending mass and talking about Catholicism, much to the dismay of some of his old Protestant friends. Yet, he found American Catholic churches very parochial and bland after what he had experienced in Europe: "The music was terrible and so were the sermons." He tried to stay with it for several years but was never satisfied.

He finally began to ask himself, "What's the closest to European Catholicism I can find in America?" After some searching, he found an Episcopal church with a beautiful liturgy and a good preacher. It felt as if he had come home, circling back to the Episcopalianism of his late childhood, but at a more informed adult level. He joined the choir and began singing again. He also joined singing groups outside the church and became known as "The Great Crooner" for his velvet voice and perfect pitch. He worked hard as the community-relations officer for his company during the day and sang his way into the best of Washington social life at night and on the weekends. A full decade was spent this way. Then Charlie began drinking more and more and playing around with a lot of different women. He wasn't settling down. Increasingly he drifted away from church life in his late thirties and early forties.

The summer of 1972 changed his life. He was forty-five years old—a successful businessman with lots of friends and lovers. Yet, for the first time he was beginning to sense his own mortality. He could actually die! Heart attacks and cancer had taken people he knew in their forties. What had he really been living his life for? What would give real meaning to the rest of his life as he faced the creaks and groans of middle age?

One July night he was on his third round of drinks in a bar with a woman friend, Joan, when a character named Scooter sat down next to them. He was hilarious. As he told stories, though, he kept using the word "spirit." Charlie thought to himself, and later said to Joan, "That's very odd." Even odder, he thought, was that she hadn't noticed it. The next evening Charlie went back to try to find Scooter. He was at the same seat at the bar.

"What's all this about 'spirit'?" Charlie inquired.

Scooter proceeded to tell him about a "born-again" experience he'd had after the love of his life left him. He had wandered grief-stricken and depressed into a Protestant church, wondering if it was worth living anymore. The minister saw him sitting there, spoke with him briefly, and then invited him into the office. They began a regular counseling relationship that lasted several weeks. Then one day when he was praying alone in the church, Scooter had an overwhelming sensation of Jesus next to him saying, "Come to me, and I will give you rest."

The very next weekend, Charlie and Joan went to a party in someone's Georgetown apartment. Charlie drank too much and ended up in the corner with a woman who started telling him about her father. He had been battling cancer at one of the nation's best hospitals. The doctors finally sent him home, saying his condition was incurable. They gave him only months to live. His daughter quit her job to be with him in his final days. Previously she had been just a nominal Christian, but now she started praying fervently for her father every day. Miraculously, he recovered completely and went back to work at his construction firm. That night she was in tears, thanking God in prayer, when she felt His strong hands on her shoulders. She described having been "born again" as a Christian at that moment and blessed with a rich spiritual life ever since.

Three strikes and you're out—or in. The next weekend Charlie was having some work done on his apartment. He began talking to the twenty-four-year-old carpenter, Jimmy. Jimmy hadn't been able to finish his education at the Air Force Academy because of a head-on collision with a truck in the Colorado mountains. "I was at death's door when I arrived at the hospital," Jimmy remembered. "The Presbyterian chaplain spent every minute with me, praying and praying. I saw myself going to meet my Maker. The chaplain asked me if I accepted Jesus Christ as my Lord and Savior. It was a very emotional moment. I said I did, with all my being. Suddenly it was like the first day of my life. Everything looked fresh and new. Within two weeks I was out of the hospital and on the road to recovery. Here I am today."

Charlie explains, "Now it could just have been all the attention these three people got from a family member or clergy that gave them a positive attitude and a will to live. Or maybe the 'spirit' was there after all. All I know is that I had these three conversations with unconnected people in the space of less than two weeks. When I told Jimmy about the first two, he said, 'Charlie, I think there's something going on in your life. There's a message here that you need to hear.'"

Charlie continued: "Jimmy invited me over to dinner after he finished work that day. He lived in a Christian community. I had half a dozen people thinking with me over lasagna that night about what it all meant in my life. I went home around midnight and began reading about the early Christian community in the New Testament book of Acts. Just before I went to bed, I decided to get down on my knees and pray. For a change! It had been a long time. And then I had a *very* dramatic experience. It was like the heavens opened and I was bathed in light. For the next several weeks I couldn't talk about anything else."

He related his experiences to some colleagues at work, who asked him to join a weekly prayer breakfast they had organized with the help of a minister associated with the InterVarsity Christian Fellowship. "It was wonderful. They held my hand. They helped me understand what was happening to me. Now I knew personally what it meant to be 'born again.' I've never been the same since. I'm sure not a saint, but I do try to focus all the time on having Christ in my life."

Before long he was invited by InterVarsity to talk to students back at his alma mater about his experiences. For more than a quarter century he has continued his involvement with the campus group as well as with one kind of businesspeople's prayer group or another. Meanwhile, he has been in and out of many churches.

There was a conservative Presbyterian one that "got too cultish. They thought they had the only way." He switched to a downtown Episcopal church before he found a Roman Catholic order whose small services spoke directly to his heart. Their work with the urban poor also attracted his contributions of time and money. He particularly liked the combination of conservative faith with liberal social action.

Trying to find a Catholic church closer to his home, though, he found the neighborhood parish too large. "There was no sense of community, and the only ones at the coffee hour seemed to be visitors." As a result he went back to an Episcopal church ("I always go back to the Episcopalians when I don't know what else to do!"). After six years of singing in the choir and serving on the vestry of this very formal church, though, he became tired of people saying "That's a very private question" when he asked them about their relationship to Jesus. So he found another Episcopal church nearby that called itself Pentecostal and evangelical. "It's full of young people, very multicultural, and incredibly joyous!"

That's where he is now. Maybe not tomorrow. He explains, not surprisingly, "I'm not a denominational person. What's important is the spirit of the place. It has to have a feeling of community. It has to make sense to my rational mind. And it needs to be filled with the spirit of God. I'm an enthusiast, and I will be until the day I die." What he likes best these days about his InterVarsity involvement is going on retreats with young people. "I learn from anyone, no matter what their age." His business prayer breakfasts also mean a lot because of their diversity: "There are Catholics, Christian Scientists, converted Jews, Republicans, and Democrats." He adds with a twinkle, "Actually there are too many Republicans, but that's all right as long as they aren't misinforming us about abortion and homosexuality."

I consider Charlie to be at Stage Five of spiritual development, the Interdependence stage. That's because after years of struggle between dependence and independence, he is clear about his own religious path as an evangelical, "born-again" Christian, but he is also open to dialogue and exchange with vastly different kinds of people of all ages. He is attached to no leader, yet God is no longer distant for him. He insists on using all his faculties—intellectual, emotional, and spiritual—rather than saying he has simply taken a "leap of faith." Paradoxically, he is organizationally committed to the InterVarsity Christian Fellowship but skeptical about organizations, having trouble staying in any church community for more than five or six years. He is deeply involved with his prayer group, but his religion does not put him in lockstep with most of his business brothers' and sisters' politics. He wants nothing to do with religion that seems cultish. Although he's had a mystical "born-again" experience, he is "not a saint," not yet at the Unity stage of faith development. Charlie does not yet live with a sense of the all-pervasive unity of God or of a universal community of all religions.

Siddhartha, Karen, Arvind, Barbara, Charlie, and I each picked a path and began walking. It wasn't always easy, and there were plenty of bends and curves along the way. It turned out to be most difficult for Barbara, because she didn't heed the warning signs of dangerous religious practices: deception, separation from old friends and family, a total environment occupying all her time, rigid hierarchical control, and prohibition of doubt and intellectual inquiry. The rest of us found a lot of fulfillment sooner or later. (The results may not be in yet on Karen, but she did enjoy being a religion major!) I believe our lives were changed for the better. It was liberating and exhilarating. I encourage you to take that first step. The mountain beckons.

Joining

Janet Taylor calls herself a second-generation religious skeptic. Her mother and father met at an Ethical Culture gathering in Chicago. A kind of practical philosophy, it held out the promise of an intelligent, believable religion without dogma. However, for them it just led to cynicism. While Janet was growing up, her father took her to the local Protestant church, but it seemed more a faint echo from a prior generation—how children should be brought up—than a current commitment on her father's part. She rebelled and stopped going during high school, just as her father was struggling with the painful cancer that killed him in her senior year. Her mother was always loving but felt increasingly sure that there could be no God who would allow this tragedy to happen to her husband.

Janet came to Tufts University to study engineering. When she was studying the "cold" disciplines of science, math, and engineering in the library during her freshman year, however, she found herself easily distracted by "warmer" books and journals about psychology and religion. It was the human being, not the machine, that she wanted to learn about. Dropping the engineering major, she found herself sequentially disappointed by psychology, political science, economics, history, literature, and philosophy. Religion was the candle that kept drawing her like a light in the darkness. It seemed both to provide a wide perspective on life and to stimulate close personal reflection.

Her love for humankind started to grow as she studied religion. The problem for her was that she couldn't figure out how to attach it to individual people. In her circle of friends, there were few who could talk about religion. And she could never bring herself to get involved with any campus religious groups. Maybe she'd find like-minded people by joining an organization to do community service, she thought. But, when she considered how much patience, diligence, and humility could be involved, she decided to stay on the loner track.

Her reading also became more strained and difficult. She devoured Buddhist, Taoist, and Christian texts. Each seemed to contain critical spiritual lessons. Yet, after a month or so, the teachings that had seemed so important at the time were largely forgotten. Each text tended to take her in a different direction, and nothing stuck with her. Looking back years later, she realized what her problem was: she didn't look at anything deeply enough or with enough commitment to find something lasting in it.

Writing became the next way for her to find meaning. She started keeping a journal and writing articles for the campus newspapers. At the same time she started meditating. Again, she found that she picked up each activity with great enthusiasm, and each was rewarding as she did it. Yet she had little discipline. After days of waking up early to write or meditate, she would sleep until noon. Then it would take a week or more for her to get back to the journal and the half hour of quiet sitting.

Since college, after working for a year in a New York bank to earn some money, she has started traveling outside the country. She has no immediate plans for her future employment, except teaching English as a second language and picking up other odd jobs as she goes. When friends ask what she wants to do when she grows up, she refers half-jokingly to someone who says he wants to "become a self-actualized human being." She's searching and inquiring. She's picked paths and started walking. She's literally on a journey. Yet in reality she's lost in the world, as well as within herself. She's worked hard to move from the material to the spiritual, to look deep within herself and search for meaning in the universe. For that she deserves a lot of credit, especially in comparison to people who move blindly and unthinkingly out of college into lockstep jobs and prearranged lives. What she needs most, though, is to stop flailing away alone and to find some spiritual traveling companions. It's been awfully lonely on her path for a long time. Joining with some friends could make a big difference in helping her achieve the commitment and discipline she's been longing for.

Ahmad Karim has found those trail mates. His path has been very different from Janet's, but it was only by joining with traveling companions that his religion began to work for him. He grew up in the Seattle area. His parents, both originally from Egypt, wanted him to be fully involved in American culture but also to grow up in a devoutly Muslim household. As is traditional, they prayed five times a day and maintained what he calls "an aura of religion" in their home. His mother teaches in the Seattle school system. His father is a lawyer actively involved in international human rights; he has been an election observer in Haiti, Bosnia, and Cambodia.

Although Ahmad attended a Muslim Sunday school and took Arabic lessons throughout his childhood, he remembers most of his childhood religion as "just going through the motions." His parents never pushed him or forced him in any way. He was encouraged to search, read widely, question, and understand for himself. In reality, though, Ahmad was just a normal kid who generally did what pleased his parents without thinking about it all very much. Islam seemed to involve a direct relationship between himself and God. It was carried out through a set of practices, and he didn't have a lot of doubts about it—or a lot of interest, frankly.

Everything changed dramatically when he accompanied his parents on the *hajj*—the pilgrimage to Mecca—just before college at the age of seventeen. The *hajj* is one of the "Five Pillars" of Islam, which are the minimum obligatory practices for all Muslims. They include 1) reciting the creed ("There is no god but God, and Muhammad is his prophet"); 2) praying five times daily; 3) fasting during daylight hours in the lunar month of Ramadan; 4) giving charity to the needy; and 5) making the pilgrimage to Mecca once in one's lifetime. Ahmad had always dutifully followed his parents' directives on the first four. The *hajj*, however, marked his personal commitment to Islam.

Mecca, in the country now called Saudi Arabia, is the sacred city where the prophet Muhammad was born, lived all but the last ten years of his life, and first proclaimed the word of God, which became the Muslim scripture, the Qur'an (or Koran). When Ahmad's family was ten kilometers from the city, he and his father changed the clothes they were wearing and put on a special two-piece garment, essentially like two small sheets or towels around their waist and over their shoulders. His mother traded her American clothes for an all-white garment. The symbolism of the clothing is that all people are equal in the sight of God: it doesn't matter where you come from, how much wealth you have, or what your background is.

Ahmad describes the awesome spectacle of being with hundreds of thousands of other people, all dressed alike, walking seven times around the Ka'bah, a small shrine near the center of the Great Mosque in Mecca, toward which daily prayers of Muslims all over the world are always oriented. Even more astonishing was the afternoon he unexpectedly spent walking in a valley several miles from Mecca. The bus he was riding on with his mother and father broke down, forcing them to make this part of the pilgrimage on foot. There were Muslims—literally fellow travelers on a common pilgrimage—as far as he could see behind him and as far as he could see ahead. He was filled with reverence and solidarity of a sort he had never imagined. The conversations about faith he had as he walked along brought him together with Muslims from as far away as Indonesia and as close at hand as the Arab countries of the Middle East. He talked to people from sub-Saharan Africa, the Indian subcontinent, and parts of the former Soviet Union, all of whom took him seriously as a fellow Muslim. This became *his* tradition and not just that of his parents.

When Ahmad came to Tufts, his classes conflicted with the major public prayer time on Friday afternoons, just as they had in high school. Traveling companions had become so important in his spirituality, though, that by sophomore year he made sure that this time was free of classes. He got involved in organizing and leading Friday prayers in the Tufts Islamic Center. He met Muslims from all over the world right there at Tufts and began conversations that have never stopped. This has been a great learning process for him. But the month of Ramadan that year was even more so.

During this month there are recitations from the Qur'an every night of the thirty, but the "Night of Power," on the twenty-seventh, is said to be better than a thousand months, a night when angels come down to be with people until dawn. It commemorates the night when Muhammad first received his commission from the angel Gabriel to proclaim the word of God. People get together as usual after breaking the fast at sunset, and there's a lot of praying that night. Ahmad strangely found himself ashamed in front of his friends. He didn't feel that he was reciting the Qur'anic Arabic properly, even after all his childhood years of lessons.

Why should this matter so much? Was it a question of wounded pride and bruised ego? No—the issue was much more significant than that.

Arabic was the original language of transmission from God to Muhammad; it's considered a sacred language. Also, as historian of religion Huston Smith has explained, Qur'anic Arabic has a strong emotional and hypnotic effect due to its rhyme, rhythm, and melodic cadence. The contents and the container are inseparably fused. This is why translations of the Qur'an have historically been discouraged, and why they are called interpretations, rather than renderings of the original. It may also explain why outsiders like Thomas Carlyle, reading the Qur'an for the first time in translation, have described it as toilsome and confused.[1]

So Ahmad joined an Arabic class at Tufts to learn the language better as part of his religious development. Now he feels quite comfortable reading out loud. And as a consequence, he says, he's found a lot more contemplative peace in his own prayer practice. Traveling companions brought Islam alive for him on the *hajj* and have helped him advance spiritually ever since.

The late teens and twenties are a good time to examine the importance of joining with other travelers to find one's religion. That's because this period is usually the age of tension between Dependence and Independence in spiritual development. By the time of Interdependence, well into adulthood for most of us, the significance of religious community is generally clear. Yet, when you're struggling to become independent and stand on your own two feet, companions can seem to be holding you back. To say "I'm spiritual, but I'm not religious" is to say I have my own way that's not related to some group or organization or institution. It can feel dependent to be part of a group. Won't your budding individuality be buried?

Not necessarily. In fact, companions during the Independence stage can serve as a sounding board, helping you to discover what's really you and what's not. They can challenge self-deception, help you see what you look like in others' eyes, and facilitate personal development through dialogue. They can assist you to become truer to yourself, to develop personal virtues and discipline, and to discover what really matters to you. The classic philosophical and political discussions lasting late into the night during college are usually more a sign of increasing independence than of dependence.

Companionship during the Dependence stage usually has quite a different quality, a conformist one. There's a susceptibility to fashions and fads. You tend to learn the most from respected leaders, exemplars, and models. Loyalty is paramount. You run in a pack and don't easily hold membership in multiple groups at the same time. There's not a lot of personal risk taking, unless it's backed up by the gang against outsiders. The potential of cult involvement is high, but so is that of finding a meaningful life philosophy with a respected sage to point the way.

The increasingly independent Rebecca Malkin would have left Judaism if it hadn't been for traveling companions she found after high school. She grew up in England in a family of Orthodox Jews, even though they weren't particularly observant. She went to Orthodox Jewish schools every year of her life until she got to Tufts. By that time she'd become frustrated with her tradition, even though she remained close to her family. She felt smothered by Orthodox Judaism, and she was resentful of how it seemed to belittle women. Why should men and women be segregated in worship? Why should only men be rabbis? So she began to search.

She took a year off between high school and college to work on a kibbutz in Israel. On Yom Kippur, the Day of Atonement, the holiest day in the Jewish calendar, everything came to a complete halt. Now, this should not have surprised her, given her Orthodox upbringing and the fact that this was Israel, the Jewish state, after all. But the kibbutz was populated only by secular Israelis. She had made sure of that before deciding to live there. They called Yom Kippur "The Day of Enjoyment," because all work and all schooling and everything else stopped so that kibbutz members could just have uninterrupted, unmitigated fun with each other. It was the most relaxing day of the year. She felt a new kind of freedom there she had never known before. It was not just personal freedom, either; it was communal freedom, shared and enjoyed together.

In college she took the step of checking out Hillel, the campus Jewish student organization—but not too closely, because she valued her freedom and was worried about getting mixed up in smothering "religion." However, she became intrigued by some people there who called themselves the Jewish Women's Collective. This group planned events that felt deeply spiritual to her, such as new moon celebrations. Since antiquity, she learned, Jewish women have taken this day off each month to celebrate their freedom. There was a different theme stressed at the gathering every month, such as tolerance and open-mindedness or liberation itself. Each meeting was an hour long and included poetry, singing, a creative activity, and discussion. She felt her spiritual dimension was touched in those celebrations as in no other place in her life. They had a clear feminist focus, in contrast to the patriarchal nature of so much of Judaism, including the Hebrew scriptures. She felt as if she was spreading her wings and flying, with wonderful companions at her wingtips.

The next step was attending a feminist Passover Seder in New York with six hundred attendees "from everywhere." She now describes it as a turning point for her—one of the great spiritual moments of her life. There she found not only a profound sense of camaraderie but also a learning process about how to effect change. The new moon celebrations and the feminist Seder had now reestablished her on the Jewish path, but in an entirely fresh way.

She wanted to bring her new spirituality to her family's religious celebrations and to educate her brothers and parents about Jewish feminism without insulting them or turning them off. So at the next Passover she put an orange on the family's Seder plate and asked everyone to tell a story about the orange and its significance to the Exodus story of the ancient Jews' liberation from slavery in Egypt. Wonderful, creative yarns were concocted by each member of her family.

Then Rebecca explained that opponents of women becoming rabbis had made this statement in Florida several years ago: "Women belong in the rabbinate as much as an orange belongs on a Seder plate." Feminist Seders have used oranges as a centerpiece ever since. Her family listened thoughtfully and appreciatively, Rebecca said, and saw the connection to the basic theme of Passover—liberation. She says they've become accepting of the importance of Jewish feminism, just as she's become committed in a new way to Judaism as her spiritual path. So friends helped her stay with Judaism, and her family's openness helped her widen her circle of traveling companions to include them, too.

Nathan Zuckerman in Philip Roth's novel *The Ghost Writer* was not as lucky. I've taught the book many times both to Tufts undergraduates and Harvard Business students. It incisively reveals problems with trying to go one's religion alone. The students are almost always torn, however; most of them end up wanting Nathan to maintain his independence, even if it means hurting the Jewish community around him.

Nathan is a twenty-three-year-old writer from Newark, New Jersey, finding success in 1956 publishing his first short stories. One of them is based on an old feud in his family. Before he submits it to a national magazine, he sends it to his parents "to please them and make them proud."[2] It does neither. His father considers him to have culled "the most shameful and disreputable transgressions of family decency and trust" from their past. Nathan admits as much but defends himself on the basis of artistic freedom: "Hadn't Joyce, hadn't Flaubert, hadn't Thomas Wolfe, the romantic genius of my high-school reading list, all been condemned for disloyalty or treachery or immorality by those who saw themselves as slandered in their works?" Nathan is convinced he's written a good story, and that's that.

Artistic freedom is not the issue for Nathan's father. He's concerned about religious solidarity in a world that only a decade before annihilated half of the Jews then alive. No, America is not Nazi Germany, his father knows, but the "story, as far as Gentiles are concerned, is about one thing and one thing only. . . . It is about kikes. Kikes and their love of money. That is all our good Christian friends will see, I guarantee you." From Dr. Zuckerman's perspective, Gentiles won't "think about how it's a great work of art. . . . People don't read art—they read about *people*. And they judge them as such." He continues: "I wonder if you fully understand just how very little love there is in this world for Jewish people. I don't mean in Germany, either, under the Nazis. I mean in run-of-the-mill Americans, Mr. and Mrs. Nice Guy, who otherwise you and I consider perfectly harmless."

Nathan stops speaking to his father after receiving a letter from a judge who once penned a college admissions recommendation for him. Dr. Zuckerman has put this pillar of the Newark Jewish community up to encouraging Nathan not to publish the story. Judge Wapter writes of spiritual dignity, the artist's responsibility to his community, and Nathan's personal obligation to those who have helped him become successful. A list of ten questions is appended to the long letter, including this: "Aside from the financial gain to yourself, what benefit do you think publishing this story in a national magazine will have for (a) your family; (b) your community; (c) the Jewish religion; (d) the well-being of the Jewish people?"

In his own opinion, Nathan has not abandoned Judaism. In fact, *The Ghost Writer* begins with his visiting a famous Jewish author at his isolated farmhouse in the Berkshire mountains of western Massachusetts: "I had come, you see, to submit myself for candidacy as nothing less than E. I. Lonoff's spiritual son." Nathan first read Lonoff's books "as an orthodox college atheist and highbrow-in-training" at the University of

Chicago. In the process he learned "how much I was still my family's Jewish offspring."

The problem is that Lonoff is an entirely reclusive and solitary Jew. He's married to a Gentile woman named Hope. He refuses all degrees and awards, joins no organizations, grants no public interviews, and declines ever to be photographed. He's lived out in the country at the end of an unpaved road for more than a quarter century. He won't become active in the Pittsfield synagogue. Hope feels as if she's married to Tolstoy, because Lonoff's life is utterly consumed in "turning sentences around." When he's walking with her in the woods or even just eating a meal with her, he's bad-tempered and restless, wanting to get back to his writing again.

With his mentor's spiritual isolation appearing even worse than his own, Nathan develops a bizarre, no doubt unconscious, way of proving himself a devoted Jew. He begins to imagine that an assistant of Lonoff's, a former student now helping the great man catalog his manuscripts at home, is none other than Anne Frank, who escaped from the concentration camp after all. Nathan wants to marry her and take her back home. It can't be coincidental that both Judge Wapter in his letter and his mother in a phone call have encouraged Nathan to see the recently opened Broadway adaptation of *The Diary of Anne Frank*.

The book ends with his spiritual mentor's wife running off into the Berkshire snow with an overnight bag, screaming that she's leaving for good and moving to Boston. Lonoff calls after her from the front door, "But how can I live alone?" Nathan seems fated to live alone with his writing as well, since by now the assistant has made it clear that she's not Anne Frank and has headed back to her job at the Harvard library. Instead of thinking about how to reconcile with his family and the Jewish community, Nathan starts making feverish notes about his visit for his next story as soon as Lonoff, abandoned by Hope, disappears into the cold in search of her.

Now, how could I explain to someone like Nathan or Lonoff how utterly transformative it is to have traveling companions on one's spiritual journey? I tried going it alone myself in the early years of my ministry. Five years later I learned what a difference it made to work within a spiritual community. Maybe my story can help.

I had gone to law school and to divinity school simultaneously for five years with the idea of developing some kind of community ministry within which I could use law as a tool. After graduating from both schools at Harvard in 1975, I went to work for a 150-year-old social service organization that is now called the Unitarian Universalist Urban Ministry. It's supported by more than fifty metropolitan area churches and has a tradition of freeing ordained ministers from parish responsibilities to provide "ministries at large" to the inner-city poor of Boston. I was to furnish a "ministry at law" to low-income people in the Dorchester area of the city. That meant I would represent people who couldn't afford lawyers in whatever matter they brought to me, free of charge to them. I would be paid a salary by this church organization. The ministry dimension would involve my taking the traditional role of lawyer as counselor very seriously, listening to my clients' problems in general, not just their legal issues, and helping them make sense of their lives. It didn't mean, however, that I would proselytize for my religious tradition or even discuss religion with my clients unless they brought it up.

For the first two years I served as a staff attorney in a federally funded legal services office in Dorchester. That meant I had the support of paralegals and secretaries, access to a law library and office equipment, and supervision by the managing attorney. I had my own caseload, and, like most legal aid lawyers, I quickly found myself working overtime trying to meet my clients' legal needs. I spent a lot of time in court, in the law library, and throwing acerbic paper back and forth with other attorneys. There wasn't much time to be a counselor to my clients, I learned. There also wasn't much time to notice the leaves changing colors in the fall or the flowers coming up in the spring.

Within a year I had an ulcer, and my wife of six years had left me. Neither was necessarily related to my work, but I wasn't getting much opportunity to minister to anyone, including myself. I felt like a spiritual maverick truly operating at large, doing his own thing, without any kind of religious community surrounding me or supporting me. I couldn't even maintain a worshiping relationship to a local church, because I was accepting invitations to preach in different churches on Sundays about the work they were supporting in the inner city.

So, in the third year I became the assistant minister of the local Unitarian Universalist church in Dorchester. I assisted in every Sunday service and preached once a month. I visited the sick, conducted baptisms, weddings, and funerals, helped with the religious education program, and represented the church at various community meetings. I also had a lot of opportunity to provide counseling to individuals. What was largely missing, however, was the "at law" part of my ministry. There were only a few people who came to the church needing legal help with the likes of welfare terminations and eviction notices. I also found how hard it is to have one's own spiritual needs met as one of the professional leaders of a congregation. You lead the community, but professional obligations prevent you from fully being a member of it. The senior minister was a great help, but, for all intents and purposes, I still operated very much alone.

In my fourth and fifth years I began wearing both minister's and lawyer's hats simultaneously at a state mental hospital in Dorchester. I became the acting chaplain of the institution as well as its appointed patients' rights officer. I conducted religious services for these low-income patients and visited them for counseling on the wards, while at the same time representing their interests in conflicts with medical personnel and the hospital administration. As chaplain I was usually appreciated by other staff on the wards, although not always—from some psychiatric perspectives, religion was considered an illusion, or worse.

As patients' rights officer, though, I was often perceived as the enemy. I challenged doctors' rights to cure patients by medicating them against their will. I reminded staff that, under Massachusetts law, nonviolent patients couldn't be locked up in seclusion rooms simply for infractions of rules. I defended patients' rights to keep their own clothes and belongings. I insisted that there be seats on toilets and doors on toilet stalls. I criticized attempts to limit patient access to the outside world (to lawyers in particular).

This was lonely work. I headed a corps of patient representatives throughout the hospital, but that was an add-on title to their primary jobs and they weren't legally trained. They always felt that if they were too outspoken they might risk their jobs, not to mention their daily working relationships with other staff. Few of them had much status in the hospital hierarchy. Meanwhile, I had little ongoing contact with the other clergy who would come in and out of the hospital to visit their own parishioners. On weekends I was again often preaching in a different one of the fifty churches that supported the work of the Unitarian Universalist Urban Ministry. There was no real religious community of which I was a part.

Burned out and still suffering with an ulcer after five years of ministry at large to the poor, I took a year's leave of absence for the spiritual odyssey around the world that I described in the chapter "Thinking." Although I was traveling alone most of the time, I stayed in a number of religious communities along the way. I began to relish the bonds with other spiritual voyagers. There was the Hindu ashram in Bali where I awakened for group yoga on the beach every day with the first rays of light. At a shrine in Japan a group of Shintoists spent three days preparing me for ritual purification under a 40-degree waterfall. Buddhists whom I stayed with for a week taught me parts of the Lotus Sutra to chant with them every day. I spent half months with mentors in the cities of Jerusalem and Cairo, steeping myself in Judaism and Islam before traveling around Israel and Egypt for another two weeks each. I attended a Spanish language school for a month in Guatemala with a Maryknoll priest and a Sister of Mercy nun; we talked constantly about the Christian response to the poverty and oppression of indigenous peoples in that country, where they had come to minister.

I returned to Dorchester almost a year to the day after I left, now determined to find a way to serve in religious community with others. Within six months I had founded the Unitarian Universalist Legal Ministry. In a storefront near a busy intersection, it was operated by a dedicated group of divinity students and church volunteers, including attorneys. We provided free legal information and referral services to people unable to afford a lawyer. The model was explicitly ministerial—seeing clients' legal problems in relation to their whole life situation and being as willing to pray with a client, when asked, as to read legalese on a government form. Our staff meetings were full of spiritual support for one another, as well as for our clients.

Testimony at those meetings included very personal descriptions of the kind of faith that got volunteers involved with us in the first place, and that kept them involved. More than once these words of Jesus were discussed: "Come, you that are blessed by my Father, inherit the kingdom prepared for you from the foundation of the world; for I was hungry and you gave me food, I was thirsty and you gave me drink, I was a stranger and you welcomed me, I was naked and you clothed me, I was sick and you took care of me, I was in prison and you visited me." Jesus is asked when these things were done for him, and he replies, "Truly, I tell you, just as you did it to one of the least of these my brothers or sisters, you did it to me."[3]

Some volunteers whose sense of religious faith had been weak explained how they had been fed and strengthened by their clients' faith—and by the level of caring and commitment they had seen in the relationship between staff and clients. Others described how this involvement had clarified their understanding of the Christian theological debate about the value of faith and works. We transcend our petty egos by devotion to the source of all life, which leads naturally to wanting to serve others. Jesus had cited love of neighbor along with love of God as part of the greatest commandment, on which "hang all of the law and the prophets."[4] The letter of James was also quoted in our staff meetings: "Faith by itself, if it has no works, is dead."[5]

I was thrilled, and totally renewed, by the Legal Ministry. Not only was there a religious community among the staff, but churches in which I was preaching on Sundays were getting directly involved with our work in Dorchester. That meant I was developing deep, faith-filled relationships with individuals I would see before and after those services. Some of them worked in our office. Others were attorneys who had volunteered full-scale assistance for clients whose problems couldn't be resolved with self-help information and conciliation attempts from our office. Church committees had been set up to stay in touch with our work, raise money, and find furniture and other items needed both in our office and by our clients. There were other church members who couldn't come to the office but were willing to write articles for local newspapers, research issues upon request, compile directories, and translate materials into Spanish and other languages. A number of them wanted to meet with me or with one another regularly to examine their own religious journeys in relation to the Legal Ministry.

How different all this was from my disconnected days as a minister on my own in the community! For example, one sixty-year-old widow, whose husband had been murdered, was counseled by the Legal Ministry for three years. She worked with a team of two office staff, two volunteer lawyers, and a church that secured a charitable grant. She was caring for a fourteen-year-old boy who had been abandoned at the age of two; a volunteer attorney successfully pursued adoption in the probate court. Her house was being foreclosed for back taxes she couldn't pay with her four-thousand-dollar annual income as a part-time health aide; another volunteer attorney stopped the foreclosure and secured a widow's property tax abatement. Two rental units in the house were empty because previous tenants had trashed them before they left; the charitable grant allowed them to be fixed up again. Office staff helped her get Medicaid benefits for the adopted son, obtain fuel assistance benefits to cover overdue heating bills, and file forms to prevent shut-offs of her other utilities.

Meanwhile, one of our staff members spent hours in pastoral counseling and prayer with her, as this widow wondered what kind of God could have wreaked so much havoc in the life of a hard-working, decent Christian woman. I was deeply touched when another staffer, who had previously spent nine years in corporate bill collection, said one day, "The Legal Ministry makes you integrate theology with life. It forces you to say, 'This is the way I know God. This is the reason I love God. How does that change the way I live my life?'"[6]

One thing missing in the Legal Ministry, though, was a sense of religious community among our clients themselves. We said in reports and articles that we worked on an empowerment model, helping organize tenants' unions, welfare rights groups, and other collective efforts to deal with common problems faced by poor people. We assisted our clients to come together in public demonstrations against homelessness and against government cutbacks in basic survival programs for low-income people. In reality, however, we did very little to promote a sense of meaningful interaction among our clients and almost nothing to help them share spiritually with one another. We never figured out how to adapt a compelling model that I'd seen in Central America during my year's pilgrimage abroad—the *comunidades cristianas de bases*, or Christian base communities, which operated in a Roman Catholic environment, unlike our more pluralistic urban setting.

I still vividly remember the large, colorful mural on a wall of Cristo Redentor, a Catholic church in San Miguelito, Panama. It portrays several Bible study groups out in the countryside, made up of peasants, workers, and indigenous people. A new church is being built on the other side of the canvas, and a priest is taking a worker's hand to show him Christ's way. Two shadowy priests in the background, with money dripping out of their pockets, are portrayed as hypocrites, betraying the word of God. More than thirty years ago this church was one of the first to develop *comunidades cristianas de bases* as part of the growing liberation theology movement in Latin America. These *comunidades* gathered traveling companions, following the path of Jesus in a new way. Their study of the Bible was directly related to their daily lives of poverty, organizing them for social justice within the context of the gospel. Christ was seen as Liberator, defending the poor and the persecuted against the "principalities and powers" of the world. Each *comunidad* consisted of fifteen to twenty people who came together for literacy training and for the mutual assistance that grew out of Bible study and prayer.

I spent two Sundays and the intervening week in and around this parish. I had also learned about the *comunidades* from Father Donald and Sister Margaret, the priest and nun I studied with for a month in Guatemala. The relationships that formed within the *comunidades* tended to be very close. The Bible came alive, speaking directly to individuals' everyday struggles. Sharing feelings about one's life in relation to the characters in scripture had a profound effect on poor people both in Guatemala and Panama, leading to solidarity against unjust landlords and bosses and unresponsive government officials, and to hope through faith for members of the *comunidad*.

In the Guatemalan context it could also mean assassination for lay leaders, as Sister Margaret reported to me one Monday morning after a weekend visit to a rural *comunidad* nearby, where two men had been murdered. They were described in government reports as communists, but they were not. Sister Margaret described how it was their Christian faith that had made them strong and had given meaning to them in their lives and to their fellow Christians in their deaths. In the center of the San Miguelito mural is a peasant stooping under the weight of a heavily laden bamboo pole he's carrying, looking for all the world like a condemned, suffering man carrying a cross, yet surrounded by friends as he lifts his eyes to the hills.

In a less dramatic context, I've found my own religious life centered and renewed for the last several years in a group of four Unitarian Universalist Christian ministers. Holy Spirit Group is the title we've given ourselves. We meet for an afternoon every two weeks for prayer, Bible study, and sharing of our lives. Jason Robbins, our spiritual director, is a Catholic in a lay order of Carmelites. Married to an Episcopal priest, he's also been trained in a Buddhist tradition called Sui-Zen. As part of his religious practice, he plays a Japanese bamboo flute called the *shakuhachi* for at least half an hour every day. Jason has used the term *Christian base community* when referring to us, drawing from the Latin American experience. From a foundation of biblically based faith and mutual support, we go out into the community to try to serve and make a difference, whether or not those we work with have a spiritual life of their own.

One of us recently had to face the gunfire death of a fifteen-year-old boy in her inner-city church's summer work program. Hardly a year seems to go by without a drive-by shooting, murder or cross-fire killing of one of Alice Alexander's young parishioners. So often, as in this case, it's a good kid—friendly, cooperative, hard-working, bright. He was just hanging out with the wrong people at the wrong time. That's hard not to do, given the realities of urban life. And how many fifteen-year-olds do we know who make the right choices all of the time? Understandably, it's terrifying to other children in the church program. Every time they think things are okay, another one of them is dead. Many have no hope. They don't expect to live; before they even reach adulthood, they have to make their peace with dying.

A huge, emotional funeral gave some release and some sense of hope to her parishioners. Yet, behind the scenes, Alice was devastated. She was deeply discouraged and depressed. The Holy Spirit Group came together around her, expressing how our hearts ached with hers. We verbalized our anger: "Children shouldn't die, and we shouldn't give them the tools of destruction, which truly they can neither control nor comprehend." We said how sorry we were and how much we cared about her. Jesus on the cross was the pervasive image for us in our prayers, knowing intense suffering but transforming it by deep love, even for those who mocked and spat upon him. We united in our sense of God's essential goodness and presence even at the lowest moments of despair.

The Holy Spirit Group has also provided a base for each of us in helping to found a new coalition of urban and suburban Unitarian Universalists lobbying for the urban poor, especially children, in the state legislature. In its first year, the Tuckerman Coalition worked successfully for the passage of two laws—providing for home visitation and parenting education for mothers under twenty-one, and ensuring summer food service for hungry children to supplement the term-time School Breakfast Program. It means a lot to roll up our sleeves and work publicly for social change together, and then to return to a private space where together we contemplatively experience how compassion flows directly out of the heart of God. As Jason puts it, the Holy Spirit Group's biweekly meetings provide "a safe place where active, compassionate people can dwell in holy stillness regularly, a place where we can drink of the eternal waters with fellow travelers."

It may be in religiously inspired political action and community service work that the value of spiritual traveling companions comes alive most clearly. I wonder how different Janet Taylor's lonely spiritual journey, described at the beginning of this chapter, might have been if her love for humankind could have been focused in a religious organization involved in social service and social action. I'm always inspired by footage of clergy and lay people linking arms to march through the streets together in the American civil rights movement of the 1960s. Similarly, many older Hindus in India tell stories of how mass nonviolent action, culminating in Indian independence in 1948, was the most personally compelling religious experience in their lifetime.

I've seen in my travels through Muslim countries how much it means for a lot of people to work together in community organizations to assist the poor, fulfilling their obligation of charity as one of the Pillars of Islam. Many Jews in the United States would say that one of their strongest connections to their religion is through organizations like B'Nai B'rith's Anti-Defamation League and charities supporting projects in Israel. Buddhists can meditate alone, but they are often drawn deeply into the *sangha*, the Buddhist community, through the social service outreach that has been one of its most important functions for millennia.

For myself, joining with other travelers on my religious path has given meaning to my work, taught me about compassionate love, created a context for deep personal change and growth, and dramatically enlivened my faith.

Crossing

⟶⟍᠌᠊⟍᠊⟋⟍⟍⟵

Sally Raman grew up Catholic in Des Moines, Iowa. Her parents come from India and call themselves Syrio-Christians. They are proud to be part of a tradition said to have begun in 52 A.D. when the apostle Thomas brought Christianity to India and was martyred there. The Christian population expanded in the sixteenth century with the arrival of Portuguese missionaries. Sally's parents are deeply committed Christians, but they say their faith is enhanced and deepened by their knowledge and appreciation of Hinduism. They have learned from religious trail crossings.

Sally's mother practices yoga and meditation, seeing them as effective preludes to Christian prayer. In their house they have statues of Hindu gods and of the Buddha, as well as several crucifixes of Jesus. Sally says all provided an air of sanctity for her as a child as she moved from one room to the next. Her family also adopts the Hindu perspective that different avatars, or incarnations of divinity, have come to different peoples in different times and places throughout the ages. Their avatar is Jesus, but they respect and appreciate their friends' commitments to other avatars, such as Krishna and Buddha.

Sally started having trouble with Catholicism when her father died in the middle of her high school years. She was devastated and blamed God. She began to see hypocrisy in her local church, too—especially in how some parishioners treated her differently because she was a person of color. She developed disagreements with certain church dogma, such as positions on birth control and abortion, and the prohibition on women's ordination to the priesthood. Mass felt stiff and formal. She stopped going at the age of sixteen.

When Sally got to college, though, she found a very different experience at the 10:00 P.M. Sunday Mass in the chapel. It was packed with hundreds of other students from many different cultures and backgrounds. The music was led by a very talented group of undergraduates, who sang and played guitars. The priest's sermons were directly relevant to her daily life as a student. The cider and doughnut reception following the Mass was a warm, welcoming time with people she had met in classes, sports, and campus organizations, without ever realizing they were Catholics.

There was also a Catholic social service organization that came to campus and caught Sally's imagination. Called St. Egidio, it is a lay movement founded in 1968 in Italy by students and young professionals. It now has chapters around the world in the Americas, Africa, and Asia, helping the poor, homeless, handicapped, and sick. Its international peace initiatives have included negotiations that ended more than a decade of civil war in Mozambique. She worked with them during the summer after her freshman year and was particularly impressed by how spiritual they were, closely connecting daily prayer and Bible study to assistance to people in need. Part of their special genius seemed to be their intense particularity as a Catholic organization at the same time that they were completely open to dialogue and cooperation with other religious groups—both to solve social problems and to deepen their understanding of Catholicism through close relationships with non-Catholics.

So Sally found a new Catholicism for herself, which increasingly she related back to the old faith with which she'd grown up. She began practicing yoga every morning as a spiritual focus for prayer and study of the lectionary (selections of scripture for each day of the year from the Old and New Testaments.) She kept statues of Jesus, the Buddha, and Lord Krishna together in a corner of her room. And she began to reach out to Muslim friends to learn more about their tradition.

On a trip to Morocco she had been struck by how few desperately poor people she found there in comparison to India. In this Muslim country, everyone always seemed to give as a matter of course to anyone who begged. She learned that almsgiving was one of the Five Pillars of Islam, and now she wanted to know more from her Muslim friends about the other four. The requirement of daily prayers helped stimulate a similar discipline for her. The month of fasting during Ramadan brought Lent alive for her. Instead of it being a drab time of "giving something up for Lent," she began to see it as a special annual time of reflection on her life and renewal as the spring approached. Also her periodic trips to visit relatives in India were reconceived as a kind of *hajj*, a pilgrimage to learn more about the roots of her Syrio-Christianity. There she examined charitable traditions in Christianity more closely, finding herself particularly moved by the communities founded by Mother Teresa of Calcutta.

In eighth grade Sally had attended Protestant youth group meetings with friends in Des Moines. She stopped going, though, after she realized that the leader was insisting that no one could go to heaven who was not Christian. She knew too many deeply spiritual Hindus for that to make any sense. Her parents were appalled by the leader's claim. They quickly explained not only that it was wrong to discriminate against other religions, but also that many opportunities to strengthen one's own Christian faith are missed without respectful exposure to other traditions. Their instruction had finally become clear for Sally in college.

Shusaku Endo is a Japanese Christian author who teaches this lesson dynamically in his novel *Deep River*. A character named Otsu thinks about becoming a Catholic priest after going to a Jesuit university in Japan. The priests there talk freely about what they've learned from Buddhism and Shinto in their own spiritual life; one priest who teaches Western philosophy to Otsu also practices Zen meditation. Although Otsu never doubts that "Jesus has me in his grasp," what he learns from Buddhism and Shinto, and later from Hinduism, brings him to see that "God is not so much an existence as a force . . . an entity that performs the labors of love."[1]

This understanding gets Otsu in trouble at the seminary he attends in Lyon, France. There his superiors claim that he's a heretical pantheist, seeing God in all things, rather than understanding Him as a Creator separate from His creation. Otsu responds that European Christianity has a limited perspective: "These people reject anything they cannot slice into categories with their rationality and their conscious minds." For example, Otsu's Christianity is informed by the haiku of Basho, the great seventeenth-century Japanese Zen Buddhist poet. Otsu feels that the European Christians responsible for his training will never be able to understand the import of a verse like this of Basho's:

when I look closely
beneath the hedge, mother's-heart
flowers have blossomed

European Christians are intent on "rank ordering all living things" and "ignore the great life force that exists in Nature," which equally causes mother's-heart flowers to bloom and grants life to human beings. His Japanese sensibility leads him to this position: "I don't think God is some-one to be looked up to as a being separate from man . . . I think he is within man, and that he is a great life force that envelops man, envelops the trees, envelops the flowers and grasses."

By the end of the book, after Otsu has finally been ordained a priest, he is discovered by a college classmate to be living in Varanasi, India, the holiest city of Hinduism on the banks of its holiest river. The ashram where he's taken up residence has welcomed him warmly. He dresses in a Hindu *dhoti* to carry the poor who are dying in the streets to a health facility and the bodies of those who have already died to the funeral pyres along the Ganges River to be cremated. As he explains to his classmate, even the most solitary, impoverished outcasts "come dragging their legs to this city with the hope of having their ashes scattered in the River Ganges."

His old friend replies, "But you're no Hindu Brahmin."

Otsu retorts, "Is that distinction so important? If that man [Jesus] were here in this city now . . . he of all people would carry the fallen on his back and take them to the cremation grounds. Just as he bore the cross on his back while he was alive."

The colleague won't give up: "In the end aren't you believing in reincarnation the same as the Buddhists and the Hindus? You're a Christian priest, after all."

Otsu explains that when Jesus was crucified, "the disciples who remained finally understood his love and what it meant. Every one of them had stayed alive by abandoning him and running away. He continued to love them even though they had betrayed him." Every time Otsu looks at the River Ganges now, he thinks of Jesus: "The Ganges swallows up the ashes of every person as it flows along, rejecting neither the beggar woman who stretches out her fingerless hands nor the murdered prime minister, [Mrs. Indira] Gandhi. The river of love that is my [God] . . . flows past, accepting all, rejecting neither the ugliest of men nor the filthiest."

Otsu's life certainly isn't pretty. When he returns that night to the ashram after talking to his friend, two or three stray dogs are rummaging through the garbage in the courtyard. The door into his tiny room falls open on loose hinges. As he turns on the bare light bulb, the smell of sweat is still strong from the heat of the day. Bathing consists of dipping a rag into a bucket of water. Lighting a mosquito coil is essential to avoid being eaten alive by insects. After kneeling in prayer he does some reading from the small collection next to his bed: a Catholic prayer book, the Hindu Upanishads, a book by Mother Teresa, and a volume of the sayings of Mahatma Gandhi. Before he knows it, sleep overtakes him and the book slips to the floor from between his grimy fingers. The next morning he arises at 4:00 to hold a private Mass in his own room before heading out to find the dead and dying in streets covered with dung and dirty water.

Soon he stumbles upon a squalid-looking woman hunched against a wall in the faint light. Her shoulders are heaving as she struggles for breath, and she peers at him through expressionless eyes. Otsu pours her a cup of water from a bottle he carries and speaks to her softly: "*Pani. Pani. Ap mere dost hain.*" ("Water. Water. I am your friend.") She has trouble drinking, but she whispers through tears, "*Ganga.*" ("The Ganges.") As Otsu prepares a sling he has fashioned to carry her on his back he says to her, "*Koyi bat nahin.*" ("There is nothing to fear.")

Walking toward the Ganges, straining under her weight, Otsu steadies his breathing and begins to pray: "O Lord, You carried the cross upon your back and climbed the hill to Golgotha. I now imitate that act. You carried the sorrows of all men on your back and climbed the hill to Golgotha. I now imitate that act." By the end of the book, Otsu has become even more Christlike, and he is fatally attacked for trying to protect both the sanctity of Hindu cremation and the naivete of a camera-toting Japanese sightseer on his college friend's tour. His classmate questions whether Otsu isn't simply a fool, throwing his life away trying to imitate Christ, "which doesn't mean that this world full of hatred and egotism is going to change!" Although Otsu is called "completely power-less," the reader is left to contemplate a Christian life full of meaning, passion, and commitment, immeasurably strengthened by Otsu's appreciation for other religions.

A fuller understanding of Hinduism could have made me a better Christian during an incident in Varanasi that haunts me to this day. At the end of the summer in which I was living with the Brahmin priest and his family, as I described in the chapter "Walking," our group of twelve American college students spent several days at Benares Hindu University in Varanasi. One morning I took a rickshaw with another American a mile or two from the tree-lined campus into the hopelessly crowded center of the city. Soon after leaving the university grounds, we saw an old, half-naked woman, barely breathing, lying in a pool of filthy water along the side of the road. Flies were buzzing around her in the hot sun.

A man was going down from Jerusalem to Jericho, and
fell into the hands of robbers, who stripped him, beat
him, and went away, leaving him half dead.

Luke 10:30

Varanasi is the city of death, I thought. *But this is terrible. No one to help her. No friends. No family. And scores of people just walking by her and around her. India is so utterly different from anything I've ever experienced. It's overwhelming. I wonder what authorities are responsible for picking her up and when they'll be along. Maybe she's just asleep. Or could she be drunk?* We continued on our way.

Now by chance a priest was going down that road; and
when he saw him, he passed by on the other side. So

likewise a Levite, when he came to the place and saw
him, passed by on the other side.

Luke 10:31–32

When we returned in the afternoon she was still there. Now clearly she
was dead. Flies and other insects covered her body. They were crawling in
and out of every orifice. As I look back on it, I know what Otsu would
have done that morning.

But a Samaritan while travelling came near him; and
when he saw him, he was moved with pity. He went to
him and bandaged his wounds, having poured oil and wine
on them. Then he put him on his own animal, brought
him to an inn, and took care of him.

Luke 10:33–34

What was wrong with me? Why didn't I stop and do something? Was
there simply too much suffering and death around, too many limbless
beggars and emaciated children? I was a foreigner, after all. Was this my
business? I think now that it's partly that I wasn't enough of a Christian,
but also that I wasn't informed and changed enough by Hinduism. It's
doubtful that this woman would have lived long in any case, but the kind
of human contact Otsu provided—a cup of water at her lips, and reassur-
ing words that she was being taken to the Ganges—would have transformed her final moments, as anointing oil and prayers might do for a
Catholic. A more deeply felt understanding of the sacred meaning of the
Ganges could have moved me to be the kind of neighbor Jesus speaks of in
his parable of the Good Samaritan, who was a foreigner too. This is not to
say that I was required to carry this woman on my back or in my rickshaw. Yet I could have turned back to the university to make some

inquiries and phone calls to help get her down to the Ganges, or to make sure the good Samaritans of Varanasi knew she was there so they could minister to her.

Learning from religious trail crossings, of course, happens in all directions. The Hindu priest with whom I lived said that Jesus' Sermon on the Mount was one of the scriptures he returned to the most for inspiration, besides the Bhagavad Gita. He had tried to live a life of action in a dual career, in business as well as religion, but always one of nonattachment and selflessness. He was the manager of a heavy machine manufacturing plant built by the Russians, where his employees' interests were always foremost in his mind. He took business ethics very seriously. The Gita counsels, "A man should not hate any living creature. Let him be friendly and compassionate to all. He must free himself from the delusion of 'I' and 'mine.'" How is one to do this? By attachment to God: "Perform every action with your heart fixed on the Supreme Lord. Renounce attachment to the fruits. Be even-tempered in success and failure."[2]

For the priest, Jesus' words expanded and amplified those of the Gita: "Blessed are the merciful, for they will receive mercy. . . . If you greet only your brothers and sisters, what more are you doing than others? . . . You cannot serve God and wealth. Therefore, I tell you, do not worry about your life, what you will eat or what you will drink, or about your body, what you will wear. Is not life more than food, and the body more than clothing? . . . Consider the lilies of the field, how they grow; they neither toil nor spin, yet I tell you, even Solomon in all his glory was not clothed like one of these. . . . Strive first for the kingdom of God and his righteousness, and all these things will be given to you as well."[3]

The priest considered his business and economics education to be a gift of which he was simply the steward; he tried to apply it conscientiously, but without ego attachment to the results. In fact, when I was living with him the machine manufacturing business was doing very badly; the plant was producing at less than half of its capacity. He was concerned and worked hard trying to improve the company's performance, while never blaming his employees or trying to protect or aggrandize his own position with the firm.

Christianity and Hinduism are major world religions whose practitioners have not always paid a lot of attention to one another, unlike Sally and her parents and the family with which I lived in India. However, there are traditions that conscientiously search out trail crossings. Travelers on those paths often spend a lot of time lingering at the intersections. Mine, the Unitarian Universalist, is a good example. It's a merger of two historically liberal Protestant Christian denominations, whose formal Statement of Principles and Purposes now asserts that we draw from many sources, including not only Jewish, Christian, and Humanist teachings but also wisdom from all of the world's religions. As our statement says, we are "grateful for the religious pluralism which enriches and ennobles our faith."

I found Unitarian Universalism after a couple years of counseling with my Presbyterian college chaplain, following my return from India. As the Brahmin priest had suggested, I wanted to figure out how to be an open, nonexclusive Christian, following in Jesus' footsteps myself while appreciating others' journeys on their own paths. My chaplain, however, had problems with the fact that I didn't accept the unique divinity of Jesus Christ. I explained that I took Jesus to be my personal avatar but that I was convinced that other historical figures like Krishna and the Buddha had been equally filled with the spirit of God. I wanted my Christian faith to be energized by continuing exposure to other traditions. He reminded me of Jesus' claim in the Gospel of John that he was the way, truth, and life and that no one could come to the Father except through him. I responded that Jesus in the same chapter of John insists that "in my Father's house there are many rooms."[4] Surely some of those rooms housed Krishna, Buddha, and other avatars.

After many discussions along this line, my chaplain introduced me to Unitarian Universalism. "Go check out that denomination!" he nearly shouted at me one day in exasperation. "They seem to think like you and talk like you. Maybe they'll have a home for you." He explained how it was a free tradition, appreciative of all the world's religions, without any dogma or doctrine binding its members. That meant there were people putting different adjectives before the words *Unitarian Universalist*—including Jewish, Christian, Humanist, agnostic, and Buddhist. They were all welcome.

I started reading about the tradition and going to a local church. I was delighted. I really did seem to have found my religion, although I wasn't sure it would sustain me beyond my questioning college days. It has, although sometimes it can seem terribly heady and too much of a potpourri of the world's religions, struggling for spiritual depth. Nonetheless, I have always found people within the tradition who challenged and mentored me, helping me respect others and gaze far out into the cosmos, as well as respect myself and plumb my own soul.

Perhaps my preparation to become a Unitarian Universalist began with my childhood neighbors across the street, who were Bahá'ís. I was fascinated by their exotic Persian faith. Their temple in Wilmette, Illinois, was also a landmark for me every time I walked along the Lake Michigan beach near my house. These people knew so much about comparative religion, and yet they were clear about their own path, devoted to the nineteenth-century prophet Bahá'u'lláh. They kept talking about how to overcome racism and promote world peace.

Since I've been organizing interfaith programs at Tufts, I've had the privilege of meeting several dozen Bahá'ís at the university and in the Boston area. One is Malcolm Smith, who recently spoke at one of my dinnertime "Chaplain's Tables." He had become a Muslim before he had ever heard of the Bahá'í tradition. His story is more complicated than that, though, and it held me spellbound.

When Malcolm was growing up in Washington, D.C., his mother was Baptist, his father was Methodist, and together they attended a large African Methodist Episcopal (AME) church. Every Sunday throughout his childhood he walked the two blocks to church with his parents, brothers, and sisters. Most of the morning he would spend in Sunday school, but to this day he trembles with fear remembering those emotional hallelujahs in the big church service before the children were sent off to classes.

His world in urban Washington was one of violence—from walking home every day from school to the refuge of his own home, which turned out to be no escape from beatings. God always seemed punitive for him, and he felt because of the violence and abuse he experienced that he must be a bad boy. He spent most of his childhood locked in depression and self-hatred, with few friends and little hope. He began praying at night in this vein: "Now I lay me down to sleep. I pray the Lord my soul to take. If I could only die before I wake. I pray the Lord, 'Not another day!'" By seventh and eighth grade he was yelling at the sky, "Why did you put me here? What am I doing here? Why have you left me here, when you could just say 'Poof!' and I'd be gone? Where's your love?"

In high school he became more philosophical and less religious. He started understanding the ravages of racism in his life as an African American. Helping others in need became an outlet for his own despair, and he became more politically radical each year. By the time he entered college, he had rejected God as a childish fantasy and become an ideological Marxist. He found a powerful, supportive community of activists and started challenging what he saw to be institutionalized bigotry within his university. He also remembers making a Catholic girlfriend cry by being fiercely and outspokenly atheistic.

A major turning point occurred near the end of his sophomore year in college, when his grandfather died. Malcolm had spent many summers with him on his farm in North Carolina, and he was the only person who ever seemed to love Malcolm without questions or qualifications. At the funeral, in a hot, noisy Pentecostal church, Malcolm was a total mess. He couldn't stop crying and didn't know what to do. The service seemed to be going on forever, and several times he thought he was going to faint. Suddenly, the pastor called him up front and asked him to give testimony through his tears.

Malcolm dragged himself up to the flower-adorned coffin and stood for a while in perfumed silence, not knowing what to do. Then he started telling the congregation about the last conversation he'd had with his grandfather before his death. When they parted at the end of each summer during his childhood, his grandfather always sat him down, told him how much he loved him, and asked him to be a good boy until they met again. On his deathbed, though, his grandfather had said, "We won't meet again now, Malcolm, until the next life. You've got your whole adulthood on this earth ahead of you. No matter what, my love will follow you every day. Believe me, though, it's harder to be a good man than a good boy. I have faith in you, Malcolm, as long as you work on living by the Golden Rule. Never forget to do unto others as you'd have them do unto you."

When he finished this story, Malcolm began to hear a voice that sounded like it was coming from the rafters of the church, until he realized it was his own. He was saying, "Grandfather, I make this vow to you, now, before everyone here and before God, that I will always strive and persevere to be a good boy and a better man." His voice locked back into place within him as he said "Amen." He instantly realized how the light from the windows had been flooding in upon him. He was completely exposed and highlighted, yet at the same time he felt bathed and refreshed. It was the first consciously spiritual experience Malcolm had ever had, immediately following the first consciously spiritual act he had ever taken, by making this sacred vow.

Returning to college, Malcolm found himself saying to his latest Marxist girlfriend, "If religion makes people feel better in times of grief, who has the right to take it away from them?" Then he began working harder than ever academically and started getting straight A's. He declared a major in peace and justice studies and soon found himself deeply absorbed in the life and works of Gandhi. He was so entranced, in fact, that he spent the next summer reading everything of Gandhi's he could find in Washington libraries. This was the first openly spiritual political activist who had impressed him, and Malcolm soon found himself having another mystical experience in reading Gandhi's favorite scripture, the Bhagavad Gita.

Ironically, Gandhi had developed his commitment to nonviolence through reading the Gita's dialogue between the warrior Arjuna, who hesitated to go to battle because he feared he might kill his relatives, and the Lord Krishna, who explained that Arjuna must charge into action but maintain at all times an attitude of nonattachment and selflessness rather than glory-seeking or self-satisfaction. This shed a very different light on the social action and political change work in which Malcolm had been involved. It had largely been grounded in his own ego—trying to compensate for a lifetime of personally experienced bigotry and violence. One sunny summer morning, as he sat on his back porch reading the Gita, he became riveted to the text and felt that Krishna's words were being addressed directly to him. He promised that he'd give up his sense of suffering and victimization for a new spaciousness of mind and for selfless action. He staggered off the porch an hour later feeling his life had been forever changed.

Gandhi had studied the Bible and the Qur'an as well as the Hindu scriptures. He wrote, "I have come to the conclusion, in my own experience, that those who, no matter to what faith they belong, reverently study the teachings of other faiths, broaden their own instead of narrowing their hearts."[5] Malcolm knew something about the Bible from his childhood, but now he wanted to know about the Qur'an. He asked his mother for a copy for Christmas. He was amazed to find that it moved him as deeply as the Gita, if not more so. He found an insistence and urgency in it that brought it even closer to him. For example, he loved reading this:

> The Beneficent God,
> Taught the Qur'an.
> He created man,
> Taught him the mode of expression.
> The sun and the moon follow a reckoning
> And the herbs and the trees do adore Him . . .
> And the earth, He has set it for living creatures;
> Therein is fruit and palms having sheathed clusters,
> And the grain with its husk and fragrance.
> Which then of the bounties of your Lord will you deny?
> . . . Soon will We apply Ourselves to you, O you two
> armies.
> Which then of the bounties of your Lord will you deny?
> . . . The flames of fire and smoke will be sent on you
> two, then you will not be able to defend yourselves.
> Which then of the bounties of your Lord will you deny?
> And when the heaven is rent asunder, and then becomes
> red like red hide.
> Which then of the bounties of your Lord will you deny?[6]

Malcolm read the Qur'an from cover to cover and then began frequenting bookstores to find books on Islam. Friends spotted him sitting on the

floor in the aisles making ecstatic noises, especially over the mystical literature of the Sufis. Those passages spoke of the oneness of creation, the
unity of humanity, and the love of God, which made for the love of all
people. Malcolm came to realize that he'd in fact fallen in love with Islam.
He resisted for a while the submission to God that is the literal meaning of
the word *islam*. Within three months, however, he had submitted, in his
first adult commitment to a religious community.

After he graduated from college and began working for one of the
Public Interest Research Groups (PIRGs) founded by Ralph Nader,
Malcolm's religion began providing more and more sustenance as he
faced long hours of work and more social isolation than he had known in
college. It was comforting to pray five times a day, physically prostrating
himself before God. He felt a strong sense of community when he joined
with other Muslims to break the fast every night during the holy month of
Ramadan. Public interest work took on a new meaning when set in the
context of Muslim charity—one of the Five Pillars of Islam.

Then, almost four years to the day since he had become a Muslim,
Malcolm found himself back in a bookstore browsing through the Middle
East section. He stumbled on a small book by Joseph Sheppherd entitled
The Elements of the Bahá'í Faith. It described a prophet named
Bahá'u'lláh (1817–1892) who grew up Muslim in Persia (now Iran) and
after a vision in 1852 founded a new religion called Bahá'í.

Malcolm was particularly struck by Bahá'u'lláh's doctrine of pro-
gressive revelation—that God has revealed Himself to various great
Messengers, such as Krishna, Moses, Buddha, Jesus, and Muhammad,
who then founded religions, but that revelation is not historically sealed.
The revelation to Bahá'u'lláh added the assertion of the essential unity of
the world's major religions. Humanity must now be understood as one
race, the world must be unified into one global society, and through an irresistible historical process to come, not only will religious barriers break

down, but so will those of race, gender, class, and nation. Bahá'u'lláh insisted that he was no more the seal of the prophets than Muhammad had been. He was only the most recent of the great Messengers from God; others would inevitably appear in the future.

Of course, denying the finality of Muhammad's revelation makes the Bahá'í faith heretical from most Muslims' perspective. The Islamic creed, repeated daily by followers, states that Muhammad is the last—the seal—of all the prophets who have come, or ever will come, to humanity. Because of his claims, Bahá'u'lláh was imprisoned in Teheran and then exiled to Iraq. Later he was exiled to Turkey and ultimately to a penal city, Acre, in Ottoman Palestine, where he died.

Malcolm was attracted to this religion, which had grown out of Islam and whose scriptures sounded as poetically beautiful to him as the Qur'an. He began seeking out Bahá'ís to talk with and was invited to "fireside" conversations in some of their homes. He knew that conversion from Islam would be a serious step, since the consequences in certain Islamic countries could be death. Yet, he was deeply touched by the Bahá'í vision of racial unity and the abolishment of class, tied to an activist commitment to roll up one's sleeves and work for social justice. Hope awakened within him. He was also attracted to the Bahá'í belief that all human beings have a basic nobility, with more potential than any of us has yet realized. Much of Bahá'í practice, he came to learn, is focused on how to develop one's best possible self.

So, on September 15, 1996, six months after discovering Sheppherd's book, Malcolm decided at the age of twenty-five to become a Bahá'í. Before he went to bed he said his Muslim prayers and then followed them with those from the Bahá'í tradition. He knew when he woke up the next morning that his Muslim friends would now see him as an apostate. Yet, Malcolm was clear for himself that he had not stopped being a Muslim. He would continue to study the Qur'an as a primary source of inspiration, recognize Muhammad as a great prophet, read Sufi poetry, and say Muslim prayers alongside those of Bahá'í. His main path would remain Muslim, just as other Bahá'ís would claim that their basic ways were Christian, Native American, Shinto, Hindu, or something else.

Now, three years later, Malcolm is more sure than ever that he made the right religious choice. A key teaching of the Bahá'í tradition is respect for and unity with parents, even for those who have badly abused one in the past. He has learned how to relate positively to his parents now—to show them a forgiveness and love that none of them had ever thought possible. He says tearfully that "Bahá'u'lláh gave my parents back to me as a gift." They too have been touched as they have seen how differently Malcolm relates to them.

Malcolm has been studying Arabic in order to understand the Qur'an more deeply and appreciate Muhammad's role as a prophet. He has worked to defend Muslims in this country from a public prejudice that sees them all as extremists and potential terrorists. His work with the Public Interest Research Group has become more fulfilling as hope has become central to his perspective. Helping hasten the historical movement toward world unity has transformed much of what he used to see as only crisis, confusion, and chaos.

The most painful dimension of Malcolm's conversion, though, bringing anger to his otherwise peaceful countenance when he talks about it, is his knowledge of what has happened to Bahá'ís in their land of origin, Iran, over the past two decades. More than two hundred Bahá'ís have been executed simply because of their faith since the Islamic Revolution of 1979.[7] Charges have included "apostasy" and being "unprivileged infidels at war with the Muslim nation" because they held Bahá'í feasts and owned Bahá'í books.[8]

Another recent dinner speaker at a Thursday night Chaplain's Table was a Bahá'í student born in Iran. Relatives of his have been imprisoned and tortured because of their beliefs. Yet, as a *New York Times* article has put it, "The adherents of this relatively little-known religion seem unlikely villains. They uphold the divine origin of all major religions, including Islam. They shun violence, abstain from partisan politics and advocate unexceptionable principles such as the 'development of good character' and the 'eradication of prejudices of race, creed, class, nationality and sex.'"[9] How can members of such a religion be so terribly persecuted?

I once delivered a sermon entitled "Is Religion Doing More Harm Than Good?" I'm so often appalled and ashamed at the dehumanization and violence wrought in the name of religion that I wondered out loud if sane people shouldn't work toward the elimination of religion on the face of the earth, or at least toward confining it deep within the walls of churches, mosques, temples, and shrines, or within the prayerful hearts of its practitioners.

No religious tradition is immune from this scourge. For example, as I've taught in a course entitled "Religion in International Relations," during the 1990s a Jew named Yigal Amir murdered Israeli prime minister Yitzhak Rabin and later said he had "no regrets" because he "acted on orders from God." He was supported by a militant religious community that had earlier spawned Dr. Baruch Goldstein, who killed thirty-five innocent Muslims at prayer in their mosque.[10] Catholics have killed Protestants, and vice versa, in Ireland, and Orthodox Christians have killed Catholics and Muslims in Bosnia, and vice versa, in the name of their religions. Hindus destroyed a sixteenth-century mosque in Ayodhya, India, because they wanted to build a temple to Rama on the same spot. The resulting communal violence and riots killed more than two thousand people.[11] Sri Lankan Buddhists have slaughtered Tamil Hindus, and vice versa, directly appealing to religion.[12]

Some have tried to explain all this in terms other than religion. They speak of politics and economics, ethnicity and race, demographics and geography. Religion is just being manipulated, so the argument goes, by politicians and others to their own secular ends. Wouldn't we have to admit that religion at its core—in its scriptures and founders and purest adherents—is inherently humane and nonviolent?

Unfortunately, there's a growing body of scholarship that seems to suggest that religion is itself a root cause of brutality and savagery. As described earlier in this chapter, scriptures speak approvingly of the Hindu god Krishna encouraging Arjuna on the field of battle.[13] Joshua enters the Jewish promised land by fighting the battle of Jericho, knocking down the walls and destroying the defending army, and then mopping up by killing all the women and children and animals and then burning the whole city to the ground.[14] Jesus Christ says at one point, "I have come not to bring peace, but a sword. For I have come to set a man against his father, and a daughter against her mother."[15] The Sikh community in India, which was founded by the gentle soul Guru Nanak in the sixteenth century, has since come to be known as "the army of the faithful" and uses the double-edged sword as its symbol.[16]

A group of scholars led by David Little at the U.S. Institute of Peace concluded in a 1994 report that "one must see contemporary religious violence as an expression of tendencies always present in the religious life of humanity."[17] It is no excuse to say that religion gets manipulated and perverted to violent ends by false prophets and unholy followers, nor that its original essence has been lost when it becomes violent.

Instead, Little and others ask us to look at how part of religion's special genius lies in its ability to provide persons and groups with a sense of identity or a "place in the universe." In doing this, it frequently divides human communities into an "in" group and an "out" group. In conflict situations, distinctions between those who are "in" and those who are "out" are often heightened to the point of demonizing the other. Bosnian Muslim, Catholic Croat, and Orthodox Serb speakers have all been heard to say that the others cannot be trusted; each tells stories of appalling atrocities performed by the "out" groups. Then armed force becomes legitimated in struggles with "out" groups, almost always framed in defensive terms, even though it might look thoroughly aggressive to an objective observer. This becomes accentuated when connected to land—to the need or "right" to dominate within a given territory, like a Greater Serbia, a Buddhist Sri Lanka, and a Jewish promised land of Israel. There have been historical occasions when both Christians and Muslims have made claims to the entire world, in direct conflict with each other.[18]

So is this all hopeless, and is religion ultimately doing more harm than good? I don't think so, because for so many of us, probably the great majority of the world, it's through our religious traditions that we actually learn what it means to be human—to be humane, caring, and loving. Our moral education comes at religious knees. Our spiritual leaders and institutions are constantly being judged against strict standards of hypocrisy and decency, in contrast to people and organizations whose moral shortcomings are often excused by their success, say, in making a profit, defending national security, or educating well. We need groups and traditions in society that can be judged by ultimate standards and not just by short-term accomplishments.

But what about the religious violence to which we all seem vulnerable at any time? What if indeed "the potential for religion to be a root of conflict is always present in human societies,"[19] as Little and others put it? This group of scholars also provides some answers. First, the desire for a secure place in the universe, which group feeling addresses, cannot be discounted, but in-group narratives of conflict can also be turned into narratives that promote mutual respect and tolerance. "Love your enemies and pray for those who persecute you," says the Jesus who tells parables of turning the other cheek.[20] "No compulsion is there in religion," says the Qur'an, and "To you your religion and to me my religion."[21] Judaism has a story of swords being beaten into plowshares,[22] and Hinduism's Bhagavad Gita tells of a Sustainer who dwells in the heart of every moral creature and is the purity of the good. Buddhist stories describe how victory can only breed hatred.[23]

Religion cannot ever ignore the social and psychological needs that violence seeks to address and must draw creatively on its own rich resources for making peace, doing justice, and providing personal security. In our low moments of seeing only the harmfulness and violence of religion, we need to remember the great heritage of *ahimsa* in Hinduism and Buddhism, for example, and of nonviolence in Christianity. We need to tell and relive the stories of Gandhi and his Muslim allies in India, the Dalai Lama in Tibet, Archbishop Desmond Tutu in South Africa, and Martin Luther King, Jr., and his Jewish civil rights partners in the United States. Then, and perhaps only then, can religion be said to be doing more good than harm.

There's one other approach I've found hopeful. It's the work of organizations like the Parliament of the World's Religions, which first gathered in Chicago in 1893 and then reconvened in the same place in 1993. The nineteenth-century parliament is considered by many to be the birthplace of modern interfaith dialogue. Some seven thousand world religious leaders and adherents then assembled in 1993 to discuss the role of religion as we enter the next millennium, including promoting understanding and cooperation among all religious communities.[24] An overlapping effort is that of the World Conference on Religion and Peace, founded in 1970 to promote cooperation between the world's religions for peace. It is a nongovernment organization accredited to the United Nations and has chapters in thirty countries and members in over a hundred.[25]

I studied with a professor at the Harvard Divinity School named Wilfred Cantwell Smith, a historian of religion, who gave me hope that there are significant counter-trends to religiously inspired violence in the world. He wrote a book entitled *Toward a World Theology*, in which he argues that humankind has now arrived at a historical moment when we can finally see clearly that all humankind is one—we are all crew on spaceship earth, our lives are interdependent, and our fate is in our collective hands. He sees an emerging consciousness around the world that we are all heirs to the entire religious history of the human race. Therefore, we must begin to theologize—that is, to articulate our faith or relation to transcendence—in terms of that entire history and not just in relation to our own tradition, whether it be Christianity, Judaism, Islam, Hinduism, Buddhism, traditional indigenous religions, individual spirituality, or something else.

Smith points out how particular groups have always participated in the religious evolution of other traditions. For example, a Christian like Martin Luther King, Jr., has used the teachings of a Hindu, Mohandas Gandhi, to develop his Christian doctrine of nonviolence. Christian missionaries have challenged traditional forms of Buddhism and Shinto in Japan, helping to breed "new religions" within Buddhism and Shinto that adopt certain Christian ideas and methods. Hell is an idea whose development can be traced from Persian Zoroastrianism through Judaism, Christianity, and Islam. The Roman Catholic use of rosary beads was adapted at the time of the Crusades from the Muslims, who used prayer beads (and still do). The Muslim practice actually followed a Hindu use. The Buddhists also took up prayer beads from the Hindus and carried them eastward through Asia and ultimately to Japan. There are many trail crossings.

Historically, we are reaching a point of convergence, where people from all traditions are starting to become aware of these connections. It's likely we can now begin participating more self-consciously in one another's traditions. At minimum, we can speak of the unity of humankind's religious history, seeing that all religious traditions are interconnected in having grown out of, having been influenced by, or having interacted with others. Buddhism grew out of Hinduism. Christianity grew out of Judaism, and Islam out of the soil of both. Obviously, even in these closely related traditions, people haven't been religious in the same way. In fact, religious life has been extremely varied. Yet, it's becoming more clear that the major religious traditions can be understood only in terms of a context in which the others form a part.

So, another antidote to religious violence could be this increasing awareness of the history of other religious communities and of world history as a whole, especially as the information revolution truly creates a global village. This doesn't mean Christians will cease to be Christians or Buddhists to be Buddhists. We can hope, though, that they'll understand the dynamic concept of a Christian strand or a Buddhist strand with its own unique color, interwoven in the common religious tapestry of the world. Then, while still maintaining their own integrity, they may be able to participate in what is ultimately the only true community—the world-wide and history-long community of humankind.

Trail crossings need not be bloody encounters. Instead they can enhance everyone's journey on his or her own path by providing perspective and new vistas within each person's own tradition when contrasted with another. Furthermore, like the blind men in the Hindu story who try to understand what an elephant is like while feeling different parts of its body, we finite beings just might learn the most about the infinite God by sharing our varying religious experiences with one another.

Sitting

——⁓——

Judaism is a communal religion: it's not as much "God and me" as "God and us." Jews are a people with some five thousand years of history. One of the reasons family means so much in this tradition is that it represents the continuity of the Jewish people. When Deborah Stein, an only child, first left her family for a few hours a day to go to nursery school, her parents made sure it was a Jewish nursery school. When she started elementary school, it was a Jewish elementary school. Hebrew lessons began at age four. She received her first prayer book at age five. Half of each school day from age six on was devoted to Jewish studies.

Needless to say, Deborah's parents were observant Jews. She remembers many days and nights of reciting words she didn't know from her prayer book about things she couldn't understand. Yet the memories are warm, because her religion was so central to the life of her family.

Deborah's world fell apart in the fourth grade. Her father moved out, and before long her parents were divorced. She felt like a pariah in her private school because everyone else's parents were married. She was ashamed and lonely, with nobody to talk to. Luckily she had a dog. Every evening she walked her golden retriever, Rusty, and they would end up at the public elementary school at the top of the hill. She would take Rusty's leash off and let him run around the baseball field. Meanwhile, she sat under a huge oak tree on bleachers overlooking the valley beyond the field.

Soon she began talking out loud to herself and the sky on those bleachers—about her school day, her parents, her friends. All of her feelings would come tumbling out—fears, anger, disappointments, hopes, dreams, and passions. She laughed and cried, whispered and yelled. It felt all right just to be herself and speak that way up there, especially as she became confident that Someone who cared about her deeply was listening. Here in the Reality stage of Deborah's religious development, God was real and He listened carefully to her prayers. Over the next ten years, well into college—until the conflict between spiritual dependence and independence began to rage within her—this became her private place of solace and prayer. Here she developed a very personal way of discussing things with God. Teachers, schools, and classmates all changed, but this relationship was always reliable. For Deborah it represented safety, confidentiality, and trust.

Sometimes she would bring her Jewish prayer book along, but usually not. She preferred her own conversation in English to her people's in Hebrew. There was plenty of time for communal prayers in her synagogue, but this was her own time. Deborah asked God for strength to face the next day. She asked for wisdom to understand her life and what was going on around her. She said "thank you" for the good things that happened to her. She'll never forget ecstatic evenings of gratitude under the oak tree when she was accepted to various colleges.

As a young working woman in her twenties now, Deborah doesn't get back to the bleachers very often. They are still there, but the view of the valley is obstructed by vegetation that has grown up across the field.

Rusty is dead. On the other hand, family problems have now subsided, and for the moment she has found some stability in her life. She is active in her synagogue, and most of her prayers have become communal again. She comes back to the hilltop now mainly to express her appreciation. Now that she's well into the Independence stage, God doesn't feel quite as much like a person anymore, either. He's become more like a force or a way, she says. Yet she senses God's presence as much as ever.

Deborah remembers how as a child on the bleachers the worst thing she could imagine was for someone to prove that God didn't exist. Her relationship with Him then was all she had. It would have been terrible to think she was just talking to herself. She had little doubt, though, that He was always there when she got to those bleachers. And still is, in a new and evolving way.

All religions have some form of prayer or meditation that is central to their practice. Part of finding a religion, I think, is finding a comfortable way to engage in some kind of personal contemplative discipline. That's not always easy for people who have gotten out of the reflective habit or never were in it in the first place. A fairly painless way to start, though, is to look at it from a health perspective, as Boston cardiologist Herbert Benson started doing more than thirty years ago.

In 1968, practitioners of transcendental meditation came to his laboratory at the Harvard Medical School, asking him to study them. Transcendental meditation had been brought to the West from India by a Hindu guru named Maharishi Mahesh Yogi a few years before, and it attracted celebrities like the Beatles and Mia Farrow. Practitioners claimed they could lower their blood pressure through meditation, and Benson was in the midst of a study on the relation between monkey behavior and blood pressure. At first, Benson politely turned them away, thinking this kind of Eastern spirituality was too "far out" for a rational Western physician to get mixed up with.[1]

The people involved with transcendental meditation were persistent, however, and eventually Benson agreed to study them, after he had met with the Maharishi to be sure their leader would cooperate with the research even if the findings proved to be detrimental to his movement. The Maharishi agreed to accept the publication of whatever results were discovered.[2]

Imagine Benson's surprise, then, when his tests proved the following benefits of transcendental meditation: a decrease in blood pressure for those with elevated levels and decreases for all people in heart rate, respiratory rate, and oxygen consumption. There was also an increase for all subjects in alpha waves, which are associated with feelings of well-being. These changes demonstrably reduced stress levels in healthy people and aided in the treatment of hypertension in patients with the disease, as long as they regularly meditated ten to twenty minutes once or twice a day.[3]

Further studies demonstrated that there was nothing unique about this particular Hindu form of meditation. Ultimately Benson isolated four elements of what he came to call the "relaxation response": 1) a quiet environment without external distractions; 2) a comfortable position, usually sitting, in which one can remain for twenty minutes without moving or falling asleep; 3) an object to dwell upon, such as one's breath, a sound, word, or phrase, repeated silently or aloud, or something to fix one's gaze on; and 4) a passive attitude, whereby distracting thoughts or feelings are allowed to drift in and then back out of one's awareness.[4]

Benson has recently written that his most significant lifelong contribution to the field of cardiology and mind/body medicine has been "in defining a bodily calm that all of us can evoke and has the opposite effect of the well-known fight-or-flight response." The irony, of course, is that what he was medically defining as "the relaxation response" already had thousands of years of history, but with a different name: prayer. Benson explains that he discovered this himself one morning while shaving: "I'd

seen that Transcendental Meditation practitioners could relax the physio-
logic mechanisms usually aroused by stress. And although at the time I
didn't know the precise formula for calling this relaxation forward, the
steps did not appear to be mysterious or difficult to learn. . . . Razor in
hand, I continued thinking. . . . And then it struck me. 'This is prayer!' I
exclaimed to my half-shaven reflection."[5]

After this insight, Benson spent two years studying world literature
and found that "there was transforming power in prayer, no matter what
the words, from a Hindu prayer to the Catholic 'Hail, Mary, full of grace,'
from Judaism to Buddhism, Christianity and Islam. There were multi-
tudes of descriptions of the peaceful state these religious practices
elicited."[6] He summarized his study of prayer in a chapter on "age-old
wisdom" in his 1975 best-seller, *The Relaxation Response*. He reviewed,
among others, the writings of Saint Augustine, Saint Theresa, and Martin
Luther on prayer in the Christian tradition; Gershom G. Scholem's writings on Jewish contemplative practice; Mircea Eliade's classic book on
Hindu yoga; H. Saddhatissa's *Buddha's Way* on meditation methods; and
Al-Ghazali's teachings on Sufi practices in Islam. He also looked at
Taoism, shamanism, and "transcendent experiences in secular literature,"
quoting from Wordsworth's "Tintern Abbey."[7] Benson has continued his
research and publishing up to the present, writing, for example, about a
faith factor and our being wired for God in his 1997 book *Timeless
Healing: The Power and Biology of Belief*.

One of the best introductions to meditation that I know is Thich Nhat
Hanh's *Miracle of Mindfulness!* He's a Zen Buddhist master, born in
Vietnam in 1926, who's lived in France and the United States and written
more than seventy-five books in three languages. He tirelessly opposed
the Vietnam War, and he was nominated by Martin Luther King, Jr., for
the Nobel Peace Prize. In *Miracle of Mindfulness!* he explains how the
Sutra of Mindfulness in the Buddhist scriptures focuses the practitioner's

attention on the breath: "Be ever mindful you breathe in and mindful you breathe out."[8] Nhat Hanh suggests that beginners sit no more than twenty to thirty minutes at a time. Sit in a comfortable position, keeping your back straight, with your head and neck aligned with your spinal column. Focus your eyes a yard or two in front of you, and, if you can, maintain a half smile, just as you see on ancient statues of the Buddha. As you begin to follow your breath, you should also relax all of your muscles, starting with the worry-tightened muscles in your face. "Let all the muscles in your hands, fingers, arms, and legs relax. Let go of everything. Be like the waterplants which flow with the current, while beneath the surface of the water the riverbed remains motionless. Hold on to nothing but your breath and the half smile."[9]

One way of following your breath in meditation is simply to count "one" in your mind as you breathe in, and then count "one" again as you breathe out. Then count "two" as you breathe in; count "two" as you breathe out. Continue up to ten, and then start over again at one. You will then notice when you've lost count, meaning that you've lost mindfulness. When this happens, he advises, simply return to "one," and keep trying. Similarly, if feelings and thoughts arise during meditation, you should try neither to get lost in them nor to chase them away. You should acknowledge their presence without becoming attached to them. For example, you may think, "It's late and the neighbors are really making a lot of noise," or "I'm feeling sad." The ideal is simply to say to yourself, "I'm thinking about my neighbors now," or "A feeling of sadness has just arisen in me," and then return to your breath.[10]

Meditation not only will relax you, according to Nhat Hanh, but will give you an overall sense of peace and well-being. As time goes on, you should be able to follow your breath, be conscious of your thoughts and actions, and be conscious of your own presence as you eat an orange, wash the dishes, or go about your work. The more mindful you become, the more you will feel aware of the miracle of life and restore yourself to a sense of wholeness. On the other hand, when you let impatience or anger interfere with mindfulness, you are sucked away from the present into the past or future, losing the significance of what you're all about.[11]

In a postscript to Nhat Hanh's book, James Forest tells a story that puts mindfulness training in a poignantly real context, testing its value. In 1968, when Nhat Hanh was in his forties, Forest traveled with him for a while. This Buddhist monk in his brown robes was then speaking to groups across America about the war in his native country. Forest reports that "after an hour with him, one was haunted with the beauties of Vietnam, and filled with anguish at America's military intervention in the political and cultural tribulations of the Vietnamese people." One night Nhat Hanh was speaking in the auditorium of a wealthy suburban church outside St. Louis. A large man stood up during the question-and-answer period and angrily challenged his "supposed compassion": "If you care so much about your people, Mr. Hanh, why are you here? If you care so much for the people who are wounded, why don't you spend your time with them?"

At first Nhat Hanh was silent. Then he began speaking quietly, calmly, and with a sense of personal caring for the man who had just condemned him: "If you want the tree to grow, it won't help you to water the leaves. You have to water the roots. Many of the roots of the war are here, in your country. To help the people who are to be bombed, to try to protect them from this suffering, I have to come here." Forest remembers the contrast between the questioner's fury and Nhat Hanh's gentleness—an overcoming of hatred by love.

After his response, though, Nhat Hanh whispered something to the moderator and quickly left the room. Forest followed him out, sensing something was wrong. He found Nhat Hanh standing on the sidewalk next to the church parking lot, struggling for breath. He looked as if he had been underwater a long time and had finally reached the surface, gasping for air. Forest waited until he had regained his composure and then asked Nhat Hanh what had happened. The monk explained how upset he had been by the man's challenge. He'd felt an almost overwhelming desire to respond to him with anger. Instead, he tried to follow his breath. He had inhaled and exhaled slowly and deeply, searching for a way to respond with calm and understanding. His practice was not yet perfect, however. Although he found a way to answer respectfully, his breathing had been too slow and too deep and he'd needed to escape into the fresh night air to regain equilibrium.

Forest asked, "Why not be angry with him? Even pacifists have a right to be angry." Nhat Hanh replied, "If it were just myself, yes. But I am here to speak for Vietnamese peasants. I have to show them what we can be at our best." Forest says this moment was an important one in his own life, one he has pondered over and over again ever since: "For one thing, it was the first time that I realized there was a connection between the way one breathes and the way one responds to the world around."[12]

The opposite of Thich Nhat Hanh's example is the title character in Leo Tolstoy's novel *The Death of Ivan Ilych*. He has no meditative practice, nor does he pray. He's a successful lawyer and judge, married with two children, living in a nice house in a cosmopolitan city, with an active social life. At work he's known to be honest and incorruptible, willing to do everything he can for others within the limits of his professional role. Then, at the age of forty-five, he contracts a terminal disease.

Tolstoy is a wonderfully perceptive writer who takes us deep inside his character's psyche in his physical and mental pain and suffering (which we desperately come to hope will never be our own). Ivan Ilych vents his anger about dying on other people, hates his doctor's professional distancing, and feels that virtually no one, not even his wife, understands or empathizes with what he's going through. The closest he gets to prayer is late in his illness, when he begins muttering "My God, My God" and crying like a baby about his helplessness and loneliness, and about the cruelty and the absence of God. "What does it mean?" he asks. "It can't be that life is so senseless and horrible. But if it really has been so horrible and senseless, why must I die and die in agony?"[13]

Prayer could have helped Ivan with several of his problems: he deeply feared death, felt alienated from everyone around him, experienced terrible pain, and was haunted by the feeling that his life was not well lived. Only at the very end, within two hours of his death, did Ivan finally open himself to prayer. Until then it was as if "he struggled in that black sack into which he was being thrust by an invisible, resistless force." But when in the midst of "screaming desperately and waving his arms," his hand fell on his son's head, "the boy caught it, pressed it to his lips, and began to cry." At that moment Ivan finally understood love, human and divine, and saw what he had been closing himself off from. He now understood what was real and right in life: "At that very moment Ivan Ilych fell through [the black sack] and caught sight of the light."

In his sudden overflowing of love for his son and his wife he realized how wretched he was making them feel by his suffering: "It will be better for them when I die." Now Ivan began acting selflessly and prayerfully for the first time: "With a look at his wife he indicated his son and said: 'Take him away . . . sorry for him . . . sorry for you too'. . . He tried to add, 'forgive me,' but said 'forgo' and waved his hand, knowing that He whose understanding mattered would understand."

Ivan then wondered what had happened to his pain. As he turned his attention back to it again, he said to himself, "Yes, here it is. Well, what of it? Let the pain be." He then confronted death: "He sought his former accustomed fear of death and did not find it. 'Where is it? What death?' There was no fear because there was no death." In place of death, Ivan now found light: "'So that's what it is!' he suddenly exclaimed aloud. 'What joy!'"

Imagine how different Ivan's life might have been if he had been able to maintain a prayerful attitude and a relationship to God throughout all his days, not just the last. But how does one do that, realistically? For many people who have lost their religion, or never had one in the first place, prayer seems like the last thing they can imagine doing. It's especially hard for people at the Independence stage of spiritual development, in which God is usually imaged as quite distant and impersonal—as spirit or soul at best.

A social worker I know has come to use Ignatian prayer as a way out of this problem. Janice Brown has gone to a number of retreats where she has been taught about the spiritual exercises of Saint Ignatius of Loyola (1491–1556), founder of the Jesuits. It all started in her thirties, when she was a single parent struggling to complete her M.S.W. (Masters of Social Work) while working full time. She had grown up as a Jesus-loving Methodist who asked for a Bible for her tenth birthday; yet, by high school, in her Dependence stage of faith development, she was spending time with a fast crowd of peers who were drinking a lot. God didn't exist for her anymore. Just to make sure, she drunkenly swore at the sky one night after a terrible date, "I don't believe in you. Get the hell out of my life!" She still imagined God as a parent, even as she disavowed Him.

Now in her thirties, Janice was searching for something again—for some kind of spiritual center in her divorced and disassembled life. A professor referred her to the Institute for Spiritual Development in Houston, where she was living. There she saw a Jesuit priest, Francis, who was ten years older than she. Janice made it clear that she was not a Catholic and had no intention of becoming one. She also explained that she didn't have any language for God. The only terms she would use, typical of someone in the Independence stage, were the abstract and impersonal ones of theologian Paul Tillich's: "Source of Ultimate Concern" and "Ground of Being."

Francis started her off reading Psalm 25. It says, "Make me to know your ways, O Lord; teach me your paths." Later it affirms that "all the paths of the Lord are steadfast love." He gave her this method of prayer to try out until their next meeting: "Find a quiet space and make yourself comfortable. Think briefly about what you most desire. That is, what do you really want, or what are you looking for? Then slowly read the psalm to yourself. As you do, stay with any imagery that catches you. Try not to think about it intellectually or figure it out. Instead, just let it 'pray you'— flow over you and through you. Pause and savor whatever draws you or moves you."

Janice at first was struck by words like these: "Turn to me and be gracious to me, for I am lonely and afflicted." This verse spoke to her: "Consider how many are my foes, and with what violent hatred they hate me." She found solace in an image that came to her of her feet being plucked out of a net. She felt both longing and the hope that she would "abide in prosperity," and her child would "possess the land" as she lifted up her soul. This was the line she found herself repeating the most: "All the paths of the Lord are steadfast love."

There were a lot of passages that disturbed her, too. They didn't ring right or true. For example, one line said that "the friendship of the Lord is for those who fear him," and another asked God to "pardon my guilt, for it is great." Fear and guilt! This was exactly what she didn't want to hear. This was why she had stayed away from churches as an adult. Besides, she was very uncomfortable with all of this "Lord this" and "God that" language. She reported all this to Francis in her second spiritual direction meeting. He gently asked her to let everything go that repulsed her: "Just stay with the words that touch you and comfort you. Enter into them. Contemplate them. Don't worry. Just listen quietly. Just be."

This started working for Janice. During the next few days she set aside twenty minutes each morning after her daughter had left for school and before she went off herself to work or to classes. She sat on her feet in a sunny chair in the living room. The Bible lay open on her knee. She read until she found a phrase that touched her. Then she took a deep breath, closed her eyes, and let it percolate down from her head to her toes. This was such a different kind of prayer than she had previously imagined she was "supposed to do." There was no need to think about some man somewhere to whom she should be speaking. She was not sending off petitions that she hoped would be answered.

Yet, sometimes she pondered the kind of graciousness and steadfast love that would ease her loneliness and pain. It was so hard not to think of herself as a failure after the breakup of her marriage. It was tough facing herself when she often felt so worthless. Sometimes she would envision being wrapped in strong, caring arms, lifted up, and carried into a bright new day.

However, the day before her third meeting with Francis, she once more felt isolated and distracted. She was far behind in her schoolwork and had just this one morning to read a book by sociologist Max Weber. She kept reading the same page over and over again without being able to pay enough attention to understand it. The more the minutes ticked by, the more anxious she became, and the more difficult her reading became. It didn't help that she had just quit smoking. After an hour she looked up and saw her face in a mirror across the room, staring back at her. Filled with sudden self-hatred, angry at herself for her inability to concentrate, Janice exploded with fury at her image, throwing a shoe directly at the mirror. The face burst before her, and she was left with scores of shards on her white carpet.

As she crept over to survey the damage, she was appalled to see the same face, now multiplied a hundredfold, staring back at her in every fragment. For the first time in her life, Janice actually felt suicidal. Any of those sharp pieces of glass would do—just a quick, deep slice across her wrist. She bolted from the room before she could get one in her hand. But she kept stumbling around the house in agony—almost physically wrestling against her desire to do herself harm—imagining her head in the oven, her body under water in the bathtub, her neck broken after a dive from the attic window onto the driveway.

What saved her was not any instinct of self-preservation. It was the sudden clear awareness that her daughter, Carol, would come home from school and find her mother dead in the house. She pictured her daughter's face—so different from what Janice had seen in the hundred mirrors. It would be horrified, aghast, utterly devastated. All of Janice's maternal instincts awakened. She wanted to hold Carol, rock her, tell her everything was all right. She visualized picking her up, carrying her upstairs to bed, telling her how much she loved her, and singing her to sleep.

The next day she told it all to Francis. His immediate response was: "Thank God for Carol!" Janice experienced Francis's words as a total surprise. It became clear he didn't mean "Thank God Carol is in your life and you have something to live for beyond yourself." Instead, he meant "Thank God Carol is in your life; in that moment God loved you through her. God wants to save you and wants you to live, not only as the mother of Carol—certainly God desires that you care for her—but God also loves *you*, absolutely, apart from any role or action you might take in life. In fact, you might say that God loves you in the way that you love Carol. And the pain that you felt—imagining how terribly you might have hurt someone you love so much—is an infinitesimal amount of the pain that God would feel if something happened to you."

As Francis spoke, Janice felt God crash through her life to redeem her. In what seemed to be a religious experience, she felt a sense of profound consolation that she—her very own unworthy and unlikable self—was unconditionally loved and had a uniquely important place in the universe. This put a very different face on Janice's discomfort with personifying

God. *The fact is,* Janice thought to herself, *in that suicidal moment Carol's face became the face of God to me. And now, even more strikingly perhaps, I see God in the face of Francis as he cries out with such feeling, "Thank God for Carol!" God is another word for love personified. Love saves. God saves.* Francis again reminded Janice of the line that meant the most to her in Psalm 25: "All the paths of the Lord are steadfast love."

She began to see that if God is the life force itself or the creative spirit behind all that is, then God can be imaged in many different ways—in as many ways as there are people, plants, animals, earth, atoms, and stars in the universe. I would add that of course no one image is "right" or "complete" any more than finite numbers bear any resemblance to mathematical infinity. That's always the risk of idolatry: something becomes an idol when it's treated as ultimate and infinite itself, rather than as simply a pointer to that which is much greater than it.

Over the next few months, Francis taught Janice more about Ignatian prayer, helping her see how concrete and full of faces it really is. As she has described it to me, "You make free use of your imagination to put yourself right in the midst of the Bible passage upon which you're concentrating. For example, as you read the Gospel story of Jesus meeting a Samaritan woman at the well in John 4:1–42, you might use all your senses to imagine the noonday sun burning your skin, the sound of Jesus' voice breaking the silence, the sight of sweat-stained clothes and dusty sandals, the smells of sheep and goats in the vicinity, and the taste of cool water from the well."

Recounting the story to me, Janice continued: "You could also imagine how the Samaritan woman progressively comes to see the face of God in Jesus. First he's just an exhausted foreigner passing through her land. Then he's a man talking to her—inappropriately to a woman in public and to a non-Jew in asking her to share water with him. He begins to speak of the living water he brings, which is different from the well water.

The woman takes his words literally and sees him as a purveyor of easily accessible and totally thirst-quenching water. She asks him for some so she won't have to keep coming back to the well every day to draw water. Next, though, he miraculously sees into her life, noting that she has had five husbands, while the man she lives with now is not her husband. The woman starts viewing him as a prophet. Jesus speaks of a new day coming when Jews and Samaritans will worship the one God not in special sacred places but simply 'in spirit and in truth.' She says that she knows the Messiah is coming, and then all things will come clear. Jesus responds that he *is* the Messiah. After bringing other Samaritans to spend some time with him, she and they come to believe he is 'truly the Savior of the world.'"

This particular Bible story had a lot of power for Janice, as she entered into the words and let them "pray her" during several weeks of early mornings in her living-room chair. It was the image of living water that provided the greatest comfort. As Jesus said, "Those who drink of the water that I will give them will never be thirsty." Francis also encouraged her to enter into her own imaginative conversation each morning with Jesus inside the story. She remembers asking him, "What am I going to do with my own emptiness?" She then visualized Jesus turning to her with deep brown eyes and a voice like a bell. "There is no emptiness," he said. She had expected him to say, "I'll fill your emptiness with my living water." What could Jesus' response mean? Well, why not ask him? So she stayed within her imaginative dialogue and did. He responded: "There's nothing inherently wrong with you. You're okay. You're not empty."

Janice described all this to Francis in their next meeting. She ended by saying, "It was so strange! Of course, this was all in my imagination. But then the make-believe conversation got beyond me. An answer came back that I didn't anticipate, and worse yet, didn't understand. But I stayed with it and asked another question. I know I couldn't have made up that answer myself, so it was like a revelation." Janice wondered if her imagination was more powerful than she thought. Maybe she was just accessing some of her unconscious. Francis's response was: "Stay with that. Pray with that. Ask God's help in discerning what's His voice and what isn't."

Janice went on: "The darnedest part of it is that this actually felt like what I think prayer is supposed to be. I felt like I was having a real conversation with Jesus, and he was answering." Of course our imagination can be powerful when we begin to give it free rein. On the other hand, the Christian claim is that it's possible, and desirable, to reach beyond ourselves and our own minds to have real dialogue with God in the person of Jesus. Part of what's so valuable in working with scripture in prayer, according to Janice, and then having personal spiritual direction with someone like Francis, is that it can help to sort out what's just one's ego and what's coming from beyond or from deep within one's own soul.

Janice is more than a decade older today. She has worked with three different spiritual directors over the years. She's still a Protestant, and now she goes to church regularly. She served as a social worker in inner-city Houston for eight years and then was named associate director of an antipoverty agency. In her prayer life, she has clearly found a "God speak" that's not herself. She recounts the "amazing process of talking to God" since her first days with Francis: "There hasn't been one time when God wasn't present to me in the critical times in my life—thinking about suicide, grief over my mother's death, fear of teenage clients with guns and knives, the joy of getting this job I have now." She's been keeping a journal, so there's an ongoing record of that "still, small voice" as well as the magnificent transcendent one. Now she goes on annual one- and two-week prayer retreats, during which her spiritual life is enormously deepened and renewed.

In case it's not clear, I'd like to affirm here that personal and impersonal forms of prayer and meditation don't need to be viewed as contradictory.

They can very fruitfully be practiced together, especially by people in the Interdependence stage of religious development, in which God or Ultimate Concern is viewed paradoxically. People in this stage have a high tolerance for ambiguity and live in a dialectical world.

I know a Lutheran minister from Minnesota who has an active prayer life with God as person—both privately at home and publicly as he leads worship services—but also has made yoga central to his own spirituality. In his thirties, Raymond Soderberg started practicing yoga to stay in shape (*hatha*, or physical, yoga, that is, to distinguish it from the other forms of yoga in Hinduism, which are ways to God not primarily through the body but through knowledge, devotion, action, and meditation—*jnana*, *bhakti*, *karma*, and *raja*). He had always been athletic, but team sports were now in his past, and fitness centers were still far in the future. He wasn't particularly systematic about yoga, but he read a lot of books and went from teacher to teacher in Minneapolis before abandoning it for more than a decade.

In his early fifties, Raymond was called to a church in San Francisco. By this time he found that his body was getting pretty creaky. He was having trouble sleeping at night. So he talked with several people he trusted who practiced yoga and had shopped around for teachers. He made the rounds and checked out four or five teachers himself. Finally he chose a man about his age who had been teaching since the age of twenty.

The realm he now entered was light years removed from his practice of yoga in Minnesota, which involved stretching and strength building. This new practice provided a way of approaching his spiritual center through his body. He began taking classes at least once a week, practicing at home three to five days a week, and going on weekend retreats whenever he had a free Sunday. He was no longer just a thoughtful, sensitive minister, open to the world around him; spiritual awareness now began within himself through awareness of every little muscle, every little joint, and even organs like his heart. Yoga slowed down this busy man, helped him feel his way toward his soul, and enlivened him in a quiet way he had never known.

However, some conservative members of his church began raising questions after hearing about his yoga practice: "This can be demonic," they said. "It leads away from God. It comes from an idolatrous, polytheistic religion in India." Reverend Soderberg could have responded that this was just physical exercise for him. But in fact it had become a deeply spiritual routine. So one morning he preached a sermon about the road to prayer.

"Be still and know that I am God!" Raymond began his sermon with this line from Psalm 46, which was the inspiration for Martin Luther's famous hymn "A Mighty Fortress Is Our God." He explained that prayer at its best comes out of deep stillness. How are we to still ourselves in preparation for prayer? There are many possibilities, but the best Raymond had found for himself was yoga. It is active, in that the body is settling into different postures just on the edge of pain. Yet, it progressively helps concentrate attention, from all the busyness and business of the world, just on one's body. Raymond explained that at the end of each yoga session, when his concentration has moved just to his breath, he settles for ten to fifteen minutes into one *asana*, or posture, usually the cross-legged lotus position. Yoga merges into meditation. Finally, after that, he becomes still enough to attempt a significant conversation with God in prayer.

In his sermon Raymond told stories of life in monasteries. Many methods have been devised over the centuries to help monks and nuns move into deep prayer, often centered in the body. In recent decades, there's been a lot of monastic exploration of Eastern methods as well, including yoga. He urged his congregation not to fear yoga and meditation as alien forces in their own spiritual development, but instead to embrace and use them.

He ended with these verses from Psalm 46: "God is our refuge and strength, a very present help in trouble. Therefore we will not fear. . . . Be still and know that I am God." Raymond, now in his mid-sixties, still serves that congregation. And he still practices yoga.

If all the spiritual exercises in this chapter sound too daunting, or at least not irresistible, I offer this parting advice. No matter what else you do, every so often try to take time to sit under a tree, literally. For three summers of the last five I've been able to do that every morning for fifteen minutes before starting my work day, and they may have been the three best summers of my life. The setting was magnificent, and of course that makes a big difference. Yet virtually all of us can find a suitable tree nearby, or can bring one inside to sit next to as the Japanese do with their miniature bonsai trees in pots.

I was teaching at the Tufts campus in the French Alps. The European Center is an eleventh-century Benedictine priory that was given to Tufts some twenty years ago. There's a walled garden behind it overlooking the cleanest lake in Europe, Lake Annecy. The lake is rimmed with mountains, some of which retain snow on their peaks well into June. A great ash tree outside the garden overhangs its northwest corner.

I invited any interested students, faculty, and staff to join me under the tree in a semicircle of lawn chairs facing the lake each weekday at 8:15 A.M. I asked everyone to sit comfortably in silence for the first five or ten minutes. Close to us was a riot of red, white, pink, and yellow flowers. The vista beyond the wall revealed another great spreading tree to the left, plunging cliffs to the right, the blue-green lake ahead, two razor-backed mountains beyond, and a palatial sky overhead. With the changing weather, the tableau kept shifting its elements and emphases like a kaleidoscope.

We always had an avian symphony. Many species of birds populated that tree, and they all seemed to sing together. It was the first time in my life that I had heard cuckoos outside of Swiss clocks. Buzzing bees fertilized the flowers before us. Rays of sun slanted over the priory to warm our backs on some days, and on others we bundled against the early chill or hooded ourselves in a gentle mist. Even on days when we had to sit inside next to priory windows, because it was raining too hard outside, the birds serenaded us as always. And the sweet, fresh smell of the flowers drifted in on the breeze. The quieter and more receptive each of us was, the more enthralled we became.

I would break the silence with five minutes remaining and ask if anyone had a favorite poem to read. Most often it would be nature poetry: Walt Whitman, Jean-Jacques Rousseau, Annie Dillard, e. e. cummings, Denise Levertov, Langston Hughes. Sometimes offerings were from specific religious traditions, usually related to nature as well: the mystical writings of the Muslim poet Rumi, scripture from the Hebrew Bible and the Hindu Vedas, prayers of the Christian Saint Francis of Assisi, sayings of Buddhist lamas. The Native American tradition was appealed to more than any other. Contented smiles from those fifteen minutes often lasted all day.

Although it's very nice there, it is not necessary to go to the Alps to sit under a tree. Deborah Stein found one near her baseball field bleachers. Herbert Benson would counsel that any quiet environment will do. A single flower in a winter bedroom can be the tree of life. What's important is simply to stop every so often, be still, and thankfully appreciate our presence in the universe.

Suffering

Many people leave religion because they can't understand why God would allow so much suffering in the world: "What kind of God could have let my child die?" "Hitler's holocaust of six million Jews proves there's no justice in the universe." "What could possibly be blessed about being poor?" "What's the use of being good when bad things happen to me and the wicked prosper?" Others find religion through suffering, or discover with gratitude that powerful resources are available to them within religious traditions to deal with anguish and torment. What seems to be universal, whether we like it or not, is that suffering exists as an inevitable part of the human condition. Perhaps the first of the Buddha's Four Noble Truths puts it most bluntly by saying, in effect, that life hurts. All religious traditions take suffering very seriously and have a lot to say about it.

When you're on a path up a mountain, you can count on some kind of pain along the way. It may come in the form of body aches and cramps, a sudden injury or other unexpected emergency, a dramatic change in the weather that soaks or freezes you, sickness, equipment failures, relationship problems, or any number of other occurrences. Something will happen. The only question is whether it breaks or strengthens you and your party. Is it a disaster or an opportunity? Does it end your trip or strengthen you to continue, perhaps in a new direction? Even if you have to go back a bit, are you better prepared for another attempt? Are you diminished as a person or group or are you enhanced? And what makes the difference?

A psychotherapist I know with two healthy children lost his third, a daughter who was born prematurely. He was utterly devastated. His Christian faith didn't provide much solace at first, nor did the Buddhist practice he had started in his thirties and continued into his forties. Over the months that followed, though, with help from some friends and family, his Christian understanding deepened and changed. Not only did he come to terms with his daughter's death, but he redirected his own life, and it became more fulfilling than he could have ever imagined. Here's his story.[1]

Robert A. Jonas was born in 1947 and grew up in a strong Lutheran culture in Wisconsin. Some of his earliest memories are of his grandmother's bedside prayers, said both in German and in English. By the time he went to college at Dartmouth, though, Jesus had ceased to be part of his life: "My own Christian religion seemed hopelessly anachronistic, its ideas and practices unable to bear the exciting promises of modernity, the depths of psychic and psychedelic experiences being uncovered daily, and the political catastrophe of Vietnam's escalating horrors." As a young adult he was drawn both to Eastern practices, especially Buddhist meditation, and to the mystical traditions of medieval Christianity. Yet his doctoral work in education and psychology at Harvard ultimately led him into a secular psychotherapy practice.

By the beginning of 1992, Jonas (as he prefers to be called) was feeling depressed and unsure about his career. Worse, he'd been sick a lot and become haunted by a fear of his own death. His midlife crisis had arrived!

But everything had changed dramatically by the next summer, when he and his wife, Margaret, were expecting a baby. It was the second trimester of pregnancy, medical tests indicated a girl, and they had already decided to name her Rebecca. Jonas wrote in his diary, "Even though I am tired and was sick a lot this past winter, I feel optimistic. . . . Our lives are graced, as if the rails have been greased, and everything good is rolling along through us without resistance."

On July 21 Margaret went into labor. Her mother had been prescribed diethylstilbestrol (DES) when she was pregnant with Margaret in the 1950s, a drug that doctors believed would lower the risk of a miscarriage. It has since been discovered that daughters born to DES mothers often have "incompetent cervixes," leading to premature births of their children. This was true for Margaret. A drug injection stopped the dilation of her cervix at one centimeter, and she was put on bed rest until her November 17 due date. Early on July 29, though, her water broke, and at 8:23 that evening Rebecca arrived, weighing only one pound, eight ounces. The baby had been in utero twenty-four weeks, and her statistical chances of survival were between 5 and 10 percent.

Jonas first saw Rebecca two and a half hours after her birth under the bright, hot lights of the premature infant intensive care unit. She was spread-eagled on a white blanket with IV needles stuck in her right leg and left arm. Her left lung had "popped" from the artificially provided oxygen that was necessary to her survival. The pediatrician explained, "We'll do everything we can to save her, but in the end it depends on her, whether she has the physical strength to pull through this crisis. We'll just have to wait and see what is in the cards for her." Jonas brought his face near hers, stroked her forehead, and said, "It's your daddy." A nurse standing nearby asked him if he wanted to baptize her. Jonas was shocked. "Pardon?" he asked. The nurse repeated the question and he found himself instinctively saying yes. A minute later she came back with a glass of water.

Of course, he didn't know what he was doing. He wasn't an ordained minister or priest. *Is there some official phrase for baptism?* he asked himself. He couldn't remember. *By what power can I do this?* He didn't know or care. So he just did what came naturally. He dipped his right thumb in the water and then brushed it lightly over the soft skin of her forehead, making the sign of the cross. He said, "I love you. Your mother loves you. Christ and God love you. God bless you and keep you. Father, Son, and Holy Spirit." Then he tried to say the prayer Jesus taught his disciples, "Our Father Who Art in Heaven." But he couldn't get through it, wanting to concentrate all his attention on her. If he was going to have only a brief time with Rebecca, he wanted to get as much of her as he could, remembering every detail of how she looked. He kept whispering in her ear, "This is your daddy. I'm right here. I love you."

Rebecca's mother had been through an emergency Cesarean section operation to get Rebecca out; the umbilical cord had been lying across the cervix and being squeezed hard enough to cut off Rebecca's oxygen. Margaret was still in the recovery room, but she was wheeled down to the preemie ICU about half an hour later. By that time, though, the doctor had indicated that Rebecca was going to die. For about forty-five minutes they held her, wrapped in a delicate cotton blanket. Then Jonas asked again if there was any hope at all. The physician explained that they could keep her alive by machine for some time, but she wasn't getting enough oxygen, and at best there would be great damage to her lungs or brain, or both.

Finally, Jonas asked the pediatrician if he, Jonas, could be the one to take the oxygen tube out of Rebecca's throat. Thinking back, he wonders, "I'm not sure why I asked. Perhaps I ached for some way to participate directly in her life and death. Feeling helpless to save my daughter, perhaps

I thought I could help her die quickly, in peace." Margaret asked whether Rebecca would experience any pain. The doctor said she was sedated and would not suffer. Jonas describes what happened next: "Slowly, lovingly, I peeled the white medical tape off her mouth and pulled the tube out of her throat. Slowly, imperceptibly, her breathing quieted. Almost immediately she began turning gray. Rebecca died in our arms, on Thursday, July 30, at 12:07 A.M."

Rebecca's death forced Jonas to face ultimate questions in his grief: How can I survive the pain of losing a child? Is life worth living? What is the meaning of life and death? If loving someone always ends in loss, what sense does it make to love? At the funeral in an Episcopal church, the rector gave a short sermon about Christ's love, and Jonas imagined Rebecca being received into the Body of Christ—"This is my beloved daughter, in whom I am well pleased. Welcome to the community of the Beloved." But another voice was working within Jonas's imagination as well: "Being a Christian is magical and foolish. Maybe we're all caught up in a collective psychosis. Dead is dead, period."

For months after Rebecca's death, Jonas was on an emotional roller coaster: "I could never know ahead of time when I needed to cry. The feelings would suddenly strike in different parts of my body. Some days, the body was numb; on other days, body sensations flowed in eddies of intensity, pleasant and unpleasant, one after another. On still others, I lay almost paralyzed in gut-wrenching pain. In my mind's eye, I often saw Rebecca on the hospital table trying to breathe." He also experienced a lot of anger, often pounding his fists on pillows, beds, and the ground, cursing and yelling "No!" in angry protest.

Trying to make sense of it all and to find some equilibrium for himself, Jonas spent some time turning to Buddhist resources. He appreciated what seemed to be a lack of dogma, creeds, or other required beliefs in Buddhism. It also helped him get out of his head, intellectualizing about life and death, and into his body, simply sitting in the midst of pain and confusion. Buddhism's healing power came through nonjudgmental awareness in meditation rather than through rational answers stated in propositional form. Yet, it didn't seem to have room for the passionate emotions, loving attachments, and devotional reverence that Jonas also felt.

Of course, Buddhism is not free of ideas either. At a Buddhist-Christian conference Jonas attended just after Rebecca died, a cheerful young Asian Buddhist suggested that Rebecca had been born and died in order to be reborn quickly. Jonas found this thought very depressing: "If everything was foreordained by destiny or God, why do anything? My efforts to understand, to improve myself, to create something new, and to love and help others were irrelevant." It reminded him of the Christian Calvinist doctrine of predestination that he had rejected as a teenager. Instead, he began to muse on a contrary idea: "Perhaps surprise is one of God's essential attributes. Maybe even God doesn't know how it will all turn out. I preferred to think that God suffered, hoped, and delighted with us, that God too was sometimes astonished, saddened or pleased by the course of events."

In fact, as the weeks passed after Rebecca's death, Jonas began to discover new dimensions of Christianity that became deeply sustaining for him. His discoveries originated from feeling totally vulnerable and out of control; there were friends and family members who came around to support him and Margaret in ways he could never have imagined. For example, he was struck by something as simple as a fellow therapist saying over lunch, "Please consider us as members of your community. We're here for talking, visiting, telephone calls, anything you need." Jonas realized that nobody had ever said anything like that to him before, or (more likely) he had never allowed himself to acknowledge the need for such support from others before.

Through the attention and help of others he began seeing how small, fearful, and greed-driven his personal ego had been. Healing love was not his to possess or channel. It comes freely from others and ultimately from God by what Christians call grace. Yet one has to be open enough to be willing to receive it, and then to let it pass through oneself to others who need it too. "Right in the heart of grief shimmered *a field* of grace," Jonas could now say. "I could stand in this field and look all around to see grace bringing new life everywhere. Or I could walk in the field and meet others, some of whom were also aware of the incredible miracle of life."

Then Jonas and Margaret started meeting other people who had lost their children. They felt an immediate, intimate bond with those parents, often spontaneously hugging and crying together as they told their stories to each other. Even though each parent's story was unique, the qualities of tender love and profound loss seemed infinite and transcendent of the particular people involved. The depths of Jonas and Margaret's personal grief opened into the presence of others who were grieving and then into grief itself. Sometimes it seemed as if there was only one grief, and Jonas wondered how very private emotions could connect him so intimately to other people and ultimately to all people and creation as a whole.

There were Christian parents who described this by saying they were participating in the Body of Christ. The message Jonas came to articulate was this: "If we saw rightly, we would see that our hearts participate in God's eternal heart and that our brief historical presence participates in God's eternal time." He began to understand that the time-bound, earthbound dimension of his love was trying to keep Rebecca alive for himself in this life, while the larger, timeless dimension set her free for God and others.

Jonas explains that while family and friends helped him find himself and his spiritual path after Rebecca's death, one of his most important mentors turned out to be a medieval Dominican friar named Meister

Eckhart. His writings touched Jonas deeply; it felt as if they had begun a dialogue as real as that between any two living people. Love lay at the center of Eckhart's teaching, but he felt that true love is always wounded and suffering, just as Jesus' love for the world was. To be alive, feeling, and loving is to be mortally wounded, because life is always imperfect and broken in some way. The problem is not in undergoing pain as such, Eckhart writes, but in clinging to private, self-pitying suffering that isn't surrendered to the universal Great Suffering symbolized in Jesus' passion on the cross. This latter kind of suffering is ultimately transformed by the perfect love of God the Creator for all of creation.

When Jonas was despairing after Rebecca's death, he remembers a cold, dark voice within him counseling, "Sure, you loved Rebecca. Your love *feels* as if it is the final truth, as if nothing could be stronger. But hope is deceptive and illusory. You will die, and that's it, period. People's personal love dies with them. Everything disappears without a trace. Feel your feelings or don't feel them; it doesn't matter. Nothing matters." As Jonas got to know Eckhart, though, another voice arose within him to challenge the cold, dark voice: "Wrong. Authentic love really participates in something greater, something that lives eternally. If we keep loving, right through death's doorway, new life springs up. But we must hold nothing back. To love in the presence of death is to cultivate divine *humus*, the ground that brings new life. And the ground is God, ever new. God brings all things into existence and receives them when they pass out of existence. Get out, Death! You have no power here anymore. *You*, death, and *You*, meaninglessness, are the ultimate illusions."

Over time, Jonas realized that Rebecca's death had thrown open a doorway in his soul: "My little ego had thought that its self-centered view of things was the way things really are. But suddenly I was standing in the midst of a great unknown Source from which proceeded all meaning, life and death. I couldn't see that Source directly—my senses were mediating

Something to me. But I trusted Jesus' and Eckhart's vision that this benevolent Something was really there, within me and among us in creation."

Jonas also learned that this insight came only in bits and pieces. Except for being open to it, he had no control over when and where grace would come. He described it as a matter of glimpses, morsels, and touches in the dark: "In those graced moments I saw, heard, and touched everything— fellow adults, children, cats, trees, rocks, rivers, pews, and pencils as extraordinary manifestations of God's presence. While the night and the pain remained, infinite Light and consolation poured into me and into everything and everyone around me. Just as Jesus' death on the cross had released the Holy Spirit into all things, earth's winds had distributed Rebecca's ashes and beautiful presence everywhere."

The suffering that taught Jonas about love and set him on a new Christian path also ended his midlife crisis and redirected his career. First, he began thinking less about what to do and more about who he was and what he felt drawn to. Then he realized that as a psychotherapist he needed to let go of his ego-connected habit of trying to "help" his clients; instead, he needed simply to appreciate and love them. After all, each of them was a fellow traveler with mortal wounds. He became less interested in applying psychoanalytic theories and more interested in accompanying clients in their emotional struggles, keeping his heart open, and looking for where love was blossoming or not.

Jonas has begun sitting with clients with this question in mind: "How are we going to get out of this difficulty?" If someone is feeling hopeless, he might say to himself, *She's right—it's hopeless.* He empathizes with her and feels stuck with her. "But because we sit together in an invisible atmosphere of love, we often arrive at hope without going anywhere. Even when sessions end with no answers, a deeper dimension of hope cradles us." This is how Jonas explains it in his new Christian language: "I realized I am most effective when I let-go-in-love with my clients, allowing myself to be broken with them, in God's presence. Turning toward God inwardly, in the presence of others, allows me to see them as God sees them, setting them free." Jonas has been born into a new life through the death of his daughter, and he hopes that he is participating in the liberation of others each day.

Jonas's Christian worldview now seems solidly settled in the Interdependence stage of faith development. Through his experience of suffering, he's reached a "second naivete," in which a religious symbol like the cross and a theological concept like love have become reenlivened for him. His self-pitying suffering was transformed through consideration of the accepting suffering of Jesus on the cross, and his wounded love brought with it a depth of feeling and understanding he'd never even imagined. It's all a far cry from the Reality or Dependence stage views of Christianity that he rejected during college as hopelessly anachronistic, full of ideas and practices that could not support modern realities. In fact, it took the insights of a medieval mystic in the final stage of Unity, Meister Eckhart, to bring him to his new awareness, as well as to a paradoxical understanding of God as both person and life force present in all of creation. Finally, while Jonas is able now to affirm himself unambiguously as a Christian, he continues to grow through Buddhist meditational practice and interfaith dialogue.

Alison MacKinsey also rejected her childhood view of Christianity, but suffering in her case brought her squarely into the Buddhist tradition. She remembers herself as a "religious little girl." Both of her parents were active in the Congregational Church—her father as a deacon, and her mother as a choir member when she wasn't teaching Sunday school. At home, she says, it seemed as if "ministers were always at our table." With other children of the church, Alison used to collect money and supplies for missionaries in China, and when she was in third grade they sent off a shipment of Bibles. Looking back, there's a kind of eerie prescience in a letter that arrived for her one day from China. It was from a missionary, enclosing her baptismal certificate, which he had found in one of the Bibles the Sunday school had provided. The gist of its message was "Thank you for all your help, but you've sent too much to China! I don't want you to lose your articles of faith!"

Five years later, when Alison was thirteen, her mother was struck by lightning and died suddenly and unexpectedly at the age of thirty-eight. At the funeral, the minister tried to comfort Alison by saying, "Your mother's happy now. She's with God." Instead of feeling solace, Alison was utterly devastated: *If God wants to snatch my mother when I need her, I don't want to have anything to do with Him ever again!* she said to herself. The minister seemed to be viewing her mother's death as a good thing in some way. Alison was crystal clear that there wasn't anything good about it to her. From that day on she fell silent on religion and tried to attend church as little as possible. Whenever she did, a deep sadness washed over her and she couldn't stop crying. As an adult she's had the chance to travel to Europe a lot, but she's never set foot inside one of the great cathedrals on any of her trips. "I just didn't want the tears to come," she says sadly.

After high school Alison turned rebellious and participated in the sixties to the hilt. Instead of going to college, she hung out in Washington's Dupont Circle, tried every drug she could find, hid draft dodgers in her two-room apartment, and learned everything she'd ever want to know about sex. It took her six years to get to college at the State University of New York at Stony Brook. There she also found a therapist, who, after several years, gave her a book on Buddhism, saying only, "You might be interested in this." Alison instantly recognized herself: "Oh, that's what I am, a Buddhist!" She identified a spiritual nature—Buddha nature—in herself. At first, she couldn't believe it; she had thought her spiritual self had died with her mother.

She was comfortable with Buddhism because it didn't posit a God, so there was no Supreme Being intervening in the affairs of the world or drawing people to greater happiness with Him after death. Buddhism for her was about relying on oneself. The first of the Buddha's Four Noble Truths affirmed that pain, from the smallest irritation to the greatest agony, is inherent in being human. The issue is simply what one is going to do about it. The tradition seemed honest and forthright, putting the practitioner face-to-face with truth. It had a pragmatic and psychologically compelling view: overcome ego attachment and your pain can recede. It had a method: practice meditation. And it promoted a way of life embodied in the Eightfold Path, which included basic ethics, mindfulness, care in speaking, and seeing work as a means rather than an end in itself. The promise was that by relying on her own internal resources, rather than some God "out there," she could grow the seed of her own Buddhahood that already lay in her heart.

In 1978 she formally became a Buddhist by "taking refuge" in the Buddha, the dharma, and the *sangha*. That meant that she adopted the Buddha as her teacher, committed herself to his teachings as truth (dharma), and joined the community of Buddhists (*sangha*). In a formal ceremony, she also received a Buddhist name, Chime Sheltron (which translates as "Deathless Crystal Torch"). She interprets this name to mean that she has a brightness within her that will never die (as we all do, but she had lost sight of this). Her naming certificate has remained framed over her bed ever since, even though she retains her birth name in daily life.

The year 1978 also marked the completion of her degree work at Stony Brook. Armed now with an M.Ed. in research and statistics and an M.B.A. in business policy, she went to work for a small research firm specializing in the creation and use of new knowledge, just as personal computers were emerging. Then in 1986 she was hired by a start-up investment company involved primarily in computer industry financing. By 1990 she was on the fast track to partnership in a major Wall Street investment banking firm: "I became driven 150 percent by ambition. Nothing would stop me. No matter what I was asked to do, I did it. I worked around the clock, ignored all my friends who kept telling me to get a life, and by September of 1995 I had made it. Partner! Master of the Universe!"

To her utter shock, though, by that winter Alison was in a deep depression. In fact, she was suicidal. Objectively, she seemed to have everything that anyone would ever want. She was making half a million dollars before bonuses, dressing beautifully, living in a luxurious penthouse, and traveling around the world. It was shades of Siddhartha Gautama, the man who would later become the Buddha, living the high life as a prince as his great discontent set in. As Alison puts it, "Not only did I have the golden egg; I had the goose too!" Yet, she felt empty at her very core. So she checked into a mental hospital during a two-week vacation. She still wanted to die. She felt utterly helpless and lost.

Those two weeks in the hospital made a difference. After her stay, she was able to get back to work. Alison thought she had developed a good cover for her unhappiness. But she learned differently in February, when she was working for a California software company on a public offering of stock. After a presentation to senior executives, one of them pulled her aside and said, "Do you realize that your hands were shaking throughout that whole presentation? I've known you for a couple of years now, and you've never been nervous or had any kind of tremors. Are you all right?" Cover blown.

Then she was saved by China. On a Tuesday in March 1996, she was reading one of the dozen or so business journals she carried in her briefcase every week. A story about economic development in China caught her eye. She began to read that despite any economic gains the country was enjoying near the coast, the status quo reigned supreme in the vast heartland. There was a vignette about one small family, headed by a man named Mr. Wong, who was raising his two daughters alone. They lived in a simple hut with no electricity or water. Mr. Wong worked the unforgiving land by hand. A picture of him and his two daughters broke Alison's heart as she saw their plaintive faces staring out at her. Alison started weeping gently, then crying. "My heart was touched in a way that it's never been—by any person or any thing," she explains. (Even now, she can't describe the article and her reaction without tears coming to her eyes.)

The next day, Alison faxed the reporter in Shanghai who had written the article. She pleaded, "Do you know these people? Can I get in touch with them? How can I help?" The village had also affected this seasoned reporter, and he offered to serve as translator and intermediary between the Chinese peasants and the New York investment banker. She learned that in this desperately poor mountainous village in central China there were many children, like Mr. Wong's daughters, who couldn't even go to school because they were unable to pay for the basics—pencils and paper, not to mention books, book bags, and warm sweaters for the unheated classrooms.

Soon Alison was helping fifty children to attend school, including Mr. Wong's two daughters. Six months later, supplied with fifty tissue-paper letters and a photo of the children in front of the school, Alison had left her hard-earned partnership and investment banking for good. "It was a terribly hard decision," she says quietly. But once I'd seen the eyes of those children, I knew that I was not going to spend my life blood sixty stories above Wall Street."

Now, while still sending money to China, Alison runs her own nonprofit operation, helping people in the corporate world find *their* hearts. It supports individuals in defining their own spiritual path and then in keeping them on that path amid the ringing phones, budget deadlines, and constant business meetings that shape so many people's working lives (and still, to her chagrin, shape Alison's significantly, even in her new work). Her enterprise also deals with organizational culture and values, examining how particular business contexts either impede or stimulate spirituality. Finally, this nonprofit agency helps with organizational learning, promoting corporate change to reduce employee alienation and enhance morale.

Halfway through her last summer at the investment banking firm, Alison spent a week of vacation at a Buddhist retreat center in New England. She spoke to her teacher there about how important her Buddhist practice had been to her during her eighteen years as a businesswoman: "It's as if I've been holding on to a golden string, a connection to my spiritual life, as a lifeline through all these years as a blue-suited professional." Then tears began streaming down her cheeks. "But, really, I've wasted all these years. I've done meditation all along, but how much, really, have I fulfilled the vows I made when I took refuge in the Buddha, dharma, and *sangha?* How much compassion have I shown for others? How much time have I spent in community with other Buddhists?" Her teacher's answer was simple: "Those eighteen years brought you here, now, to this Buddhist community and to supporting fifty schoolchildren in China. Imagine where your life may go next."

Alison's Buddhism in the past few years has indeed become a much more active part of her life; likewise, it's taken a more activist form. She speaks of Buddhism now as a road toward wholeness, both for the individual and for larger parts of society. First, though, Alison had to understand suffering deeply—both as a reality and as a motivator. At the foundation of Buddhist teachings is an awareness of suffering as an integral aspect of all conscious lives, despite our attempts to cling to material possessions and personal dreams as bulwarks against suffering. Understanding the possibility of release from the "prison of ego" through medi-tation and mindfulness practice allowed Alison to see the false dichotomies of the self as separate from the world. The next step was commitment to action, not just as something she *does* but as something she *is* in her own nature (and in everyone's true nature). Learning compas-sion as a way to act in the world, as much of the time as possible, reminded Alison that she's neither alone in her own suffering nor alone in her concern for the world in which she lives. She can now act out her Buddhist principles during her working day—as well as help others find wholeness, regardless of what their spiritual path may be.

My own experience with people who have undergone a lot of suffering is that they often mature faster than their counterparts who haven't, as well as demonstrating considerably more empathy with others. It's also amazing how many of them later claim to be grateful for their suffering, because it deepened them and helped them appreciate life so much more. In my own case, my life was radically changed when my first wife left me, I developed an ulcer, and I began to burn out in my work. At first I cer-tainly didn't see all that in a positive light. In fact, I felt as if I had fallen over a cliff into a void that had no bottom. However, as certain friends came forward and buoyed me up, I began to feel transformed. It all led to my spiritual pilgrimage around the world, a new conception of my work as part of a religious community, and a happy new marriage that pro-duced two wonderful children.

My ability to counsel people with marital problems, health problems, and job difficulties improved dramatically as a result of my own experi-ences. The late priest, pastor, and professor Henri Nouwen has written of the value of being a "wounded healer,"[2] one who is vulnerable and open to his or her own suffering in helping another. That doesn't mean seeing another's hurts as the same as one's own, or focusing on one's own prob-lems when with another. Instead, it means being compassionate, in the sense of feeling like this, in Nouwen's words: "I am your brother; I am your sister; I am human, fragile, and mortal, just like you. I am not scandalized by your tears, nor afraid of your pain. I too have wept. I too have felt pain."[3]

Suffering also stimulated a move for me from one stage of spiritual development to another. Prior to the life changes I've described, which occurred around age thirty, I would describe myself as having been in the Independence stage of faith. I was not following any teacher, and I was not part of any religious group other than my denomination in general. I thought of God impersonally as a life force. My favorite way of describing divinity was in the terms William Wordsworth had used in his poem "Tintern Abbey":

> . . . A sense sublime
> Of something far more deeply interfused,
> Whose dwelling is the light of setting suns,
> And the round ocean and the living air,
> And the blue sky, and in the mind of man;
> A motion and a spirit, that impels
> All thinking things, all objects of all thought,
> And rolls through all things.

But after my crisis I found great sustenance in the writings of teachers such as Gandhi and the liberation theologians of Latin America. I stayed in many religious communities during my travels, which helped me to realize how valuable other people were for personal support and spiritual deepening. After my return I developed a communitarian religious action and service model through the Unitarian Universalist Legal Ministry.

Does this sound like I was revisiting the Dependence stage of development? I don't think so, because I was not being led by peer pressure or particular loyalty to a leader, nor was I being pulled into a specific group. On the contrary—I was more open than ever to the unique assets and resources of the major religions of the world. Nor did I begin an unambiguously personal relationship with a parental type of God. Although I certainly was more compelled by imagery of God as person, it coexisted with my sense of God as motion and spirit that rolls through all things. This new awareness, paradoxical and multilayered, seems to bear the earmarks of the Interdependence stage—a dialectical worldview in which one is able to tolerate ambiguity and enjoy complexity.

Alison was at a critically dependent time in her spirituality when her mother died. As she understood her Congregational minister, God as a sort of superparent had taken her human parent to be happy with him. She needed her mother desperately to be with her as a real parent at this pivotal time of transition to adolescence. She viewed God as the person who had deprived her of her mother, and she found this unconscionable. As a result she was furious; from that day on she spurned God in her life.

The discovery of Buddhism marked the fullness of the Independence stage for Alison. Here was a religion without God that was all about relying on herself alone, as she saw it. If she was experiencing pain, it was her sole responsibility to deal with it. *Get your butt on a cushion and start meditating,* she would tell herself. *If I'm not happy, I've got no one to blame but myself.* She hit the wall with this kind of self-reliance almost twenty years later after making partner at her New York investment banking firm. She had pulled herself to the top by her own bootstraps and now could have anything money could buy. Yet she literally wanted to die. It was not until after the Wongs had fortuitously pushed her beyond herself in compassion and outreach and she was in sitting with a teacher in Buddhist retreat that she was able to remember the rest of her original Buddhist vows—to be an active member of a community.

Alison's newly found sense of Interdependence allowed her to develop a fresh career direction more consonant with values of compassion, community, and wholeness. Although Buddhism has been the driving force to remake herself, she now feels that she can help others on different religious paths through her work. She's also begun appropriating the word *God* for herself now in a much broader context, no longer seeing God as the parent figure who took her mother away. And she's even been able to spend time in Christian churches—doing adult education and participating in worship services—not only without crying but also with genuine spiritual connection.

Each of the major world religious traditions has unique resources for dealing with suffering, and each promises that practitioners can become stronger and wiser through distress and anguish in life. Take Hinduism as another example. I teach a course in the Department of Comparative Religions at Tufts, helping students understand different religious traditions and their ethical perspectives through works of fiction. I teach a novel called *Jasmine*, by Indian American author Bharati Mukherjee, in which the title character experiences one catastrophe after another.[4] Her husband is killed by her side in a radical Sikh terrorist attack in India. She immigrates to America, only to be brutally raped by the boat captain her first night in the country. She leaves a good job in New York for the cornfields of Iowa after making the terrifying discovery that her husband's killer has been tracking her. Finally, the banker she ends up living with in Iowa is shot and paralyzed from the waist down by a disgruntled borrower.

Jasmine's worldview is informed by the Hindu doctrine of karma. She speaks of a war within her between her fate and her will. She largely presumes that "fate is fate" and "what is to happen will happen," as an astrologer told her as a child when he predicted her widowhood and exile, based on the morality of her behavior in previous lives. Yet, she also thinks that she can "reposition the stars," based on her current behavior and her initiative. Alternatively put, she believes that she's been many different selves during this one life, with her karma in effect changing each time she takes action to survive a near-death experience. By the end of the book, the reader can see her as an audacious inheritor of the American Dream, "greedy with wants and reckless from hope," at age twenty-four happily pursuing her potential as a human being. She still views herself, though, from within a religious perspective as beginning a new reincarnation—now as lover of a divorced New York man on his way to California.

Jasmine also develops through three stages of faith during the book. As a seven-year-old child she lives in a cause-and-effect universe in which the future can be foretold based on the law of karma; one's next life will also be defined by how one acts in this one. Then, when she marries at fifteen, the adolescent Jasmine is "ready to be led" by her twenty-four-year-old husband. He's a modern man of the city and an idealist who wants her to be his equal rather than the feudal vassal she seems to expect to be. She learns his litany of independence and self-reliance by heart, but at first, ironically, only as a matter of obedience and loyalty to him.

In this Dependence stage, God too is very much like a parent to her—but one she thinks she can escape along with his rules of karma if only she can get far enough away. Her husband suggests moving to America, his studying at the Florida International Institute of Technology, and their starting a new life away from the "backward, corrupt, mediocre fools" with whom he feels surrounded in the two jobs he works. Jasmine remembers the astrologer's prophecy in her childhood and thinks that in America, "We'd be on the other side of the earth, out of God's sight." That means "all fates would be canceled. We'd start with new fates, new stars. We could say or be anything we wanted."

In fact, though, the astrologer's predictions are fulfilled before the couple can leave. Jasmine is widowed when the terrorist's bomb explodes. Then she is exiled when she leaves for America, intending to immolate herself in the flames of her husband's kerosene-soaked clothes on the grounds of the Florida campus. In the New World, Jasmine begins the Independence stage of her spiritual development. Ironically it starts with her rape, before she can get to the Florida International Institute. She manages to kill her rapist, but only after he's torn open her suitcase and so defiled her husband's belongings that she feels she can't properly fulfill her own suicide mission. Instead, she is picked up penniless on a Florida highway by a Quaker woman and a week later transported by Greyhound bus to New York City, where the woman's daughter lives. Finding work through her as an au pair for a Columbia University professor's child, Jasmine falls in love with the glow of this academic world—"its ease, its careless confidence and graceful self-absorption." Over two years in New York she becomes an adventurous American individualist. By the last page of the book, after four years in Iowa and as she gets ready to head for California, she feels completely in control of her own destiny: "Watch me reposition the stars, I whisper to the astrologer who floats cross-legged above my kitchen stove."

My final example of gaining strength through suffering highlights Judaism. Vivian Cooper's father committed suicide when she was three, leaving her mother, Susanne, a widow in Charleston, South Carolina, at the age of twenty-four. Although she remarried three years later, Susanne was embittered for life. She became a virulent alcoholic and chain-smoker. Vivian remembers her mother as a mean and angry person—emotionally unavailable and to be avoided if at all possible. As a result, Vivian spent little time at home, instead visiting friends, walking the dog, or going to the local library.

Besides two years in a Southern Baptist private school, she had little religious involvement during her childhood. Sometimes she went fishing with her stepfather on Sundays. He called it his religion. He'd say, "I'd rather be out here enjoying the beauty of the world God has given us than sitting in a stuffy room with a bunch of people in suits." Her stormy home life caused her to wonder about God and religion, however, and to look for answers to the questions of why she had to lose her own father, why she did not have a loving mother, and why there was so little joy in their family life. She read extensively about suicide and wondered if her father had been justified in his action.

Two clues emerged in her high school world literature class. There she became best friends with a classmate who was the son of a reform rabbi; she began to spend a lot of time at his house, enjoying long talks with the rabbi about the meaning of life. She also read several works of the classic existentialists, including *The Plague* by Albert Camus. The doctor in this book who has the miserable task of treating dying plague victims says he does so because there is honor in "the daily round" of his patients. He keeps at it because he can and feels he should, rather than giving up in despair. She remembers sitting at the rabbi's kitchen table discussing this book, the existentialists, and God. Her father's suicide had been his choice, for whatever reasons, but it was not a choice she wanted to make. As the rabbi told her, "You have so many gifts and so much to do."

In her junior year she began the long process of converting to Judaism. She'll always remember her stepfather's reaction when she told her parents about her plans: "Jews have gotten a bad rap throughout history. Is that really a group you want to be part of? Don't forget about Hitler." As a result, she read every book on her rabbi's shelf and in the public library about Hitler's Holocaust. The courage and fortitude of so many Jews in the face of that level of suffering made her even more certain that this was the faith for her. Given her own extended childhood suffering at home, she was profoundly respectful of a religion that affirmed life so strongly in the midst of death and destruction.

She continued to participate in synagogue life throughout her college years and well into her twenties. What was most compelling and transformative for her was the sense of community that lay at the heart of Judaism. As best-selling author Rabbi Harold Kushner has inquired, "Does any other people celebrate the special moments of life, the births and birthdays and weddings, with as much food, as much laughter and as many tears, as Jews do?"[5]

Vivian remembers reading Kushner's book *When Bad Things Happen to Good People*[6] the first year it came out. Spurred by the death of his fourteen-year-old son from a rare aging condition, he wrote "a book that would affirm life." He explained: "It would have to say that no one ever promised us a life free from pain and disappointment. The most anyone promised us was that we would not be alone in our pain, and that we would be able to draw upon a source outside ourselves for the strength and courage we would need to survive life's tragedies and life's unfairness." Founded in the story of a people liberated from slavery in ancient Egypt and brought through the wilderness to a promised land, Judaism has always been a communal religion. Acts, including deeds of steadfast love and peacemaking within the community, have always been more important than beliefs. As Kushner puts it, "doing Jewish" as "something that happens between you and other people" is more important than "being Jewish" as "a state of mind . . . something that takes place inside you."[7]

Therefore, Vivian was particularly disappointed when she moved to a suburb of Baltimore just before turning thirty and couldn't find a welcoming synagogue. She was blonde and blue-eyed and therefore didn't "look Jewish." People who learned she had converted were puzzled by the fact that she had done so for personal, spiritual reasons, and not to marry a Jewish man. Being single in such family-oriented environments was difficult, and after several attempts, she drifted away from regular synagogue participation. She eventually married a nominally Christian business executive, Gus, who never went to church. Two years later, they had a daughter, Jessica.

By the time Jessica was old enough for some kind of religious education, Gus had lost his job and joined a Christian men's group that met at a local hotel on Tuesday mornings for breakfast. He soon came home with a long list of networking contacts, golf dates, and a wallet-sized card that said he had personally accepted Jesus Christ as his Lord and Savior. He began saying grace and reading Bible verses aloud before dinner. Vivian was pleased, as she thought the newfound Christian commitment might ease the tension, angry outbursts, and violence that had become part of their life. Her hope was that embracing this religion—founded on God's love—would bring him peace and happiness.

However, the pressures of the new position Gus ultimately found simply made the domestic situation worse. He blamed the stress of his job for his foul temper and abuse. He also quit attending the Christian men's group, saying prayers, and reading the Bible. After a particularly bad episode, Vivian found a job in Philadelphia and moved out with Jessica. She speaks cynically of the difference between "talking Christians" and "doing Christians." Finding a community of spiritual people who focused on "doing" became more important than ever.

Soon after leaving her husband, Vivian saw a television program about the Holocaust. The commentator remarked on the random acts of violence that characterized the era. Vivian experienced a transformative moment of awareness, understanding clearly that her initial attraction to Judaism had come specifically through her identification with the people of the Holocaust. Her mother's violent behavior, and her stepfather's tacit support of it, made her feel a profound bond with the Jewish victims of the Holocaust and with their religion, which had the spiritual resources to cope with such havoc and brutality. Now, though, she spent some time soul-searching, as she faced the decision of how to raise her daughter. Her hope was to introduce her daughter to Judaism in a joyous way, not as a by-product of unhappiness and abuse.

As fate would have it, Jessica began to be invited to programs at the nearby United Church of Christ by children in their new neighborhood. Vivian began attending some church activities with the children and with neighbors. She found the community to be very supportive, active in community service, and filled with activities celebrating holidays. Jessica wanted to join the children's dance group—at the invitation of the dance group leader, who said the purpose of the program was to dance as a way of enjoying the bodies God has given us. Eventually, Vivian and Jessica became regular churchgoers, sitting with their friends, participating in community service events, and enjoying themselves.

For Vivian, the United Church of Christ has been an experience of learning from trail crossings. She continues to light the Jewish Sabbath candles every Friday night at home with Jessica. In December they light Hanukkah candles, but now they have added Advent candles as well. Vivian has been reading more about Christianity, both to provide a context for Jessica and for her own understanding. She has not rejected Judaism, which has provided such a great source of strength and way of being in the world for her; instead, she says her Judaism has gotten bigger as she's learned about Christianity.

For example, a friend gave her a copy of Marcus Borg's *Meeting Jesus Again for the First Time,* which among other things has helped her understand the Jewishness of Jesus. As Borg explains, Jesus was thoroughly Jewish and never meant to start a new religion: "His Scripture was the Jewish Bible. He did not intend to establish a new religion, but saw himself as having a mission within Judaism. He spoke as a Jew to Jews." Borg also emphasizes the joy experienced in Jesus' presence, tied to his Jewish understanding. No doubt he observed and celebrated the great Jewish holidays, including those "marked by much music, feasting, and dancing." Discipleship, symbolized in his Last Supper with those closest to him during the Passover season, "means eating at his table and experiencing his banquet."[8]

Rabbi Kushner's writing has helped Vivian again, too. A dozen years after his book about his son's death, Harold Kushner wrote about what it means to be Jewish in *To Life!* Like Borg, he discusses how Jesus was born and lived as an observant Jew and how all of his apostles were Jews. Kushner hopes to enrich Christian commitment, as well as Jewish self-understanding, in helping modern Christians and Jews to rediscover the heritage they hold in common. These are the words, then, that best express the Judaism that Vivian now longs to live:

> *To life*—these two words represent so much of what Judaism is about. They suggest first that Judaism is about how to live. . . . As the traditional Jewish toast over a glass of wine, *To life* conveys a sense of exuberance, a readiness to enjoy the pleasures of this world. It removes from wine, and from other pleasures, the taint of sin and self-indulgence, and invites us to look at all that God has created and find it good. The sages teach us that "in time to come, everyone will have to account for all the good things God created which he refused to enjoy."[9]

Rejoicing

—◦◦◦—

"Stuff Happens." That's the first line of eighteen on a T-shirt entitled "Religions of the World," which I was given on my forty-ninth birthday. Actually, a scatological word was used on the T-shirt, signifying "bad stuff," but we are talking about religion here, after all, and "stuff" will do. Another way that suffering can be transformed, beyond what was discussed in the last chapter, is through humor. Jokes about religion, and within religion, are legion. "Stuff happens" is attributed to Taoism on my T-shirt, which goes on to describe Hinduism as "This stuff happened before." Catholicism is "If stuff happens, I deserve it." Islam becomes "If stuff happens, it is the will of Allah." Judaism asks, *"Oyvay!* Why does this stuff always happen to me?" Buddhism is characterized as "When stuff happens, is it really stuff?"

Much of religion is actually about celebrating and having fun. The root of the word *holiday* is "holy day." On the seventh day of creation, according to the Bible, God rested, and the Ten Commandments ask us to rest every seven days too. Singing and dancing and feasting all have roots in religion, as does much of drama and the fine arts. To eat, drink, and be merry, says Ecclesiastes, is a gift of God.[1] There's a proverb that explains that "a merry heart is a good medicine; but a downcast spirit dries up the bones."[2]

A Harvard Divinity School professor of mine, Harvey Cox, wrote a book on festivity and fantasy thirty years ago, entitled *The Feast of Fools*. In it he laments how we modern Westerners have lost a lot of our capability for celebration. We are working too hard and seem to have too little time. In our scientific age we are obsessed with facts and dominated by our ever-evolving technologies.

Cox lists three reasons why he thinks it is critical that we regain our capacity for festivity and fantasy if we want to survive and flourish: The first is that by nature we are creatures who not only work and think but sing, dance, tell stories, pray, and create holy days to celebrate. No other animals relive legends of their ancestors and blow out candles on birthday cakes. As we lose this ability, we dehumanize ourselves. We treat ourselves and everything around us as objects, becoming automatons ourselves and poisoning our natural environment. Second, human survival is also tied to the capacity to change. Festivity breaks routines and opens us up to our rich wealth of experience from the past, while fantasy opens the door to the future that simple calculation ignores. Cox explains that "when a civilization becomes alienated from its past and cynical about its future, as Rome once did, its spiritual energy flags. It stumbles and [falls]."[3] Finally, without the ability to celebrate, we lose the sense of ultimate meaning and purpose in life. Celebration allows us to grasp our lives within a larger historical and cosmic setting, rather than being like gnats without either origin or destiny.

Many of the biblical psalms are drenched in words of praise like this: "O sing to the Lord a new song, for he has done marvelous things. . . . Make a joyful noise to the Lord, all the earth; break forth into joyous song and sing praises. Sing praises to the Lord with the lyre. . . . With trumpets and the sound of the horn. . . . Let the floods clap their hands; let the hills sing together for joy."⁴ Sura 34 of the Qur'an echoes this enthusiasm: "All Praise is due to God, Whose is what is in the heavens and what is in the earth, and to Him is due all praise in the hereafter. . . . O mountains! sing praises to Him, and the birds."⁵ In the modern era, one of my favorite transcendent celebrators is e. e. cummings, in this poem:

> i thank You God for most this amazing
> day: for the leaping greenly spirits of trees
> and a blue true dream of sky; and for everything
> which is natural which is infinite which is yes
>
> (i who have died am alive again today,
> and this is the sun's birthday; this is the birth
> day of life and of love and wings: and of the gay
> great happening illimitably earth)
>
> how should tasting touching hearing seeing
> breathing any—lifted from the no
> of all nothing—human merely being
> doubt unimaginable You?
>
> (now the ears of my ears awake and
> now the eyes of my eyes are opened)⁶

Cox distinguishes having fun in a religious sense from having fun in a mindless sense by reminding us that religious festivity is neither superficial nor frivolous. It recognizes tragedy, and perhaps this is why I've found that those who seem very oppressed can also appear to be having a lot of fun in their religious lives. I've watched impoverished *campesinos* in *comunidades de base* (base Christian communities) in Central and South

America, after backbreaking work in the fields for negligible wages, get together around a few instruments and sing hymns with enormous spirit and thanksgiving. I remember the North American civil rights movement in the 1960s being drenched in the joy and emotion of African American gospel music. Passover is historically a celebration of liberation from slavery in Egypt, and a reminder now that Jews everywhere must continue the struggle for liberation. That's because crusades, inquisitions, pogroms, and holocausts don't seem to stop, even (or perhaps most especially) in the modern age of the twentieth century. Easter for Christians comes only after forty days of repentance and self-reflection during Lent. The triumphant resurrection of Jesus comes only after the ghastly suffering of his crucifixion and the loss of his followers' hope for three days following his death.

It's the juxtaposition of tragedy and joy in religious celebration that has made these words of the Hindu poet Tagore favorites of mine at funerals: "Life as a whole never takes death seriously. It laughs, dances and plays, it builds, hoards and loves in death's face. Only when we detach one individual fact of death do we see its blankness and become dismayed. We lose sight of the wholeness of a life of which death is part. . . . The truth is, death is not the Ultimate Reality. It looks black, as the sky looks blue; but it does not blacken existence, just as the sky does not leave its stain upon the wings of the bird."[7]

Besides funerals, the other great rites of passage at which I officiate occur around the times of birth, coming of age, and marriage. They are usually a lot of fun, even as they signify deep commitments. For example, I'll never forget a baptism I did in a river in Vermont for two girls I had known since their birth, although they were by then well into childhood. It was one of those hot late-July cricket-stitching days along the edge of a hay field, with green mountains above and a crystal-clear stream below. Two dozen family members and friends had gathered, and it was all very informal; some of us were in bathing suits and T-shirts (although not with "stuff happens" inscriptions). I began by asking the parents and godparents a number of questions about their commitment to the girls' spiritual and moral nurture. Then I spoke about the concept of baptism. In Greek, the word literally means "to dip in water," and water has almost universally been a symbol of vitality, nourishment, and renewal. Baptism has a history going back well before the Jewish ritual described in the New Testament when John the Baptist dipped Jesus of Nazareth in the Jordan River.

Similar rituals along the banks of the Nile River in Egypt and the Ganges in India predate the Jewish and Christian practices. The two girls were to be immersed in this Vermont river, whose water symbolized the very stream of life—water that ultimately touches every shore and nourishes every race and people, all animals and all plants. By my words, I was to welcome them into the family of God and dedicate them to the good of all humankind, to lifelong respect for nature, and to their own fullest growth.

Physically, the ceremony involved full immersion—by my tilting them gently backward as they stood in water up to their waists, lowering them into the water, and then briefly dipping their heads under as they looked skyward. They had played in this river and gone swimming here a hundred times since they were babies, but today was different. People were watching, there was a lot of formal buildup, and they were in someone else's control.

What I found forever memorable was the look on each of their faces as their heads came up out of the river: stunned, wide-eyed, and awake as they suddenly caught their breath. And then laughing. Laughing at their own surprise. Laughing at how different it felt from any other time they'd been in this river. Laughing as they looked at their parents and friends, who were smiling and clapping and laughing with them. They were renewed at that moment and they knew it. Something very special had happened.

That evening after everyone had dried off, we lit a campfire to cook our dinner and roast marshmallows for dessert. Lots of stories were told. The adults drank wine and the children fruit juice. There were games and swinging and roughhousing in the hammock. At the end of the night everyone joined in singing folk songs—on and on, soloing and harmonizing, raucously and gently. This too is religion. Don't forget to have fun.

Of course, religious merrymaking can get out of hand. There's the hilarious wedding reception scene in Philip Roth's novel *Goodbye Columbus:* "We ate, we drank, we danced," explains Neil, the narrator and main character, who was attending because his girlfriend was the sister of the groom. People at the noisy head table "ate a fantastic number of rolls" as they proposed toasts and "burst into wild song." At one point Brenda, the girlfriend, "who'd been drinking champagne like her Uncle Leo, did a Rita Hayworth tango with herself." Her younger sister, Julie, "fell asleep on some ferns she'd whisked off the head table and made into a mattress at the far end of the hall." The groom's uncle, Marty Kreiger, the Kosher Hot-Dog King, was "an immense man, as many stomachs as he had chins, and already, at fifty-five, with as many heart attacks as chins and stomachs combined." Neil observes that "when the photographer came by to take pictures, Marty put his hand on his wife's pancake breasts and said, 'Hey, how about a picture of this!'" Brenda responded with phallic imagery when asked by a friend of her brother's what she had been doing all summer.[8]

Such excess at major rites of passage may simply be an age-old, archetypal part of the world of festivity to which Cox is calling us back. In fact, he lists "conscious excess" as one of the three essential ingredients of festivity. Festive activity should be revelry, during which we "live it up" and "overdo it" on purpose: "We stay up later, eat and drink more, and spend more money than we ordinarily would. Perhaps we laugh or cry or both. In some cultures conventional sexual mores and food taboos are temporarily relaxed." A second essential ingredient of festivity for Cox, "juxtaposition," is related—festivity must display contrast in being noticeably different from "everyday life." By his third essential ingredient, "celebrative affirmation," Cox means that festivity always involves "saying yes to life." It entails joy in the deepest sense, even in the face of issues such as failure and death. This is what distinguishes it from mere frivolity, which is superficial and usually cynical, despairing of making any sense out of life, rather than springing from a joyous confidence in life's ultimate goodness. The spiritual power of festivity lies in affirmation, as well as transcendence of the momentary, the ordinary, and the frivolous.[9]

Festivity can link us directly to the archaic and primordial in human life, whether we recognize it or not. Cox explains that the "New Year's Eve party demonstrates the vestigial survival of forgotten feasts and rituals."[10] This may be even more true for the great personal rites of passage from birth to death.

A wonderfully comical illustration of the archaic and primordial is available in the novelist Mordecai Richler's portrayal of a bar mitzvah in his book (and movie by the same name with lead actor Richard Dreyfuss) *The Apprenticeship of Duddy Kravitz*. Duddy has been contracted to produce a bar mitzvah film, and he is present at the point in the novel when the director shows it to the boy's family and friends.

This is the narrator's voice-over at the beginning of the film, as the thirteen-year-old Bernie is studying Hebrew and learning Torah tunes with his grandfather: "Older than the banks of the Nile, not so cruel as the circumcision rite of the Zulus, and even more intricate than a snowflake is the bar mitzvah." The synagogue service is then shown, with the Ark being opened and the Torah passed to Bernie. Before long, though, the service is interrupted on the screen with a montage of other images: an

African tribal dance, a jungle fire, the slaughter of a cow, lightning and rain, a jitterbug contest, fireworks, and an advertisement for Maidenform bras. A family viewer almost faints.

The film cuts back to Bernard being led up the aisle by the rabbi to read from the Torah; then faces are panned in the synagogue. Close-ups of a baby being circumcised are interwoven in the footage as Bernie says blessings and reads from scripture. Before long, other bizarre images are appearing on the screen. The narrator relates the bar mitzvah ceremony to Aztec sacrifice, ancient priests' initiation rites, and becoming a fully accepted member of a tribe. There are images of soldiers marching, a James Thurber cartoon, a venereal disease warning in a public urinal, a hand on a woman's breast, and more. By now the sickened relative has left the viewing.

The camera then pans over a table of gifts, while the narrator says, "They came with tributes for the boy who had come of age." Included are a fishing rod, a prayer shawl, a rubber dinghy, lots of checks, six sport shirts, fifty silver dollars in a velvet-lined box, a chemistry set, gift certificates and a savings account book, three toilet seats, five subscriptions to *National Geographic,* and much, much more. Next, the rabbi is seen talking to Bernie in his office at length, concluding by autographing a copy of his book *Why I'm Glad to Be a Jew.* The film finally ends after a lot of footage of merrymaking at the dinner and dance that follow the service. None of the viewers speak. Silence reigns. The first to break it is the rabbi, who has been sitting in the audience and watching the film carefully, especially to see how much screen time he got (a lot). "A most edifying experience," he pronounces. "A work of art."[11]

Making fun of clergy is an age-old religious ritual in itself. Jesus called many in his day hypocrites, because they didn't practice what they preached. As an engrossing speaker himself who certainly knew how to turn a phrase, Jesus seemed to be a master of hyperbole and absurdity when skewering clergy. "Blind guides!" he said. "You strain off a midge, yet gulp down a camel!"[12] In another droll commentary on religious officials, he exclaimed, "How can you say to your brother, 'Brother, let me take out the speck that is in your eye,' when you yourself do not see the log that is in your own eye? You hypocrite, first take the log out of your own eye, and then you will see clearly to take out the speck that is in your brother's eye."[13]

Hypocrisy remains an active generator of clergy jokes today. Here's one offering from a great compendium of entertainment within the Jewish tradition, *The Big Book of Jewish Humor*:[14]

A man was boasting about the piety of his rabbi.

"My rabbi, may he live to be a hundred and twenty, is so pious that he fasts every day—except of course, for Saturdays and holidays."

"How can that be true?" asked his friend. "Why, just this morning I saw your rabbi eating breakfast."

"That shows how much *you* know," replied the first man. "You see, my rabbi is very modest about his piety. If he eats, it is only to hide from others the fact that he is fasting."

Money and sex generate a lot of modern jokes about clergy hypocrisy. Fallen Protestant televangelists are easy targets, for example:

"Did you know that Bakker and Swaggert are starting a new magazine?"

"No. What are they going to call it?"

"*Repenthouse*, and it will have a Praymate of the month."[15]

But perhaps any minister has his or her price:

A woman called on the Presbyterian minister and asked him if he would preach a funeral for her dog who had died.

"I can't do that, ma'am," he said. "Why don't you try the Baptist preacher?"

"All right," she said, "but can you give me some advice. How much should I pay him—three hundred dollars or four hundred dollars?"

"Hold on," he said, "I didn't know your dog was a Presbyterian."[16]

Perhaps not surprisingly, my favorite clergy jokes show them to be very wise. I particularly relish a series about Zen Buddhist masters called *Zen Comics* by Ioanna Salajan. Here are a few (without the pictures):

The disciple asks, "Master, how is it that you see things so clearly?" The Master, sitting cross-legged in a posture for meditation, answers: "I close my eyes."

The Disciple asks, "Master, is there any special way to be disciplined in the Tao?" The Master answers, "Yes, there is. When you're hungry—eat. When you're tired—sleep."

Two novices are talking. "Look at that monk over there, standing on the hill. I wonder what he's doing?" says one. The other responds, "Probably waiting for someone." The first disagrees: "No! It seems more like he's looking for something." A quarrel ensues, with each arguing his position. Finally they decide to ask the monk: "Excuse me, old monk," the first disciple begins, "Would you tell us what you're doing?" The monk's reply is brief. "Sure, I'm just standing on this hill."

The Disciple asks, "Master, what happens to the enlightened man and to the man of illusion after death?" The Old Monk responds, "How should I know?" The disciple is surprised: "Because, Master, you are an enlightened man." The Old Monk concludes, "That may be, but I'm not a dead one."[17]

Here's one from the Jewish tradition in the same vein:

A rabbinical student is about to leave Europe for a position in the New World. He goes to his rabbi for advice, and the rabbi, a great Talmud scholar, offers an adage that, he assures the younger man, will guide him throughout his life: "Life is a fountain."

The young rabbi is deeply impressed by the profundity of his teacher's remarks, and departs for a successful career in America. Thirty years later, hearing that his mentor is dying, the younger man returns for a final visit.

"Rabbi," he says to his old teacher, "I have one question. For thirty years, every time I have been sad or confused I have thought of the phrase you passed on to me before I left for America. It has helped me through the most difficult of times. But to be perfectly honest with you, rabbi, I have never fully understood the meaning of it. And now that you are about to enter the World of Truth, perhaps you would be so kind as to tell me what these words really mean. Rabbi, why *is* life like a fountain?"

Wearily, the old man replies, "All right, so it's *not* like a fountain!"[18]

By good luck, as you know from the Introduction, I had a college roommate who became a cartoonist. Garry Trudeau has had a lot of fun caricaturing clergy over the years in *Doonesbury,* often portraying them more as naive than wise. Some of the adjectives one might use to describe his Rev. Scot Sloan character are simplistic, earnest, jargonizing, and presumptuous. Yet, this character is also idealistic, passionate, hopeful, and kind. A couple of times during my chaplaincy career at Tufts I have delivered sermons entitled "The Gospel According to *Doonesbury*" (I and II), because in having fun with religion, Garry also conveys a profound spiritual message, wittingly or unwittingly. It's that summarized by the prophet Micah in the eighth verse of chapter six: "What does the Lord require of you, but to do justice, and to love kindness, and to walk humbly with your God?"

I got the idea of a *Doonesbury* Gospel from reading a book by Robert Short called *The Gospel According to Peanuts*, which finds spiritual meaning in Charles Schulz's cartoon strip. Schulz once said, "If you don't *say* anything in a cartoon, you might as well not draw it at all. Humor which does not say anything is worthless humor. So I contend that a cartoonist must be given a chance to do his own preaching."[19] Garry always *says* a lot in his cartoons (well beyond the words and deeds of his Rev. Scot Sloan), and in my opinion he's a great preacher.

First of all, in many ways *Doonesbury* has become the conscience of the nation. Day in and day out in the morning newspaper it makes morality a public and objective matter, not just a private and subjective one. It manages to hold us all to account, often through the classic mechanism of revealing hypocrisy. Second, it brings very diverse people together, both in its panels and in its readership—conservative and liberal, Christian and Muslim, Black and White. Third, it gores everyone's ox, revealing all of our vulnerabilities and foibles in such a way that we can smile at and empathize with each other, remembering our common humanity. The Gospel of *Doonesbury* is threefold: Ethics and the struggle for a better world really matter (do justice). We are all in this together (love kindness). Let none of us take ourselves too seriously along the way (walk humbly with your God).

One of the cartoons I have on my wall at home dates back to January of 1972, a little over a year after the strip was launched. The first two frames read: "Good morning, Brother! Welcome to 'The Exit,' the coffee-house where people can really relate! Reverend Scot Sloan's the name. Perhaps you read about me in 'Look.' I'm the fighting young priest who can talk to the young." Addressing a helmeted college football player and fraternity man, B.D., Rev. Scot goes on in the third frame: "My specialty, of course, is setting up dialogues. Often I am successful in getting people to look at themselves honestly and meaningfully." In the final frame, B.D. speaks for the first time, saying, "Good for you, Sweetheart. One black coffee to go."[20]

In the prior day's strip, Rev. Scot had been discussing plans for his cof-feehouse with Michael Doonesbury: "It's just a hunch, see, but I can't help feeling you youths need someplace to come when you feel like relax-ing. This coffeehouse can be the perfect milieu. Dynamic, exciting, now. And the good Lord willing, perhaps it will even turn a profit." Doonesbury asks what the profits will be used for. Rev. Scot's idealism and naivete are linked as he responds, "To wipe out poverty, hunger, hate, war, frustration and inadequate housing." All Doonesbury can say at that point is "Oh."[21]

In the past three decades, every American president, Democrat and Republican, has been subject to *Doonesbury*'s moral rapier, from Nixon's impeachment proceedings to Clinton's, from Carter's peanut politics to Reagan's Iran-Contra dissembling. Some have taken it more personally than others. President Ford explained, "There are only three major ve-hicles to keep us informed as to what's going on in Washington: the elec-tronic media, the print media, and *Doonesbury*—not necessarily in that order." President Carter recalled that "even when it hurt to be criticized, I listened to him." President Bush once said, "I had the personal feeling that I wanted to go up and kick the hell out of him, frankly."[22]

As a modern prophet calling us to do justice, Garry has challenged the failings of business as much as government. One relatively recent cartoon has the cigarette figure Mr. Butts conducting a town meeting in China when he is asked, "Mr. Butts, what kind of impact are U.S. cigarettes having in Asia?" The answer is: "Dramatic! Before trade barriers were lowered, only adult men smoked. But thanks to American advertising and promotion, all that's changed. Today, throughout Asia, women are now smoking in growing numbers. In Korea, for instance, the number of teenaged girl smokers jumped *450%* in *one year!* We're proud of that!" The questioner picks up on this: "So you're promoting fairness?" Mr. Butts replies, "Bingo! Girls were missing out on the glamour."[23]

Doonesbury has also been a consistent critic of cultural trends that dehumanize us all. For example, Rev. Scot is walking with Michael Doonesbury behind his country house one day in the mid-1980s. The minister says to Mike, "You keep telling me you can't believe there's as much hunger in America as the reports say. Well, I'm going to show you. There are an estimated 20 million people who suffer from hunger today. It's time you met a few of them!" Doonesbury responds, "Hey . . . Where are we?" Rev. Scot explains: "In your own backyard. And these are some of the people I work with every day, people who simply don't have enough to eat!" Doonesbury, not seeing anything beyond his yard but a meadow, lake, trees, and mountains, is confused: "These are the hungry? Right here?" When Rev. Scot replies, "Yes," Doonesbury exclaims in the last frame, "But they're . . . They're invisible." Rev. Scot retorts, "See what I'm up against?" and a caption out of thin air reads "Maybe we should carry signs, Man."[24]

In terms of preaching point number two—loving-kindness and our all being in this together—the following strip is representative. In the late 1990s two homeless people, Alice and Elmont, are being interviewed by a radio talk show host, who asks, "Okay, even though you kids don't get food stamps, what do you think of the welfare bill?" Elmont answers,

"We're quite excited by it!" The radio host cannot believe it: "*What!* Why?" Alice explains, "There's no more 'Welfare State'—The Gingrich Revolution is over! We're no longer wards of the Democrats. Poverty has been bipartisanized. We're *everybody's* headache now!" The radio host starts saying, "So the cruelest bill in memory . . ." when he is interrupted again by Alice: "A cause for celebration!" Elmont adds, "Nothing fancy— A quiet dinner of muscatel and cat food!"[25]

Collections of *Doonesbury* comics have been introduced by commentators across the cultural and political spectrum, including Garry Wills, William F. Buckley, Jr., Gloria Steinem, and Studs Terkel.[26] What medium other than *Doonesbury* could have put a stars-and-stripes-forever American soldier into a fast friendship with a Vietcong terrorist during the Vietnam War? In one panel, when the Vietcong explains how he longs for a bowl of his mother's rice and laments how she's worried sick about him, the American soldier responds, "Amazing . . . I didn't know Commies *had* mothers."[27] Who other than Garry Trudeau could have a juror explaining his feelings after a trial this way? "At first it seemed cut and dried. After all, these guys were tobacco executives! Pariahs! Case closed! But then I thought, hold on! They're not tobacco executives, they're *human beings!* They have families and friends! They have feelings and dreams just like *other* human beings! But then I thought, hold on! They're not human beings—they're *tobacco executives!*" The panel ends with his wife saying, "Heavens! What a pickle!"[28]

Finally, *Doonesbury* preaches humility. In early 1980, Rev. Scot is heading off to Iran and Michael Doonesbury asks him, "So what exactly are you planning to do in Tehran, Scot?" The minister responds, "Well, my main mission is to visit the hostages, of course, to offer them comfort and let them know they haven't been forgotten." In the next frame Rev. Scot explains, "Also, if the opportunity arises, I was thinking of overpowering one of the guards and holding off the others until I could radio for another rescue attempt." In the final frame, Rev. Scot reconsiders: "But I dunno. People might see that as just a big ego trip." Doonesbury ends the panel by saying "Yeah. You have to guard against that."

Perhaps the ultimate humility for me in writing this book on finding your religion is illustrated by a mid-1990s cartoon depicting Michael Doonesbury and his wife, J.J., talking to their school-age daughter about church. Doonesbury says, "Alex, honey, Mom and I have been talking and we've decided it's time for us to start attending church as a family . . ." His daughter replies, "Church? Church is *boring!*" Doonesbury has an answer: "Well, we thought you might say that. All kids think that . . ." Alex asks, "Didn't *you* think church was boring when you were a kid?" Doonesbury rejoins, "Well, sure, I hated going. But church was good for me, so my parents made me stick it out. You may end up hating church, too, but you have to come by that feeling honestly. You have to put in the pew time, like Mom and I did." "Oh," says Alex, looking thoughtful. Then she wonders aloud: "What if I like it?" Doonesbury looks shocked: "Like it? What do you mean?" Her mother ends the conversation by declaring, "We'll cross that bridge when we get there, honey."[29]

A lot of Americans, perhaps like Doonesbury and J.J., are Christmas-and-Easter Christians. Those are the only two days of the year they darken the door of a church. One of the reasons may be that these two days are the most fun in the Christian year (perhaps substituting Christmas Eve for Christmas Day in many families, since everyone is too busy having fun with gifts on the day itself to go to church). Many clergy and devout churchgoers lament this phenomenon. I would rather return to what Harvey Cox said about festivity and fantasy: Many modern Westerners have lost a lot of their capability for celebration. Why can't there be more fun in religious life all the time, not just twice a year?

When I spent a couple of months in Guatemala during the early 1980s, I was amazed by the joyful way religion pervaded routine experience there. Sometimes it seemed as if almost every day was a Catholic saint's day or a feast day. That was partly due to the large size of the indigenous population—half of the population is said to be of Mayan ancestry—who wear brilliantly colorful clothes, mix their celebration of Christian, traditional, and local festivals, and seem never too far from their flutes, drums, and marimbas. I remember well how within a week of my arrival in early October, a larger-than-life-size image of Saint Francis was being borne on men's shoulders through highland streets, led by a flutist and drummer and followed by a huge crowd. Then a ritual dance in costumes and masks (with no tourists around) portrayed the coming of the Spanish *conquistadores* some 450 years ago. I saw a fiesta calendar for patron saints that listed activities for a third of the days in an average month. And generally there seemed to be more going on inside and outside of the main church than anywhere else in town.

Cox emphasizes juxtaposition as one of the three essential ingredients of festivity. Festivals must contrast with ordinary life to be festivals. Holy days and holidays must be juxtaposed or set apart from common days and work days. The Sabbath is honored because it's different from the rest of the week—a day of rest after six of toil. Even in Guatemala, the majority of time each month is *not* fiesta time, and there's plenty of exhausting labor being done. Yes, Christmas and Easter *are* different and special and should be so. I'm afraid, however, that increasingly North Americans are forgetting even how to celebrate them—or other winter solstice and vernal equinox holidays, to universalize this discussion.

It's not coincidental that Christmas, Hanukkah, and Kwanza (an African harvest festival celebrated by many African Americans since the 1960s) cluster around the date of the longest night of the year. It's a depressing time in the northern hemisphere, with all of us having to face the long, cold season ahead. So what can we do? Come together as families and friends, light candles, tell stories, and sing songs. That is, if we are on a religious path. We can have a good time, right in the face of the darkness. In our secular society we have a lot of holiday parties, also, but many people complain that we've become too rushed, frenetic, and commercially oriented to savor them very deeply. Hangovers and weight gain are the main effects of these holidays for many of us.

All three of these religious celebrations also bear the theme of joy in liberation. As Cox reminds us, religious jubilation is different from frivolity in that it recognizes the relationship of delight to adversity. Christmas celebrates one who is born to free humanity from corruption and alienation—usually referred to as sin and death. Jesus comes with the promise of eternal salvation. In the Latin American *comunidades de bases* I have described, Jesus is also seen as a liberator from political, social, and economic oppression. Hanukkah commemorates the successful Maccabean revolt of the Jews against the Syrians in the second century B.C.—a guerrilla war of national liberation. In the book of First Maccabees, the struggle is compared to the Exodus liberation from the Pharaoh of Egypt. Kwanza is a celebration of Black pride and self-determination in the face of enduring racism. One of its seven principles, with indigenous religious roots—*kujichagulia*—is "to define ourselves, name ourselves, and speak for ourselves, instead of being defined and spoken for by others."

The longest and hottest days of the year were the hardest times when I was in Cairo, Egypt, one summer during the month of Ramadan; the daytime temperature never fell below one hundred degrees Fahrenheit. In this predominantly Muslim country, virtually everyone was fasting every day—including not drinking a drop of water—until nightfall. Yet, as soon as the sun sank below the horizon and a cannon was sounded on the Nile River (and shown on TV), joy was abundant everywhere. Families and friends gathered over special foods. Then as the darkness deepened, a kind of carnival atmosphere seemed to prevail, with more activity than ever in and around the mosques.

The religious center of Cairo, the place that in medieval times was its physical center, is the Mosque of El Azhar. Many evenings I walked around the nearby bazaar area of Khan el Khalili, which was brightly lit with colored lights and full of decorations and music. The celebrations there went on from dusk to dawn, with people pouring in from outside Cairo, coming and going from the mosque, and sleeping in the streets. I was quite struck by the combination of individual self-reflection and collective enjoyment intermingled throughout the month of Ramadan, not only from day to night but also throughout those nighttime hours. There was no doubt that Ramadan was juxtaposed, in Cox's sense, as a distinctive month in the year (which over time migrates through the seasons, based on the lunar calendar). Egyptians were particularly aware of their religion during these twenty-eight days—the discipline of fasting brought with it a sense of both communal festivity and personal transformation that would be unlikely to happen at any other time.

Juxtaposition—and the opportunity it gives for having fun within religious practices that also have deep seriousness of purpose—becomes clear to Jewish children at a very early age when they participate in their family's Passover Seder each spring. Just as Christmas and Easter are the most celebrated Christian holy days, Passover is the most widely observed Jewish holiday.[30] There are lots of child-friendly customs during the Passover meal, such as hiding the special piece of the unleavened bread, called the *afikomen,* which will end the meal, and rewarding the child who finds it. As early as three or four years of age, Jewish children memorize a passage beginning "*Ma nish-ta-na ha-laila ha-zeh mi-kol ha-lei-lot?*" Translated from the Hebrew, it means "Why is this night different from all other nights?" Four answers follow in the Haggadah, the Seder service, which distinguish everyday meals from the Passover meal: for example, "On all other nights we eat leavened and unleavened bread, but on this night only unleavened bread." Jewish practice provides lots of opportunities for sacred time, set apart from the ordinary, from lighting the Sabbath candles at home every Friday night to the solemn fast day of Yom Kippur, which comes at the end of the ten days of reflection and repentance each fall after the new year commemoration called Rosh Hashanah—as well as another half dozen holiday periods, including the wonderfully lighthearted and comical revelry of Purim late in the winter.

A recent book on Jewish humor by Rabbi Joseph Telushkin, though, insists that Passover still inspires more jokes than any other holiday.[31] One is related to the tradition that the youngest person at the Passover table recites the Ma Nish-ta-na from memory—and usually works very hard getting ready to do so! Consistent with the premise of this book that many modern people lose their religion during adolescence, though, for many adult Jews the Ma Nish-ta-na is the sum total of Hebrew that they remember. Rabbi Telushkin ends his book with this story:

An English Jew, a prominent novelist and intellectual, is informed that he will be knighted. The queen's protocol officials prepare him and other knights-to-be for the ceremony. He is informed that, when he stands before the queen, he is to recite certain Latin words just before being knighted.

On the day of the ceremony, the man is very nervous and, sure enough, when he approaches the queen, he forgets the Latin expression. As precious seconds tick by, the only non-English words that he knows pour out of him: "*Ma nish-ta-na ha-laila ha-zeh mi-kol ha-leilot?*" The queen, confused, turns to her protocol officer and asks, "Why is this knight different from all other knights?"[32]

In summary, mountain climbing should be fun, whatever else it is—energizing, challenging, difficult, exciting, eye-opening, and awe-provoking. I have always been struck by the half-smile on the Buddha's lips as he is portrayed in statues and paintings. Sometimes he's depicted as a laughing Buddha, apparently consumed in mirth. His expression is a continual reminder that spiritual life should never be a deadly serious affair. A sense of humor is one of the most important ingredients for successful trekking and climbing. Enthusiasm is another—maintaining an attitude of eagerness and delight, which can ultimately lead to ecstasy at the top of the mountain. Enthusiasm can also bring appreciation of the small everyday joys along the way that renew us and fulfill us. One of my favorite professors at Tufts is fond of reminding me that the etymological root of *enthusiasm,* from the Greek, is *en theos,* "God within."

There's one more joke I can't resist to end this chapter, in the service of having fun at trail crossings as well as on your own religious path:

A rabbi and a priest were discussing their professions.

"Do you ever get ambitious?" asked the priest.

"Well," said the rabbi, "I suppose I could always move to a larger congregation. What about you?"

"Well, I suppose I could become a Cardinal."

"And then?"

"Well, it's theoretically possible that I could become the Pope."

"And then?" asked the rabbi.

"And then?" repeated the priest. "Isn't that enough? Do you want me to become God?"

"Well," said the rabbi softly, "one of *our* boys made it."[33]

Conclusion

———⏤〜⏤———

So finally, what's the point of it all? To reach the top of the mountain? To see God face to face? To become enlightened and attain Nirvana? If so, most of us will fail. There are those who will achieve the state of Unity, which I described in the "Opening" chapter as the final stage of spiritual development. Yet, they are few and far between. Generally these are the great mystics—from spirit persons[1] such as Buddha, Jesus, and Muhammad, who founded the major religions, to prophets such as Moses and Gandhi, who acted under divine inspiration, to contemplatives such as the Persian poet Jalalud-din Rumi and Spanish Carmelite nun Saint Theresa of Avila.

But, so the rest of us can have some inkling, what does it look like at the top of the mountain? Well, this is how Saint Theresa describes the highest stage of prayer, which she experienced regularly after years of training and practice:

> Here there is no sense of anything but enjoyment, without any knowledge of what is being enjoyed. The soul realizes that it is

enjoying some good thing that contains all good things together, but it cannot comprehend this good thing. All the senses are taken up with this joy so that none of them is free to act in any way, either outwardly or inwardly. . . . How what is called union takes place and what it is, I cannot tell. . . . The soul sometimes leaps out of itself like a burning fire that has become one whole flame and increases with great force. The flame leaps very high above the fire. Nevertheless it is not a different thing, but the same flame which is in the fire. . . . If a person reads in this state he can scarcely make out a single letter. . . . He hears but does not understand what he hears. . . . It is the same with the tongue, for he cannot form a word, nor would he have the strength to pronounce one. . . . Anyone who has experienced this will to some extent understand. It cannot be expressed more clearly, since all that happens is so obscure. I can only say that the soul conceives itself to be near God, and that it is left with such a conviction that it cannot possibly help believing.[2]

Hesse's Siddhartha finally reaches the Unity stage, as he stares into the water one day, after decades of meditational practice:

The river flowed on toward its goal. Siddhartha saw the river hasten, made up of himself and his relatives and all the people he had ever seen. . . . Siddhartha listened. He was now listening intently, completely absorbed, quite empty, taking in everything. He felt that he had now completely learned the art of listening. He had often heard all this before, all these numerous voices in the river, but today they sounded different. He could no longer distinguish the different voices—the merry voice from the weeping voice, the childish voice from the manly voice. They all belonged to each other: the lament of those who yearn, the laughter of the wise, the cry of indignation and the groan of the dying. They were all interwoven and interlocked, entwined in a thousand ways. . . . [W]hen he did not bind his soul to any one particular voice and absorb it in his Self, but heard them all, the whole, the unity; then the great song of a thousand voices consisted of one word: Om—perfection.[3]

While few of us attain these mystical states regularly, it's been my experience that almost all of us are briefly surprised by them—blindsided, if you will—at least once or twice in our lives. That means we have a window into Unity, with or without all the years of training and practice. We have a hint of what the world looks like for those travelers on the spiritual mountain who have managed to follow their religious paths to the very top. I remember being blindsided this way one night on a Florida beach. Since then, I've had no doubt that ordinary daily life is not the whole picture.

During college I was spending a spring break visiting my grandmother, who lived a couple of hours north of Miami. I'd come home from a party around midnight, and I decided to take a walk and look at the ocean before going to bed. After scrambling down some steps in the seawall, I found myself alone on a wide stretch of sand. The moon was supposed to be full that night, but the sky was covered by high clouds that transmitted the moonlight as if through a diaphanous veil. Large, smooth ocean swells were slowly breaking on the beach. I walked halfway down to the water and stood for a long time, mesmerized by the rhythmic sound of the waves, the white line of surf that appeared and disappeared, and the sweet, warm breeze rustling my shirt.

Suddenly the moon burst through the clouds with a single shaft of light, focused directly on me. As if in a Cecil B. deMille movie, I was at the center of a drama, with the surf beginning to sound like music and the air electrified with anticipation of what was going to happen next. Unconsciously

I stretched out my arms at my sides, palms up. I could feel my heart beating within my chest. It seemed timed to the breaking of the waves. The moonlight appeared to pulsate with the same rhythm. The breeze became one with my own breath. The moon hole in the clouds kept widening until the whole beach was bathed in white light. Everything throbbed with connection.

It was all too much, too charged. I fell to my knees and rocked back on my heels. *Harmony, fusion, fullness*—words like these filled my mind. I had a strong sense of presence: of my being fully present in the world and the world being utterly present to me. Was there something more? A divine presence? Was God going to speak to me from the clouds? I tried to listen. Hyperaware, I also looked, and smelled, and felt. As I did, I noticed that a dark shape was beginning to form along the white line of surf. It became larger and larger. Slowly, I realized it was moving. Toward me. Although I had no real point of perspective, it looked big and round.

It may have taken ten minutes to get close enough for me to identify what it was. Meanwhile, the clouds had covered the moon again and nature had returned to its component parts. Now I realized that a huge sea turtle was approaching me, measuring some four or five feet from head to tail and weighing hundreds and hundreds of pounds. Its progress was slow and ungainly as it dragged all of its weight up the beach on four paddlelike flippers. It didn't seem concerned that a human animal was on the beach too. In fact, it advanced single-mindedly right up to where I was on the dry part of the beach. It stopped dead, not more than ten yards from me.

For several minutes there was silence and stillness. Then the turtle began swiping at the sand with its front flippers. Soon all four flippers were violently trashing about, throwing sand in all directions, occasionally sprinkling me. I sat and watched. It kept digging, for a long time. Half an hour later it had created a pit a couple of yards across and several feet deep.

Next, the turtle carefully scooped out sand from the middle of the pit, a cup at a time, to make a deep hole into which it finally lowered its tail. Then eggs began dropping—dozens and dozens, maybe a hundred by the time she was done. I became very moved by what was going on. *So this is it!* I thought. *The great cycle of life is being elucidated for me—and only for me—on this big wide beach, here and now.* Why? Was this just a random moment? Was it a coincidence that a shaft of moonlight had aligned everything around me just before this turtle emerged? Was it simply happenstance that with so much Florida shoreline available, this turtle had dragged herself up to within a few yards of where I was kneeling?

I didn't have any answers, but I felt very grateful to have been visited in this way. Whether my conscious mind liked it or not, it all seemed miraculous. I sat in awe as one white egg after another filled the hole. When she was done, the turtle gently raked sand into the hole to cover the eggs and packed it down with a flipper. Then the violent thrashing and slinging of sand began again, filling the large pit back in. Ten minutes later the surface was level, and the turtle turned back to the water. She lumbered down the beach and straight into the surf. For a couple of minutes a round, dark shape could still be seen as the water receded between waves, and then she disappeared for good.

The beach scene now looked just as it had when I came: high clouds covering the moon, smooth ocean swells, and a warm tropical breeze in the middle of the night. Had anything really happened? Had I hallucinated all of this? Had I had too much to drink at the party? All I knew was that something had knocked me to my knees and kept me there. And a clearly marked path lay before me in the sand.

That night the curtains were parted briefly, and I glimpsed the world where mystics live most of the time. Sooner or later, many of us have this kind of experience. Yet, most of us don't stay very long at the top of the mountain. Note how British climber Frank Smythe describes Mount

Everest above 26,000 feet: "It was cold. Space, the air we breathed, the yellow rocks were deadly cold. There was something ultimate, passionless, and eternal in this cold. It came to us as a single constant note from the depths of space; we stood on the very boundary of life and death."[4] The great religious masters have learned how to live at the summit, braving the cold at the cusp of life and death in order to breathe ultimacy and see into eternity. The rest of us at best are trekkers much farther down on the mountain.

One of the students in the class I taught at Tufts on finding a religious path described hiking with her parents in the Great Smoky Mountains of Tennessee. Along their way they came to a gorgeous waterfall. She stood transfixed, overcome with its beauty and something about the way the water fell. She was not sure that God exists, but she felt spiritually filled that day. Another student spent a summer working at a dude ranch in Wyoming, leading clients on horseback along trails in the Teton mountains. She described feeling a Zenlike joy as she savored the pink colors of the range, lightning in the distance, and the rivers and fields and trees. A professor who teaches each summer at Tufts' European Center in the Alps speaks of how appreciative he's become of the wildflowers he sees as he hikes: "They're spectacular! I'm imagining now a huge meadow of bright blue gentians. And I've heard the hue from them went into the blue dyes used in cathedral windows in France. God must have been pleased to see his gift to us used to give us a better view of him."

The rabbi at Tufts has also taught in the Alps, and he's spoken about wildflowers too: "Lots of people think about mountains, and they think about big, massive things, expanses of rock and great, open vistas. But one of the amazing things that I love about mountains is the incredible small details you find there. I invented a game for when we hike. You stand in one space and you see how many different wildflowers you can identify. (I'm not talking about Latin names. I mean little white ones here and droopy purple ones over there, and so forth.) I think my record was twelve varieties spotted from one stance. The beauty and intensity of that small area is as impressive as the vast expanse you see from the top. As the French say, God is in the details."

God is also in all stages. This is important to remember when using a mountain-climbing metaphor for the spiritual life, which might imply that it's better to be higher up on the mountainside than lower down. It's not. There is beauty and there is truth at all stages, just as there is on all paths. Children know things adults don't. They love the experience of climbing trees and jumping in leaf piles. They can spend hours playing with dolls or action figures, envisioning worlds with which adults have long since lost touch. They have secret places and imaginary friends to which they will never be able to return as adults. What happens, though, if they are hurried, forced to miss all the enchantment of childhood?[5] What if they are always scheduled by adults, activitied by adults, and reality-tested by adults? They miss a wonderful part of human experience.

Spiritual development is a process, just like the rest of human growth during the life cycle. Would you give up your twenties because someone claims it's better to act as if you were forty? It can work the other way, too. Would you condemn someone in their sixties for not acting as if they were forty? Maybe certain people would in the youth culture of America, where it seems to be considered best to be forever young.

For some reason, religion is often perceived through nondevelopmental lenses as something you either have or don't, either get or don't. Then, once you have it or get it, it's never supposed to change or "you've lost your anchor." Looked at developmentally, though, religion is a process, not a product. It's a journey, not a destination. What happened to me in a month of chugging across Russia during 1980 on the Trans-Siberian railroad, visiting towns along the way, was much more important than the fact that I made it from the Pacific coast to the Baltic Sea.

We need to beware of judging other people's spiritual development on the basis of our own. It is instructive that Jesus said that children are "the greatest in the kingdom of heaven."[6] Not only should they not be judged for their children's faith, but he exclaimed, "Whoever welcomes one such child in my name welcomes me."[7] The theory of faith stages should not be thought of as a template or a way to pigeonhole other people. Instead, it should be a way to free ourselves from becoming stuck religiously and to free others from the imperialistic view that only our way is right.

Instructive here is the Hindu parable of blind men feeling an elephant—a metaphor for God or Ultimate Reality. The man who is holding a tusk claims the elephant is like a cold stone. The one feeling the hide argues that it's actually like rough tree bark. Another, at the tail, relates instead that the elephant is like a soft broom. A fourth blind man, at the mouth, insists that the animal is the site of a warm spring. None of the blind men alone can ever gain perspective on the whole elephant, which is much larger than each of them—just as we finite beings can never presume to experience and articulate the totality of the Infinite. Yet, their understanding would be dramatically increased if they would stop insisting on their own truth, learn from one another, and begin to construct a composite picture.

Community is a very important part of a full spiritual life. We eat and drink together around our religious tables, and we celebrate together the great holidays and rites of passage. None of these experiences work very well alone. Our tables and our celebrations usually consist of people at quite different stages of faith development. They have been walking at different altitudes on the spiritual mountain, and these are good times to broaden our own understanding by learning about what they've seen and heard (and touched and smelled and tasted!). These are often family times, and, by definition, families include people at various developmental stages. My examples of people alone in nature, including myself on the beach, can be misleading if they leave out the reality of how much we grow and change through our interconnections with others—in caring, friendship, and love. We also do that as much, if not more, in cities and workplaces and schools and homes—as well as churches, temples, and mosques—as we do in the great outdoors.

Getting on a path—represented by a religious tradition—is also critical to making spiritual progress up the mountain. The view is the same at the top no matter how you get there, as the mystics tend to tell us, but it's very hard to gain much altitude without getting lost when you're not following any trail. A student in my Tufts class liked a different analogy but made the same point. He explained that if we wander around in a thick forest, picking fruit and nuts off the lower branches of this tree and that, we remain in the dark. Things only begin to brighten up when we pick one tree and start climbing higher and higher. If we're lucky enough to reach the top, we'll see the sky. And that's not to condemn others for climbing tall trees of different species. For indeed, if we look around, we'll realize that others have the same view from the top that we have.

A surprising conclusion for many of my students at the end of the course was that they found themselves circling back to the religion of their childhood in order to begin their mountain climbing. As one put it, "I had come to see Judaism as an all-or-nothing proposition. Moving back toward it was the last thing I expected when I took this class. Now I understand that even if I'm not Orthodox like my parents, I can still find a comfortable place within the Jewish tradition." Another wrote in her journal, "Perhaps the most inspiring thing that I have gotten from the class is the idea that it is okay, even beneficial, simply to use the Christian religion that I have grown up with as a starting place. I used to think that I had to explore and understand fully all religions before embarking on my journey; now I realize that this can come as I travel up the mountain."

The most important thing to remember is that you can do it. Each of us has a rich, complex, dynamic story of our own to tell and develop. Each of us can perceive the mountain in the distance, open ourselves to the possibility of mountain climbing, approach it, pick a path, and start walking. It may be a familiar path from an earlier time in your life, or it may be a brand-new way for you. As you start climbing, other travelers will help you along. You can also learn a lot about the mountain from people who have been on other paths. Taking time to develop some spiritual practices like prayer or meditation will make a big difference. And it won't always go smoothly. There will be tough times ahead, but they can strengthen you. Finally, you'll find a lot of joy on that mountainside. If you keep your sense of humor and your willingness to celebrate, the journey will enrapture you and change your life. The mountain beckons.

APPENDIX A

❦

Reading for the Next Steps on Your Path

COMPARATIVE

Diana Eck. *On Common Ground: World Religions in America* (CD-ROM). New York: Columbia University Press, 1997.

Here's an ideal way to learn all about the world's religions—at your own speed and in your own way. Diana Eck, a professor of comparative religion at Harvard, has put together a superb CD-ROM with the help of her students and lots of colleagues. To teach about Hinduism, for example, there are minimovies on the likes of *puja* worship and temple building in America. There is a time line with small clickable essays about the history of Hinduism throughout the world since 2500 B.C. and in America since 1780. You can examine Buddhism, Christianity, Islam, and Judaism in just the same way, along with a number of other traditions. There is a directory of temples, mosques, synagogues, churches, and other religious organizations all over America, complete with pictures and commentary, so one can start visiting and experimenting today. An extensive index, glossary, and bibliography are also at your fingertips. A preview is at www.fas.harvard.edu-pluralism

Huston Smith. *The World's Religions.* San Francisco: HarperSanFrancisco, 1991.

I have found no better survey of the major world religions. I have used this book in class after class at Tufts, and students always like it. There are chapters on Buddhism, Christianity, Confucianism, Hinduism, Islam, Judaism, and Taoism. Professor Smith simultaneously gives one a bird's-eye view of each religious tradition and helps one stand in the shoes of practitioners so that the world can be seen through their eyes too. The stories and examples are wonderful. Each faith comes alive and sparkles on the page. It can be used as a reference or read straight through.

Bahá'í Faith

Colette Gouvion and Philippe Jouvion. *The Gardeners of God: An Encounter with Five Million Baha'is.* Oxford: Oneworld Publications, 1993.

A couple of French journalists interviewed Bahá'ís from many different backgrounds for this book. The authors present both the principles of the faith and also the way they are lived and experienced in this rainbow religion, which seems comfortably to include all races and nationalities. The founder's story is told and set in historical context, and it is followed by descriptions of more than a dozen current Bahá'ís' "roads to belief." Persecution of Bahá'ís is also recounted, and there's a chapter on how Bahá'ís are seen through the eyes of followers of other religions. Leo Tolstoy, for one, appreciated how the Bahá'ís "have rejected all these monstrous hierarchies which divide the old religions and they aspire to come together into one single religion common to the whole of mankind."

BUDDHISM

Thich Nhat Hanh. *Peace Is Every Step: The Path of Mindfulness in Everyday Life.* New York: Bantam Books, 1992.

This Zen Buddhist monk, born in 1926, has written more than seventy-five books in three languages. Here, in *very* readable form, he relates Zen teaching and practice to everyday life—like walking, driving, eating, talking on the telephone, and washing the dishes. He gently probes anger and suffering, as well as love and compassion. I like the way he eases one into meditation and a meditational attitude toward all of life, helping one to live more in the present moment. Yet, he is no navel-gazer and world-renouncer. Thich Nhat Hanh actively and tirelessly opposed the Vietnam War, and he was nominated by Martin Luther King, Jr., for the Nobel Peace Prize. He gently encourages each of us to stay active in the search for world peace and justice.

CHRISTIANITY

Marcus J. Borg. *Meeting Jesus Again for the First Time.* San Francisco: HarperSanFrancisco, 1994.

I identify closely with this thinker who grew up Christian, almost left his faith for good, and then discovered an adult version of it that has changed his life. His early years were spent in a conservative Midwestern town of Protestants and Catholics. Every Sunday he went to church with parents who were pillars of his Protestant congregation. He became "enlightened" with a scientific worldview in college. His doubts about religion deepened during seminary, where he rejected Jesus as God on biblical evidence. He became a secular scholar of the New Testament, teaching at a state university. Ultimately, in his forties, he awoke as a brand-new Christian, with a radically different view of Jesus, God, and religious life itself. Most of the book describes the form of Christianity he's found.

HINDUISM

Diana Eck. *Encountering God: A Spiritual Journey from Bozeman to Banaras*. Boston: Beacon Press, 1993.

Hinduism here is seen through the eyes of an American seeker who became a scholar of comparative religion as a result of her study of Hinduism. She reports how her faith journey from Montana to India led her to understand her own Christian faith differently and more clearly (as did my own faith journey from Illinois to India). In a very Hindu way, affirming that there are many ways up the spiritual mountain, Eck spends much of the book describing encounters between the religions in the modern era. She insists on the importance of following a path (and has plenty to say about the Hindu one), yet she also comes to a vision of worldwide religious interdependence. You'll learn a lot about Hinduism in this book, but you may learn even more about the spiritual mountain as a whole.

ISLAM

John Renard. *Seven Doors to Islam: Spirituality and the Religious Life of Muslims*. Berkeley: University of California Press, 1996.

This beautifully constructed book tries to cast a net around the everyday spiritual lives of the world's Muslims, who differ tremendously from one subtradition and one culture to another, just as Christians and Buddhists do. There are sections on scripture, devotion, heroes, art, community, education, and mysticism. A companion volume, published in 1998, presents texts from the Qur'an and the sayings of Muhammad (*hadith*), poetry and devotional literature, and great teachers through the centuries. It's called *Windows on the House of Islam: Muslim Sources on Spirituality and Religious Life*. Several dozen illustrations in each text aid significantly in appreciating the world's second-largest religion.

JUDAISM

Harold S. Kushner. *To Life: A Celebration of Jewish Being and Thinking.* New York: Warner Books, 1994.

Many people have heard of Rabbi Kushner's best-selling *When Bad Things Happen to Good People*. Passing through airports, I've picked up other great paperbacks he's written for the general reader. This one, though, is directed to Jews—in particular to those for whom their childhood faith has lost its meaning. ("It will continue the conversation that was abandoned years ago, but this time on an adult level.") It's also written for people from other backgrounds who have developed a serious interest in Judaism as adults. Kushner is a joy to read. He's engaging. He tells good stories about himself and others. He answers all your questions. And he writes clearly and directly.

UNITARIAN UNIVERSALISM

John Buehrens, F. Forrester Church, and Robert Fulgham. *A Chosen Faith: An Introduction to Unitarian Universalism.* New York: Ballantine Books, 1998.

Several of the most insightful minds in modern Unitarian Universalism collude here to present a storied overview of the religious movement. They tell their own stories, those of people they've met, and those of historical figures—such as the nineteenth-century transcendentalist Margaret Fuller and the modern social prophet James Luther Adams. Along the way the tradition comes clear, including why it's "the one church to have, if you're having more than one." The book is structured according to the sources of Unitarian Universalist faith enumerated in denominational principles, including direct experience of transcending mystery and wonder, words and deeds of prophetic men and women, wisdom from the world's religions, love of God and neighbor, and guidance from science and reason.

APPENDIX B

_ᘓ ᕔ_

Contacts for the Next Steps on Your Path

COMPARATIVE

Association for Religion and the
   Intellectual Life
College of New Rochelle
New Rochelle, NY 10805–2339
(914) 235–1439
www.aril.org

BAHÁ'Í FAITH

National Bahá'í Centre
536 Sheridan Road
Wilmette, IL 60091
(800) 228–6483
www.us.bahai.org

BUDDHISM

American Buddhist Congress
933 S. New Hampshire Avenue
Los Angeles, CA 90006
(213) 739–1270
www.wgn.net/~abc/abc

CHRISTIANITY

Eastern Orthodox
Greek Orthodox Archdiocese of
   America
8–10 East 79th Street
New York, NY 10021
(212) 570–3600
www.goarch.org

Protestant
National Council of Churches
475 Riverside Drive, Room 850
New York, NY 10115
(212) 870–2227
www.ncccusa.org

Roman Catholic—Higher
  Education
Catholic Campus Ministry
  Association
300 College Park Avenue
Dayton, OH 45469–2515
(937) 229–4648
www.udayton.edu~ccma/

Roman Catholic
National Conference of Catholic
  Bishops
3211 4th Street, N.E.
Washington, DC 20017–1194
(202) 541–3000
www.nccbuscc.org

HINDUISM

Hindu Students Council
P.O. Box 9185
Boston, MA 02114–0041
(617) 698–1106
www.hindunet.org

ISLAM

Islamic Society of North America
6555 South 750 East, P.O. Box 38
Plainfield, IN 46168
(317) 839–8157
www.isna.net

JUDAISM

General—Higher Education
Hillel International Center
1640 Rhode Island Avenue, N.W.
Washington, DC 20036
(202) 857–6560
www.hillel.org

Conservative
United Synagogue of Conservative
  Judaism
Rapaport House
155 Fifth Avenue
New York, NY 10010–6802
(212) 533–7800
www.uscj.org

Orthodox
Union of Orthodox Jewish
  Congregations of America
333 Seventh Avenue
New York, NY 10001–5072
(212) 563–4000
www.ou.org

Reform
The Union of American Hebrew
    Congregations
633 Third Avenue
New York, NY 10017–6778
(212) 650–4000
www.uahc.org

UNITARIAN
UNIVERSALISM

Unitarian Universalist Association
25 Beacon Street
Boston, MA 02108
(617) 742–2100
www.uua.org

Notes

_⁀ᏅᎧ‿_

OPENING

1. Donna Radley is not her real name. Stories throughout the book are based on fact, but people's identities have been disguised and certain elements of their stories changed or embellished to protect their confidentiality.

2. My stages are derived most directly from theirs. See chapters by Fowler and Oser, for example, in Oser and Scarlett, *Religious Development in Childhood and Adolescence*. Another very helpful resource is Parks, *The Critical Years*. My own understanding of faith stages, as described in this chapter and its two charts, has been tested and modified through my counseling experience during almost twenty-five years of ordained ministry.

3. See, for example, Erikson, *Childhood and Society* and *Identity, Youth, and Crisis*.

4. See, for example, Piaget, *The Origin of Intelligence in Children* and *The Early Growth of Logic in the Child*.

5. See, for example, Kohlberg, *Moral Stages* and *The Psychology of Moral Stages*.

6. See, for example, those collected and referred to in Oser and Scarlett, *Religious Development in Childhood and Adolescence*.

7. For another conceptualization of the stages of Dependence, Independence, and Interdependence, see the "Maturity Continuum" in Covey, *Seven Habits of Highly Effective People*, especially pp. 49–53.

8. Luke 2:41–52.

9. Harvey Cox, as quoted in Fowler, *Stages of Faith*, p. 181.

10. Paul Ricoeur, as quoted in Fowler, *Stages of Faith*, p. 197.

11. See Fowler, *Stages of Faith*, pp. 188–197.

THINKING

1. Eliade, *The Sacred and the Profane*, p. 38.

2. See Exodus, chapters 19–34, and Deuteronomy, chapters 4–11.

3. Exodus 24:17.

4. See, for example, Deuteronomy 11:26–28.

5. Bernbaum, *Sacred Mountains of the World*, p. 97.

6. Qur'an, 23:20 and 95:2.

7. See, for example, Qur'an, 2:51–55; 7:143–154.

8. See, for example, Qur'an 2:87–89; 23:44–53.

9. Jung, *Memories, Dreams, Reflections*, p. 7.

10. Hall and Nordby, *Primer of Jungian Psychology*, p. 28.

11. Jung, *Memories*, pp. 77–78.

12. Jung, *Memories*, p. 42.

13. The story of Jung's First Communion, which follows, may be found in his *Memories, Dreams, Reflections*, pp. 52–56.

EXPERIENCING

1. Information in this chapter about the *kecak* dance is taken from Levine, *Bali*, pp. 109, 118–119, 123, 134–135.

2. Quotations are from my diary entries from books I read in the library of the Bali Canti Sena Foundation (bibliographic references were not preserved).

3. See the works of Wilfred Cantwell Smith; in particular, *Towards a World Theology*, pp. 113–114, 147; *Faith and Belief*, p. 12; and *The Meaning and End of Religion*, pp. 167–168.

4. Emerson, *Selected Writings*, p. 65.

5. Emerson's 1838 Divinity School Address is reproduced in a number of collections of his work. One is Emerson, *Selected Writings*, pp. 65–84.

6. van Doren Stern, *Henry David Thoreau*, pp. 4, 6, 15, 18, 22, 28–31, 34–35.

7. van Doren Stern, *Henry David Thoreau*, p. 303.

8. Thoreau, *Walden*, pp. 254, 306, 310, 452.

9. Shibayama, *A Flower Does Not Talk*, p. 17.

10. Smith, *World's Religions*, p. 137.

11. Thoreau, *Walden*, p. 309.

12. As cited in the hymnbook of the Unitarian Universalist Association, *Singing the Living Tradition* (Boston: Beacon Press, 1993), no. 556.

WALKING

1. The name of this church has been disguised, by creating a church that does not exist in the index of Melton, *Encyclopedia of American Religions*.

2. The quotes from *Siddhartha* that follow in this chapter are taken from pages 7–9, 14, 23, 28–29, 88.

JOINING

1. Smith, *World's Religions*, pp. 233–234.

2. Quotes that follow are from Roth, *Ghost Writer*, pp. 9, 11, 80, 81, 92, 94, 110.

3. Matthew 25:34–36, 40.

4. Matthew 22:36–40; see also Mark 12:28–31.

5. James 2:17.

6. As quoted in Karen Baker, "Legal Ministry: To Heal and Empower," *Harvard Divinity Bulletin* (June–July 1982), p. 4.

CROSSING

1. Quotations are from pages 64, 117–118, 184–185, 191–193, and 212.

2. Quotations are from Bhagavad Gita, trans. Prabhavananda and Isherwood.

3. Matthew 5:44, 47; 6:24–26, 28–29, 33.

4. See John 14:2 and 14:6.

5. Gandhi, *Message of Jesus Christ*, p. 43.

6. Sura 55:1–6, 10–13, 31–32, 35–38.

7. "Iran Hangs Bahai in Religion Case," *New York Times* (July 24, 1998), section A, column 6, citing U.S. State Department spokesman James P. Rubin.

8.   "Death Sentences for the Bahai," *New York Times* (December 31, 1993), section A, p. 28.

9.   R. W. Apple, Jr., "Iran's Baha'is: Some Call It Genocide," *New York Times* (February 27, 1983), section 4, p. 9.

10.   Mark Juergensmeyer, "The Terrorists Who Long for Peace," *Fletcher Forum* 20, No. 1 (Winter/Spring, 1996), pp. 1, 3.

11.   Amartya Sen, "The Threats to Secular India" (March 11, 1993).

12.   Kelsay et al., "Religion and the Roots of Conflict," p. 9.

13.   Bhagavad Gita.

14.   Joshua 6.

15.   Matthew 10:34–35.

16.   Juergensmeyer, "Terrorists," p. 7.

17.   Kelsay et al., "Religion and the Roots of Conflict," p. 10.

18.   Kelsay et al., "Religion and the Roots of Conflict," pp. 3–6.

19.   Kelsay et al., "Religion and the Roots of Conflict," p. 10.

20.   Matthew 5:38, 39, 44.

21.   Qur'an, 2:258; 109:1.

22.   Isaiah 2:4.

23.   Dhammapada 1:8.

24.   See Kung and Kuschel, *A Global Ethic*.

25.   "World Conference on Religion and Peace" (Geneva International Forum, 1997), http://geneva.intl.ch/geneva-intl/gi/egi/egi191.htm.

SITTING

1.   Benson, *Relaxation Response*, p. 59.

2.   Benson, *Relaxation Response*, pp. 59–61.

3.   See chart in Benson, *Relaxation Response*, pp. 70–71.

4.   Benson, *Relaxation Response*, pp. 78–79 and 112–113.

5.   Benson, *Timeless Healing*, pp. 16, 195–196.

6.   Benson, *Timeless Healing*, p. 199.

7.   Benson, *Relaxation Response*, pp. 74–98.

8.   Sutra of Mindfulness, as quoted in Nhat Hanh, *Miracle of Mindfulness!*, p. 15. As explained on page 7, this sutra is the Anapanasati Sutra—the 118th sutra in the Majhima Nikaya collection of sutras. It teaches sixteen methods of using one's breath.

9.   Nhat Hanh, *Miracle of Mindfulness!*, pp. 34–35.

10.   Nhat Hanh, *Miracle of Mindfulness!*, pp. 21, 38.

11.   Nhat Hanh, *Miracle of Mindfulness!*, pp. 3–6, 14.

12.   James Forest, "Nhat Hanh: Seeing With the Eyes of Compassion," in Nhat Hanh, *Miracle of Mindfulness!*, pp. 101–104.

13.   Quotes that follow are from pp. 145, 151, 152,.

SUFFERING

1.   This person is not disguised. The full account of his story is chronicled in Jonas, *Rebecca*. The story here is taken from that book (pages 1–3, 11, 28–29, 32–35, 44–45, 51, 59, 64, 73, 76, 79, 81–82, 101, 122–125, 130–131, 140–143) and from a personal interview with Robert Jonas.

2.   Nouwen, *Wounded Healer*.

3.   Nouwen, *Here and Now*, p. 105.

4.   See, for the story that follows, Mukherjee, *Jasmine*, pp. 1, 6, 9–10, 34, 44, 71, 77, 105, 107, 116, 120, 146, 151, 165, 169, 190, 214.

5.   Kushner, *To Life!*

6.   The quotations in this paragraph come from page 133.

7.   Kushner, *To Life!*, p. 301.

8.   Borg, *Meeting Jesus Again*, pp. 22, 27, 135.

9.   Borg, *Meeting Jesus Again*, pp. xi–xii.

REJOICING

1.   Ecclesiastes 3:13.

2.   Proverbs 17:22.

3.   Cox, *Feast of Fools*, p. 13.

4.   Psalm 98, verses 1, 4–6, 8.

5.   Qur'an, sura 34, verses 1, 10.

6.   e. e. cummings, *XAIPE*, edited by George James Firmage (New York: Liveright Publishing Corp., 1997).

7.   From Rabindranath Tagore, *Sadhana*, as cited in Carl Seaburg, ed., *Great Occasions: Readings for the Celebration of Birth, Coming of Age, Marriage and Death* (Boston: Beacon Press, 1968), p. 247, originally published in *Sadhana* by Rabindranath Tagore (New York: Macmillan, 1913).

8.   Quotations are from pages 106, 109, and 110.

9.   Cox, *Feast of Fools*, pp. 22–26.

10.   Cox, *Feast of Fools*, p. 9.

11.   Excerpted from chapter 6.

12.   Matthew 23:24.

13.   Luke 6:42. See also Matthew 7:4–5.

14.   Novak and Waldoks, *Big Book of Jewish Humor*. See page 198 for the joke that follows.

15.   Jones, *Preacher Joke Book*, p. 14.

16.   Guy Wesley, "Forget to Ask," in Jones, *Preacher Joke Book*, p. 33.

17.   Adapted from Salajan, *Zen Comics*, pp. 8, 58, 80–81, 86.

18.   Novak and Waldoks, *Big Book of Jewish Humor*, p. 17.

19.   Charles Schulz, "Knowing You Are Not Alone," as quoted in Short, *Gospel According to Peanuts*, p. 1.

20.   G. B. Trudeau (Universal Press Syndicate, 1971).

21.   G. B. Trudeau (Universal Press Syndicate, 1971).

22.   The presidents' quotations come from Trudeau, *Flashbacks*, pp. 84, 96, 228.

23.   G. B. Trudeau, *In Search of Cigarette Holder Man* (Kansas City: Andrews and McMeel, 1994), p. 7.

24.   Trudeau, *Flashbacks*, p. 194.

25.   Trudeau, *Planet Doonesbury*, p. 56.

26.   Respectively in *The Doonesbury Chronicles* (New York: Holt, Rinehart and Winston, 1975); *Doonesbury's Greatest Hits* (New York: Holt, Rinehart and Winston, 1978); *Doonesbury Dossier: The Reagan Years* (New York: Henry Holt, 1984); *Doonesbury Deluxe* (New York: Henry Holt, 1987).

27.   Trudeau, *Flashbacks*, p. 25.

28.   G. B. Trudeau, *Doonesbury Nation* (Kansas City: Andrews and McMeel, 1995), p. 27.

29. Trudeau, *In Search of Cigarette Holder Man*, p. 66.

30. Telushkin, *Jewish Humor*, p. 190.

31. Telushkin, *Jewish Humor*, p. 190.

32. Telushkin, *Jewish Humor*, p. 191.

33. Novak and Waldoks, *Big Book of Jewish Humor*, p. 96.

CONCLUSION

1. This term is used and described by Marcus Borg in relation to Jesus in his *Meeting Jesus Again for the First Time*. He explains how spirit persons are known cross-culturally as "people who have vivid and frequent subjective experiences of another level or dimension of reality" (p. 32). They also become "mediators of the sacred" to the rest of us, whether they name it as Yahweh, Brahman, Atman, Allah, the Tao, Great Spirit, God, or something else.

2. Saint Theresa of Avila, *The Interior Castle*, as cited in Happold, *Mysticism*, pp. 352–354.

3. Pp. 110–111.

4. F. S. Smythe, *Camp Six: An Account of the 1933 Mount Everest Expedition*, second edition (London: Hodder and Stoughton, 1938), p. 243, as cited in Bernbaum, *Sacred Mountains of the World*, p. 239.

5. See Elkind, *The Hurried Child*.

6. Matthew 18:4.

7. Matthew 18:5.

Bibliography

Barry, William A. *Finding God in All Things: A Companion to the Spiritual Exercises of St. Ignatius*. Notre Dame, IN: Ave Maria Press, 1991.

Beckerlegge, Gwilym, ed. *The World Religions Reader*. London: Routledge, 1998.

Benson, Herbert. *The Relaxation Response*. New York: William Morrow and Co., 1975.

————. *Timeless Healing: The Power and Biology of Belief*. New York: Scribner, 1996.

Berger, Peter. *A Rumor of Angels: Modern Society and the Rediscovery of the Supernatural*. New York: Anchor Books, 1990.

Bernbaum, Edwin. *Sacred Mountains of the World*. San Francisco: Sierra Club Books, 1992.

Bhagavad Gita. Translated by Swami Prabhavananda and Christopher Isherwood. New York: New American Library, 1954.

Bible: New Revised Standard Version. Iowa Falls, Iowa: World Bible Publishers, 1989.

Borg, Marcus J. *The God We Never Knew: Beyond Dogmatic Religion to a More Authentic Contemporary Faith*. San Francisco: HarperSanFrancisco, 1998.

————. *Meeting Jesus Again for the First Time*. San Francisco: HarperSanFrancisco, 1995.

Buber, Martin. *I and Thou*. New York: Simon & Schuster, 1996.

Campbell, Joseph. *The Power of Myth*. New York: Doubleday, 1988.

Camus, Albert. *The Plague.* New York: Vintage, 1991.

Covey, Stephen R. *The Seven Habits of Highly Effective People: Restoring the Character Ethic.* New York: Fireside, 1990.

Cox, Harvey. *The Feast of Fools: A Theological Essay on Festivity and Fantasy.* Cambridge, MA: Harvard University Press, 1969.

Cummings, E. E. *Selected Poems.* New York: Norton, 1994.

Eck, Diana. *On Common Ground: World Religions in America* (CD-ROM). New York: Columbia University Press, 1997.

———. *Encountering God: A Spiritual Journey from Bozeman to Banaras.* Boston: Beacon Press, 1993.

Eliade, Mircea. *The Sacred and the Profane: The Nature of Religion.* New York: Harcourt, Brace & World, 1959.

Elkind, David. *The Hurried Child: Growing Up Too Fast Too Soon.* Reading, MA: Addison-Wesley Publishing Co., 1981.

Emerson, Ralph Waldo. *The Selected Writings of Ralph Waldo Emerson.* Edited by Brooks Atkinson. New York: Random House, 1950.

———. *Self-Reliance and Other Essays.* New York: Dover Publications, 1993.

Endo, Shusako. *Deep River.* New York: New Directions, 1994.

Erikson, Erik H. *Childhood and Society.* New York: Norton, 1950.

———. *Identity, Youth and Crisis.* New York: Norton, 1968.

Fowler, James W. *Stages of Faith: The Psychology of Human Development and the Quest for Meaning.* San Francisco: Harper & Row, 1981.

Gandhi, Mohandas. *The Message of Jesus Christ.* Bombay: Bharatiya Vidya Bhavan, 1971.

Gouvion, Colette, and Philippe Jouvion. *The Gardeners of God: An Encounter with Five Million Bahá'ís.* Oxford: Oneworld Publications, 1993.

Hall, Calvin S., and Vernon J. Nordby. *A Primer of Jungian Psychology.* New York: Taplinger, 1973.

Happold, F. C. *Mysticism: A Study and an Anthology.* London: Penguin Books, 1990.

Hassan, Steven. *Combatting Cult Mind Control.* Rochester, VT: Park Street Press, 1988.

Hesse, Hermann. *Siddhartha*. New York: New Directions, 1957.

Holy Quran. Translated by M. H. Shakir. New York: Tahrike Tarsile Qur'an, 1982.

Jonas, Robert A. *Rebecca: A Father's Journey from Grief to Gratitude*. New York: Crossroad Publishing Co., 1996.

Jones, Loyal, ed. *The Preacher Joke Book*. Little Rock, AR: August House, 1989.

Juergensmeyer, Mark. *The New Cold War? Religious Nationalism Confronts the Secular State*. Berkeley: University of California Press, 1993.

Jung, Carl G. *Man and His Symbols*. Garden City, NY: Doubleday & Company, 1964.

————. *Memories, Dreams, Reflections*. New York: Vintage Books, 1965.

Kelsay, John, et al. "Religion and the Roots of Conflict," in *Religion and Human Rights*. New York: The Project on Religion and Human Rights, 1994.

Kohlberg, Lawrence. *Moral Stages*. New York: Karger, 1983.

————. *The Psychology of Moral Stages*. San Francisco: Harper & Row, 1984.

Kornfield, Jack. *A Path with Heart*. New York: Bantam Books, 1993.

Kung, Hans, and Kuschel, Karl-Josef, eds. *A Global Ethic: The Declaration of the Parliament of the World's Religions*. New York: Continuum Publishing Co., 1995.

Kushner, Harold S. *To Life! A Celebration of Jewish Being and Thinking*. New York: Warner Books, 1993.

————. *When Bad Things Happen to Good People*. New York: Schocken Books, 1981.

Levine, Charles, ed. *Bali: The Official Guide to the Island of Bali*. Singapore: Apa Productions, 1977.

Lewis, C. S. *The Case for Christianity*. New York: Touchstone, 1996.

Melton, J. Gordon, ed. *The Encyclopedia of American Religions*. Tarrytown, NY: Triumph Books, 1991.

Mosher, Gouverneur. *Kyoto: A Contemplative Guide*. Tokyo: Charles E. Tuttle Co., 1979.

Mukherjee, Bharati. *Jasmine*. New York: Fawcett Crest, 1991.

Nasr, Seyyed Hossein. *Ideals and Realities of Islam*. Boston: Beacon Press, 1972.

Nhat Hanh, Thich. *The Miracle of Mindfulness! A Manual on Meditation*. Boston: Beacon Press, 1976.

———. *Peace Is Every Step: The Path of Mindfulness in Everyday Life*. New York: Bantam Books, 1991.

Nouwen, Henri. *Here and Now: Living in the Spirit*. New York: Crossroad Publishing Co., 1994.

———. *The Wounded Healer: Ministry in Contemporary Society*. Garden City, NY: Doubleday, 1972.

Novak, William, and Moshe Waldoks. *The Big Book of Jewish Humor*. New York: Harper & Row, 1981.

Oser, Fritz K., and W. George Scarlett, eds. *Religious Development in Childhood and Adolescence*. San Francisco: Jossey-Bass, 1991.

Parks, Sharon. *The Critical Years: The Young Adult Search for a Faith to Live By*. San Francisco: Harper & Row, 1986.

Piaget, Jean. *The Early Growth of Logic in the Child*. New York: Norton, 1969.

———. *The Origin of Intelligence in Children*. New York: Norton, 1963.

Renard, John. *Seven Doors to Islam: Spirituality and the Religious Life of Muslims*. Berkeley: University of California Press, 1996.

———. *Windows on the House of Islam: Muslim Sources on Spirituality and Religious Life*. Berkeley: University of California Press, 1998.

Richler, Mordecai. *The Apprenticeship of Duddy Kravitz*. New York: Alfred A. Knopf, 1959.

Roberts, Elizabeth, and Elias Amidon. *Earth Prayers from Around the World*. San Francisco: HarperSanFrancisco, 1991.

Roth, Philip. *The Ghost Writer*. New York: Vintage International, 1995.

———. *Goodbye Columbus*. New York: The Modern Library, 1966.

Rudofsky, Bernard. *The Kimono Mind*. Tokyo: Charles E. Tuttle Co., 1979.

Salajan, Ioanna. *Zen Comics*. Rutland, VT: Charles E. Tuttle Co., 1974.

Schiffmann, Erich. *Yoga: The Spirit and Practice of Moving Into Stillness*. New York: Simon & Schuster, 1996.

Schuon, Frithjof. *Understanding Islam*. Bloomington, IN: World Wisdom Books, 1998.

Sharma, Arvind. *Our Religions*. San Francisco: HarperSanFrancisco, 1993.

Sheppherd, Joseph. *The Elements of the Bahá'í Faith*. Rockport, MA: Element Books, 1992.

Shibayama, Zenkei. *A Flower Does Not Talk: Zen Essays*. Tokyo: Charles E. Tuttle Co., 1970.

Short, Robert. *The Gospel According to Peanuts*. New York: Bantam Books, 1968.

Singer, Margaret Thaler. *Cults in Our Midst*. San Francisco: Jossey-Bass, 1995.

Smith, Huston. *The World's Religions*. San Francisco: HarperSanFrancisco, 1991.

Smith, Jonathan Z. *Dictionary of Religion*. San Francisco: HarperSanFrancisco, 1995.

Smith, Wilfred Cantwell. *Faith and Belief*. Princeton, NJ: Princeton University Press, 1979.

————. *The Meaning and End of Religion: A New Approach to the Religious Traditions of Mankind*. San Francisco, Harper & Row, 1978.

————. *Towards a World Theology*. Philadelphia: Westminster Press, 1981.

Stern, Philip van Doren. *Henry David Thoreau: Writer and Rebel*. New York: Thomas Y. Crowell Co., 1972.

Tagore, Rabindranath. *Sadhana*. New York: Macmillan, 1913.

Telushkin, Joseph. *Jewish Humor: What the Best Jewish Jokes Say About the Jews*. New York: William Morrow, 1992.

Thoreau, Henry David. *Walden: Or, Life in the Woods*. New York: Dover Publications, 1995.

Tolstoy, Leo. *The Death of Ivan Ilych*. New York: Signet, 1960.

Trudeau, G. B. *Flashbacks: Twenty-Five Years of Doonesbury*. Kansas City: Andrews and McMeel, 1995.

————. *Planet Doonesbury*. Kansas City: Andrews and McMeel, 1997.

Wordsworth, William. *Selected Poems*. New York: Penguin Books, 1994.

Index

~~~&~~~